cation

Improving Church Education

H. W. BYRNE

Religious Education Press
Birmingham Alabama

Library of Congress Cataloging in Publication Data

Byrne, Herbert W 1917–
Improving church education.

Bibliography: pp. 344–46
Includes index.
1. Christian education. I. Title.
BV1471.2.B93 268 79-10852
ISBN 0-89135-017-9

Religious Education Press, Inc.
1531 Wellington Road
Birmingham, Alabama 35209
10 9 8 7 6 5 4 3 2

Religious Education Press publishes books and educational materials exclusively in religious education and in areas closely related to religious education. It is committed to enhancing and professionalizing religious education through the publication of significant scholarly and popular works.

PUBLISHER TO THE PROFESSION

To my wife—Nelle
To my son—Bert
To my daughter—Betty

Contents

Contents

Foreword

Few endeavors of the church so directly influence the future as does its educational ministry. Beliefs, practices, attitudes, and understanding are but four dimensions of Christian life affected by the character of education offered to those children and adults who are in the process of becoming tomorrow's church. Herbert W. Byrne is one churchman who early in his career saw the potential of Christian education for helping the church become what it ought to be in the world. Byrne's vision seems very much in line with that part of the Great Commission in which Jesus commands the church to commit some of its human resources toward "teaching new disciples to obey all the commands I have given you." Thus in his mature years Byrne can look back upon having devoted more than three decades of his life to Christian education as a primary ministry.

The spirit of *Improving Christian Education,* this latest of Dr. Byrne's books, is not one of pessimism concerning the present so much as is one of tempered optimism concerning the future. This is not the kind of book which is likely to be hurriedly written by an "angry young man"; rather it is the kind of book which is likely to be written by an individual who has spent the necessary years trying out in practice those ideas which have surfaced through the efforts of careful research. *Improving Christian Education,* then, is a practical book aimed toward the improvement of teaching through supervision at the teaching site. Perhaps the basic question which the book attempts to answer is "How can the supervisor best aid the teacher in accomplishing the teaching task?" The images which Byrne employs to convey his answers to the reader include those of the supervisor becoming a "teacher of teachers" as well as inspirer, facilitator, and improver of the climate for growth.

HAROLD WILLIAM BURGESS
Asbury Theological Seminary

Preface

Christian education in the local church, and particularly in the Sunday school, is under fire today. Critics are saying that much needs to be done to improve the caliber of work done in the educational program of the church. Even supporters of church education recognize that much needs to be done to improve the quality of instruction. At the same time it is recognized that much progress has been made in so-called secular education to improve the quality of teaching and learning. Supervision is a relatively new form of service in general and secular education. It is a brand new form in church education, particularly at the local church level. Only in the last two or three decades has any real progress been made toward the employment of a professional worker in local church education supervision. This office is commonly known as the Director of Christian Education.

At the very outset of this work in Chapter One an attempt is made to face honestly some of the weaknesses and problems of church education but also to use these as a springboard for improvement. Quality of life and service is the standard set in the Bible for God's people. On this premise the whole work rests. Assuming that improvement is possible, Chapter Two is devoted to a discussion of the character of a program of improvement and supervision in the local church. Purpose, process, and product comprise the threefold aspect of evaluation. Chapter Three focuses on the person and work of the supervisor himself. He is a person of high professional attainment and Christian character and functions in the capacity of a group leader rather than that of "boss."

At the heart of supervision and at the center of improvement lies the matter of evaluation. In Chapter Four the nature of the evaluation process is revealed and how it can be applied at the levels of philosophy, objectives, standards, and the implementation of needed changes.

In Chapter Five the procedures of evaluation are applied to the total church program of education in the local church and directions are indicated on what needs to be done in improving the total program with its constituent elements.

The whole matter of improvement and supervision comes to sharpest focus when applied to the improvement of teaching and learning. In the classroom is where the teaching ministry reaches its height. Much attention is given to the matter of improvement of instruction and what individual and group methods are employed to this end in Chapter Six. Product evaluation in terms of individual growth and development highlights the importance of pupil learning. Attention is focused on how this can be evaluated and improved. The chapter closes with a discussion of the evaluation of the supervisor himself and that of the program of supervision.

The term "church education" is used to identify that kind of Christian education which functions in the local church. It is to be distinguished, therefore, from Christian education found on the one hand in Christian day schools and parochial schools and on the other hand at the higher levels of Christian colleges, Bible colleges, and special schools. The term "total church program" encompasses that of the Sunday school and other agencies of teaching and learning involving children, youth, and adults and weekday activities. A parallel term is that of "church school."

Conceivably, the book should be of interest to church school workers, pastors, and church leaders. It should be equally useful as a textbook in college and seminary classes of Christian education. It could serve as a guide for study by individuals and groups, such as workers' conferences. Several illustrations of actual and practical materials used in church work by supervisors are given in the appendices. Suggestions on questions for class discussions and local church group meeting discussions are given at the end of each chapter. Suggestions for research and a bibiography may also be found at the end.

The questions posed at the chapter endings should not only be found useful in discussions but might prove to be helpful in evaluation on the part of supervisors and directors of Christian education in carrying on their functions. The suggestions for research could also serve as guides to experimentation.

Most books on supervision in the field of secular education focus almost exclusively on the improvement of instruction. While this also comprises very largely the primary emphasis in this work, attention is also given to the question of evaluating and improving the total program of church education. Due to the restricted nature of teaching in most churches because of the relatively small teaching staffs involved, supervision in church education has been broadened to include program evaluation and improvement without at the same time neglecting that of teacher and learner improvement.

Acknowledgement is made to the many people and resources contributing in one way or another to the ideas and concepts set forth. Expressions of gratitude go also to publishers who granted permissions to quote from their works.

The problems of evaluation, supervision, and improvement are complex and elusive. Many variables are involved. Solutions to problems are often no more than guesses, but hopefully expert guesses. Thus, one purpose of this volume is to make church workers and supervisors more sensitive to their problems, more appreciative of the tasks involved, and more careful in planning evaluation and problem-solving efforts.

Improving Church Education

Outline for Chapter One

The Need for a Program of Improvement and Supervision in Church Education

A. Quality—the Standard

1. Quality Required
2. Quality Demanded
3. Quality Anticipated
4. Quality Secured
5. Quality Supervised

B. The Need for Improvement and Supervision

1. Complexity of the Educational Task
2. Changing Demands of Society
3. Criteria of Values
4. Challenge to Supervision

Questions for Class Discussion

Questions for Local Church Use

Notes for Chapter One

CHAPTER ONE

The Need for a Program of Improvement and Supervision in Church Education

A. Quality—the Standard

1. *Quality Required.* We are living in a day when the emphasis on quality living and service is constantly emphasized. This is true no less for the church. If the church is to continue its influence on society, it must minister to society. In an age of science and technology demands are made to operate at a high level of competence.

What about the church? Paul wrote to Timothy, "Study to show thyself approved unto God, a workman that needeth not to be ashamed, rightly dividing the word of truth" (2 Tim. 2:15). Here the word "study," not only has mental implications but in the original instructs one to make all possible speed in these matters. Study—with all possible speed to

1. Be spiritual people—"approved"
2. Be singular workmen—"not to be ashamed"
3. Be skillful servants—"rightly dividing the word"

2. *Quality Demanded.* In the light of the accomplishments of twentieth century living, education has been under fire from many angles. Church education has not escaped its share of criticism. In 1957, an article in *Life* magazine by Wesley Schrader stirred up much controversy and anxiety when he maintained that the Sunday school was the most wasted hour in our lives. Additional articles

by other writers followed. Criticism of practices in church education have been numerous.

Charges Leveled

1. Inefficiency
2. Wasted time
3. Untrained teachers
4. Bad methods
5. Irrelevancy
6. Unproductive
7. Dull teaching
8. Decreasing enrollments

Weaknesses Indicated

1. In general attitude
    a. Sunday school not taken seriously
    b. Many pastors too busy for Sunday school
    c. Many pastors do not participate
    d. Adults not studying
    e. Loss of youth confidence
    f. Adult bad example
    g. Parents send children
    h. Drop-out problem great
    i. Learn little
    j. Public school caricatures the work
2. Inferior instruction
3. Total teaching time insufficient
4. Volunteer workers unqualified, untrained, and unprepared
5. Poor attendance

3. *Quality Anticipated.* Never before has the church had so many resources at hand. Blueprints and standards of church education are available. Many church groups have developed comprehensive programs and helpful guidance materials. Leader guides, curriculum materials,

audio-visual materials, leadership training aids, and suggestions for buildings and equipment have never been more evident than now. It remains only for the leadership to envision the possibilities and use the resources available.

4. *Quality Secured.* At least three criteria must be observed if quality is to be secured. A great deal of rethinking must be done:

1. We must reaccept the challenge to the Sunday school
2. We must reorient our philosophy of the Sunday school
3. We must readjust our methods in the Sunday school

The Sunday school began under Robert Raikes by rising to the challenge of the day in which he lived. The character and quality of twentieth century living demands the character and quality needed in twentieth century education. Pastors must change their minds about church education and give much time to the program. We must maintain the attitude that the work of the church can be done better when supported and directed by the work of church education. The whole church should be involved in teaching and learning. Our methods must be up-to-date, our programs must be interesting, our workers must be trained, our resources must be made available, and evangelism must permeate all that we do.

5. *Quality Supervised.* Improvement can be secured, but it is hard work. It calls for analysis, measurement, evaluation, experimentation, faith, prayer, courage, and action. The skills of supervision, when brought to bear on the needs observed in church education, will go far in securing improved quality of work. Using the knowledge available the various procedures which result in improvement may be summed up in the work of supervision. Here analyses of program activities and objectives are made and

appropriate plans made to secure the proper results. Progress is determined on the basis of the application of evaluation techniques by the supervisor and workers in ascertaining to what extent objectives are attained and procedures used are effective.

One of the great needs in church education today is to develop a new appreciation for the work of supervision in the program of church education among laymen and particularly at the level of teaching and learning the Christian faith. This volume has been dedicated to throwing light on this task.

Nothing will be of greater encouragement to church workers than to see steady improvement in the quality of the work they do. Evidences of this will be seen in greater commitment to Christ, more enthusiasm on the part of workers and pupils, greater knowledge of the Word of God, expanded activities of Christian service, more rewarding Christian fellowship, more meaningful participation in the life and work of the church, and, hopefully, an increase in resources as well as larger numbers of people involved.

B. The Need for Improvement and Supervision

1. *Complexity of the Educational Task.* Previous mention was made of the need of supervision in achieving a standard of quality education. Beyond this, however, lies a need seen in the very complexity of the educational task. In all forms of education there has developed a much broader concept of teaching and learning. Teachers not only impart factual knowledge, but they are called upon to

inculcate attitudes, develop necessary skills, strengthen loyalties, promote allegiance to our way of life, and reinforce moral codes. Church education, no less, faces a tremendous task. It affects all of life. Teaching the content of the faith, developing Christian habits and attitudes, motivating character by Christian ideals, and transforming both individuals and society is a tremendous undertaking. To expect volunteer layworkers to accomplish these things without supervisory assistance is expecting too much.

Adding to the complexity of the task are such matters as vast increases in knowledge, both inside and outside the church, expansions in size and enrollments, as well as new developments in teaching-learning techniques. All of these things place greater demands upon church educational workers to keep up, to study more, to keep informed, to do more, all of which demand supervisory services. Beginners need assistance and experienced workers need guidance. Great need is felt for the integration and coordination of activities and resources which affect the purposes and program of the church school.

Increasingly education is becoming a profession and a science. As such it is constantly drawing upon the findings of other sciences, such as psychology, sociology, biology, and research. This requires inservice training and learning, a continuous process. Professional growth is imperative to successful educators. The supervisor helps motivate workers to this end and plans the program to provide it. While the church is way behind in this aspect, the very nature of the task demands it. Some progress is being made however.

2. *Changing Demands of Society.* The twentieth century has brought with it a complex civilization, searching scien-

tific enquiry, skeptical attitudes, and undisciplined freedom, all of which have immensely increased the task of the church educator. Nothing less than the best in church education can face such demands. Largely untrained layworkers must have the assistance of supervision in meeting the demands of current living and service. In the face of this changing culture supervision can help provide coordination of effort, a sense of direction, and creativeness, in the midst of change. Most certainly supervision can help provide emotional support in the face of change.

Supervision really has a social basis. For many years now the advocates of democracy have pointed out the advantages of education in a democratic setting which leads to the exercising of democratic leadership, resulting in the releasing and coordinating of the creative energies of the members of the group. Leadership has the responsibility for helping the group reach valid commitments cooperatively and for following through on such commitments. Thus the nature of democracy and leadership call for supervisors who can devote time and talents to stimulating creative efforts toward improvement, to coordinating such efforts, and to following through on group commitments. In the church the concepts of Christian love and freedom would lead to an endorsement of this position but also under the leadership of the Holy Spirit.

3. *Criteria of Values.* The very nature of the Christian education task in the local church gives one a sense of priority and high value. In the face of evolutionary theories and influences both in society and education, supervision can assist educational workers in the church to hold firmly to a "sense of the divine" in our work and to a high concept of the pupil, not only as a creative, thinking,

intending creature, but also as a child of God redeemed and transformed by grace divine. To work with this kind of person is a high calling of God indeed!

Modern education stresses the importance of personality development. In the church this centers in the development of Christlike personality and Christian maturity. There is no greater work, in fact it is a ministry, in becoming co-workers with God to this end. In providing teachers and workers with professional assistance, supervision contributes directly to this end. The importance of the product, therefore, shows the need for and function of supervision in the church school.

The importance of Christian education in the life of the church shows further need for supervision. Traditionally, the teaching program of the church has contributed a large share of church membership, prospects for enlargement, and trained church workers. Thus, the church is coming to see more and more in Christian education a most effective mode of evangelism, a means of building Christian character, of creating the church of tomorrow, and reconstructing elements of society according to the will of God—of fulfilling the Great Commission.

The Sunday school still is the greatest single recruiting and evangelistic agency in the church, in spite of its problems and shortcomings. Aside from the home, it provides the largest exposure for providing instruction in the things of God. This fact alone should spur efforts to supervise the work and improve its quality.

4. *Challenge to Supervision.* The justification for a program of supervision in the local church lies largely within the framework of the needs present and as expressed above. The challenge comes to supervision, therefore, to

meet such needs. Here is revealed the legitimate functions of supervision, leading to judgment of the appropriateness of activities and techniques, and providing guidance derived from principles used to develop the supervisory program.

While much progress has been made in church education through the years, one must admit that the church's educational program is still unsatisfactory in many ways. Problems still exist and herein lies the challenge which comes to supervision—to solve these problems. Some of these problems were indicated in the previous discussion of the need for quality education in Section One of this chapter. Chief among these problems are the following:

1. Defective and fruitless teaching
2. Inadequate time
3. Untrained and inexperienced teachers and workers
4. Limited physical and resource materials
5. Lack of financial support
6. Low standards of pupil achievement and interest
7. Lack of parental cooperation
8. Absence of a coordinated program
9. Low level of application and appreciation of the importance of Christian education
10. Absence of good spirit and enthusiasm

In addition to such general problems there are those likewise which center in the work of the teacher who should have the particular attention and help of the supervisor. McNerney has classified such problems for public school teachers into seven categories.

1. Problems of attitude—resentment, discouragement, etc.
2. Problems of motivation—low state of pupil morale

3. Problems of administration—inefficiency, disorganization
4. Problems of evaluation—grading, measurement practices
5. Problems of curriculum—tradition, change
6. Problems of method—choice, grading, problem pupils
7. Problems of pre-service training—getting a job, orientation[1]

Many church education teachers have problems in these same areas as well as in others. The task of the supervisor is to help teachers solve these and their other many problems.

In meeting the challenge which comes to supervision, Swearingen has suggested three big areas which invite effort: (1) to serve and facilitate, (2) to stimulate creativity, and (3) to aid in the integration of goals.[2] Teachers are to be helped to be better teachers and to get better results. They need assistance in seeing the educational process as a whole, to develop a clear vision of values and ultimate goals, sustaining a clear sense of purpose. Most certainly church school teachers can learn from these things as well, and supervisors in church education should guide teachers and workers toward the realization of these matters all within the framework of the Christian faith and life of the church.

Questions for Class Discussion

1. Outline the role of the church school and its primary objectives.
2. How can teachers help achieve the objectives of the church and church school?

3. Discussion of the Scriptural basis of Christian and church education.
4. Discussion of the meaning of teaching and learning from a study of the original languages of Scripture.
5. Is there a legitimate basis for the criticisms leveled at Sunday school work today?
6. What arguments can be given for or against the hypothesis that the effectiveness of the educational program of the church can be determined by a continuing appraisal of characteristics and behavior of pupils both in the church school and daily life?
7. Interview several Sunday school teachers and summarize their reactions to the question, "what do you expect in the way of supervision?" Then interview several beginner teachers and find out what they expect. Compare the two groups of answers.
8. How can church people be aroused to a sense of real concern for quality Christian education in the local church?

Questions for Local Church Use

1. What is the role of the church in society?
2. Study places where the local church needs to improve.
3. Do we need a supervisor in our church?
4. Discuss the reasons that may underlie the inability to achieve maximum effectiveness in teaching. How do these reasons reveal the need for supervision?
5. Discuss ways and means of arousing the church to an appreciation of its educational task.
6. Define supervision as used in the local church. How can it be introduced?
7. How can the strengths and weaknesses of local church education be discovered?
8. What are the highest values that should motivate work for God?
9. Do you think criticisms of the Sunday school are justified?

Notes for Chapter One

1. McNerney, Chester T., *Educational Supervision* (New York, McGraw-Hill, 1951), p. 2ff.
2. Swearingen, Mildred E., *Supervision of Instruction* (Boston, Allyn and Bacon, 1962), p. 13.

Outline for Chapter Two

The Character of Improvement for Church Education

A. The Nature of Supervisory Behavior

   1. Background of Supervision
   2. Definitions of Supervision
   3. Terms and Ideas of Supervision
   4. Concepts and Types of Supervision
   5. Supervision in Public Education and Church Education
   6. The Dimensions of Supervision

B. The Process of Supervisory Behavior

   1. The Problems of Supervision
   2. The Purposes and Functions of Supervision
   3. The Processes of Supervisions

C. The Principles of Supervisory Behavior

   1. The Significance and Principles of Supervision
   2. The Principles of Supervision in Church Education

Questions for Class Discussion

Questions for Local Church Use

Notes for Chapter Two

CHAPTER TWO

The Character of a Program of Improvement and Supervision in Church Education

A. The Nature of Supervisory Behavior

1. *Background of Supervision.* The practice of supervision is a relatively new thing in all kinds of education. Early supervision in secular education was characterized by rather authoritarian policies and practices. Strict conformity to arbitrary standards was required. While these practices continued into the nineteenth century, a shift from lay to professional responsibility for inspection was noted. With the great expansion of education all along the line, the latter part of the century saw the call of largely inadequate teachers for assistance. Thus, with the opening of the twentieth century the professional literature revealed a shift away from authoritarian methods to more cooperative ones.

After 1935 supervision in the secular schools was molded by the principles of cooperation, creativity, and democracy. Previous to this, emphasis was placed on efficiency rather than on growth. Afterward, stress was placed on goals, the nature of the pupil, values, human relations, and democratic processes.

With the development of psychology as a subject matter discipline, a new concept of child nature, new definitions of teaching and learning, and new developments in curriculum produced a revolution in education. Consequently, supervision has undergone drastic changes. A new appreciation for democratic ideals led to the concept of supervision as the cooperation of teachers, administrators, and supervisors in solving the problems of improving instruction. Currently, such factors as leadership, cooperation, coordination, growth, guidance, creativity, wholeness, and improvement are stressed.

Probably a formal approach to the problem of supervision in the church arose from a sense of need to improve the quality and practice of church education. Perhaps no point in history can be cited to show the inception of supervision as a practice in church education. It can be observed, however, that with the rise of the office of director of Christian education, and in the face of developments in a departmentalized Christian education program for the local church, the need for supervisory service was recognized. Since that time church leaders have drawn largely from the developments of supervision in public school education. Principles and practices, thus borrowed, are evaluated in the light of biblical and theological principles and adapted for use in the program of church education.

2. *Definition of Supervision.* There are many definitions of supervision, but perhaps the most common one of all centers in "the improvement of instruction." What seems to be commonly held is helping the teacher on the job. In church education, supervision is broadened to include, not only the teacher, but the whole educative process. Supervision is something done to help workers carry out assignments and responsibilities properly. More specifically, supervision is a planned program for the improvement of instruction, a service concerned with instruction and its improvement. It stresses teacher growth and creativeness, but does not single out the teacher as incompetent. It plans

to help workers carry out their own plans by focusing on the total elements which affect learning. We conclude, therefore, that supervision is a complex and multiple task often intangible in nature, but it most certainly is one of the functions that is essential to the operation of a good church school.

3. *Terms and Ideas of Supervision.* An educator asked a group of teachers to list several words that come to mind when the term "supervision" is mentioned. Among the terms listed were:

Advisor	Dictator
Helper	Counselor
Helping Teacher	Friend
Coordinator	Visitor
Consultant	Resource Person
Leader	

In some circles there has been the tendency to generalize about the term "supervision" and thus confuse it with that of "administration." It is recognized that there are similarities and overlapping in function here. Basically the difference between the two lies primarily in the *reason* for an activity. For purposes of clarity the two terms are contrasted as follows:

Administration refers to	Supervision refers to
1. Determination of aims	1. Stressing improvement
2. Establishment of policies	2. Seeking quality
3. Overseeing operation	3. Realization of goals
4. Management	4. Leadership
5. Setting up organization	5. Leadership training
6. Worker placement	6. Highlights of teaching and learning
7. Financial program	

8. Resources
9. Maintenance

Major emphasis: breadth, scope

7. Efficiency
8. Problem-solving
9. Seeking results, effectiveness
10. Setting of standards
11. Inspection
12. Teaching process

Major emphasis: depth

Supervision, in one sense, may be thought of as a specialization within administration. It, along with administration, is concerned with management, but such management for the supervisor is on a very personal level. Supervisors deal with workers, not according to function, but as individuals.

While administration has the same goals as those of supervision, the former is concerned indirectly with program improvement through such matters as budget, facilities, etc. Supervision is concerned directly with improvement through the teaching-learning process.

4. *Concepts and Types of Supervision.* One's philosophy of education determines directly his educational practices. Different philosophies will favor varying concepts of supervision, but the particular philosophy one holds will determine directly his concept of supervision.

A study of the literature reveals several concepts and types of supervision. The following chart identifies the several concepts with their associated practices in supervision:

Supervisory Concept	*Supervisory Practice*
1. Autocratic, or Authoritarian	1. Supervision by command, coercion
2. Authoritative	2. Supervision according to plan

3. Inspectional	3. Supervision by investigation
4. Invitational	4. Supervision by request
5. Organismic	5. Supervision by integration
6. Democratic	6. Supervision by cooperation, group activity
7. Scientific	7. Supervision by measurable facts and unbiased judgment
8. Creative	8. Supervision by motivation, initiative, cooperation, originality, experiment
9. Corrective	9. Supervision by diplomatic suggestion
10. Preventive	10. Supervision by anticipation of difficulties

Perhaps no one program of supervision rests solely upon one concept. The current tendency is to be eclectic, using the best ideas to guide practices to optimum success. Almost no one would justify supervision by means of coercion or dictatorship. Most certainly Christian love would not countenance this in church education. Obviously, most successful education of any kind must be planned, even preplanned, so that authoritarianism in this way is useful.A substantial amount of authoritative leadership is necessary to any successful educational program. The values of democratic and creative ideals must be brought in however.

In considering and comparing all of these concepts of supervision one can see the strategic place of the supervisor in all of them. General agreement, however, is missing regarding the philosophy of techniques, the nature of education and the educative process. Perhaps one's concept of teaching in the final analysis determines his concept of supervision. The supervisor is really a teacher of teachers. His relation therefore is that of a teacher rather than an officer or administrator. Essentially, therefore, one might conceivably find aspects of all of the above concepts of supervision embraced in a total concept of supervision. Looking at it from this standpoint it is possible for us to conclude that supervision is teaching workers, and, particularly teachers, to achieve improvement, employing whatever agent, force, or method which is consistent with Christian principles and the Christian faith to achieve the goals of the church. We conclude, therefore, that supervision in the church school must be consistent with the program of the church and in keeping with what the church demands. In a sense supervision is also a screening agency by which new ideas, methods, and materials are incorporated into the program of the church and its school.

5. *Supervision in Public Education and Church Education.* While it is possible to borrow principles from general education, we must not lose sight of the particular situation in church education. Public school people are professionals and as such improvement is expected and demanded. In church education most workers are volunteers, largely untrained and inexperienced.

A major difference in quality is obviously apparent. While public education is largely concerned with objective elements in education, such as personality, skills, vocation, knowledge, and citizenship, church education specializes in the more subjective aspects of the pupil—his spiritual welfare and development. This adds a dimension to the work of supervision not present in public education.

6. *Dimensions of Supervision.* Supervision under church auspices should be viewed in the light of the total church

program. Attempts, however, should be made to discover the distinctives of supervision as a field of endeavor.

The purpose of a school, inside or outside the church, is to produce learning based on instruction. The goal to be held in view is the development of the learner. There are other products connected with school operation, such as pupil care, but that which holds priority is the teaching-learning process. There are several functions of a church, such as worshiping, witnessing, organization, administration, and serving others, but the main purpose of the church school is teaching and learning the Christian faith and life.

In the operation of a church several functions are apparent:

1. Proclamation
2. Witnessing
3. Worshiping
4. Fellowship
5. Celebrating
6. Teaching

The purpose of the school of the church is to provide assistance to the church in being the church and performing the work of the church, as well as to specialize in the teaching ministry.

To accomplish its responsibilities the church prepares for its work through

1. Organization—stressing structure, relationships
2. Administration—stressing management, operation, resources, service
3. Supervision—stressing improvement, evaluation, effectiveness.

Supervision, therefore, has two diminsions in church work: (1) to deepen the quality of the work of the church through its schools, and (2) to deepen and strengthen the quality of the teaching-learning process and ministry. The functions of organization and administration, therefore, can be said to be supportive in character to the work of supervision.

B. The Process of Supervisory Behavior

1. *The Problems of Supervision.* Obviously, supervision becomes a means to an end in meeting the needs of the church in its work as a body and as a school. To do its work, supervision needs to move beyond general needs to the identification of specific problems if the work is to be most effective. Areas in which representative problems arise for the church school supervisor include the following:

1. How to get a program of supervision started
2. How to carry on a program of supervision
3. Problems involving morale
4. Problems involving inservice training of workers
5. Problems involving leadership development
6. Problems involving human relations
7. Problems involving how to work together
8. Problems involving personnel administration
9. Problems involving curriculum improvement
10. Problems involving classroom instruction
11. Problems involving evaluation and measurement
12. Problems involving the improvement of worship
13. Problems involving the improvement of service training and activity
14. Problems involving the improvement of social and recreational activity

15. Problems involving self-evaluation
16. Problems involving age level categories
17. Problems involving the integration of agencies in the total program.

2. *Purposes and Function of Supervision.* Because of the comparative newness of the field of supervision in the church, few efforts have been made to list the purposes of supervision in the church school. Frank M. McKibben is one of the few who cite such purposes.

1. To guide those responsible for Christian education in studying the total program as it is being provided in the light of the most representative standards of their denomination and of Protestantism in general;
2. To lead workers into a fuller understanding of the nature and meaning of Christian nurture and of the conditions necessary for its fullest realization;
3. To aid workers in the various aspects of the program to determine the objectives they may seek in their work and to help them discover the extent to which they are being achieved;
4. To develop among teachers and leaders a willingness and ability to analyze and objectively to evaluate the procedures and materials they are using with a view to determining the elements of strength and weakness and to undertake specific measures of improvement;
5. To develop schedules and measuring instruments by which the program may be more accurately evaluated and to train workers in their use;
6. To carry forward continuously a program of enlistment, motivation, training, and placement in service of men and women who will be needed to carry forward the total program;
7. To help educate the parents and total constituency of

> the church in the necessity and importance of Christian education and to encourage and provide for their active participation in and support of the program.[1]

In the light of such purposes the functions of the supervisor are many. He is called upon to be teacher, administrator, innovator, evaluator, motivator, leader, counselor, coordinator, resource person and diagnostician.

The involvements of supervision are many. The supervisor in the church school is involved in

1. Selecting workers
2. Motivating workers
3. Teaching workers
4. Measuring workers
5. Correcting workers
6. Commending workers
7. Rewarding workers
8. Eliminating workers
9. Harmonizing workers

His job involves many procedures, such as:

1. Diagnosing difficulties
2. Tracing inefficiency
3. Prescribing remedies
4. Establishing objectives
5. Developing a comprehensive, well-balanced program
6. Evaluating teachers
7. Guiding staff relationships
8. Encouraging leadership
9. Exercising skills in human relations
10. Exercising skills in group procedures
11. Exercising skill in personnel administration.

The ultimate purpose or goal of supervision in the church school is God's glory, the accomplishment of His will and the pre-eminence of Jesus Christ. A second general purpose is to supply leadership to teachers and workers in the production of Christlike personality through the teaching-learning process, involving the Word of God and the work of the Holy Spirit. In common with general education the immediate purpose is to achieve quality in the program and teaching-learning process to accomplish the ends of the ultimate purposes stated.

It remains to supplement secular insights with those insights from the spiritual realm. In the church no proper concept of the function of supervision would be adequate without emphasis being given to the place of divine revelation in providing guidelines and standards for the supervisory program and procedures. The work of the Holy Spirit enables the human supervisor to become a coworker with God in the work. Great stress, therefore, should be laid on the quality of Christian character and qualifications for this important work.

3. *The Processes of Supervision.* A wide variety of terms suggesting the processes involved in supervision follows:

Planning Processes

Thinking
Determining objectives
Developing procedures
Scheduling
Forecasting
Programming

Leading Processes

Decision-making
Selecting people
Stimulating
Initiating
Demonstrating
Advising

Organizing Processes

Establishing standards
Resource allocating
Establishing relationships
Distributing functions
Coordinating
Delegating
Designing organizational structure
Developing policies

Controlling Processes

Directing
Expediting
Applying sanctions

Communicating	Taking corrective action
Suggesting	Dismissing people
Encouraging	Reprimanding
Innovating	Regulating
Motivating	*Assessing Processes*
Facilitating	
Illustrating	Judging performance
	Measuring performance
	Researching

For church education a recent listing of processes was made by Kenneth O. Gangel. They are:

Placement	Feedback
Observation	Resource
Evaluation	Involvement[2]

C. The Principles of Supervisory Behavior

1. *The Significance and Principles of Supervision.* From the study of the nature and process of supervision thus far it is quite evident that supervision is a very significant enterprise in the proper operation of a school. To provide aid to church school teachers alone is sufficient justification for its inclusion in the church program. The processes of studying defects and providing remedies for them is a most encouraging contribution to success. The reconstruction and improvement of the curriculum, the unifying and correlating of all educational forces together with improved methodologies all call for supervision. As someone has said, supervision is actually evangelistic in character where improvement of personnel and program stop losses and issue in the salvation of souls.

Further significance of supervision is seen in its very

process. To study, analyze, and compare what *is* with what *ought to be* and *could be* is an important enterprise. That workers may become more skillful, accurate, intelligent, enthusiastic, spiritual, and fruitful through the program of supervision is a very significant accomplishment. A study of the literature of general education reveals many statements of principles to guide work in the field of supervision. Most of such statements reflect a basis laid in the democratic way of life, modern leadership principles, processes of group dynamics, and findings of science.

2. *Principles of Supervision in Church Education.* The literature reveals that little writing along these lines has been done by church educators. The tendency has been to borrow from public and general education sources and adapt such principles to church work.

Statements among more conservative and evangelical educators have also been few. Kenneth Gangel expressed some principles in his short discussion on how supervision is carried out.

1. The effective administrator is completely open with his workers regarding his concept of the supervisory role.
2. Much time, prayer, and personal counseling are required in successful supervision.
3. The supervisor will be alert, objective, clear, and well-organized in evaluation processes.
4. The supervisor will be as positive as possible in the personal interview.
5. The successful supervisor will emphasize the *team* nature of the task and the important place the teacher has on the team.[3]

Vernon R. Kraft in his work *Director of Christian Education* gave wide consideration to principles which direct the work of this officer, scattered throughout his work.[4] In a previous volume the author likewise gave special attention to the work of the supervisor and to the nature of supervision in the program of the local church education.[5]

Questions for Class Use

1. Examine the definitions and functions of supervision presented in Chapter One. List any items you think were omitted or with which you are not in agreement.
2. What makes supervision both Christian and democratic?
3. What is the difference between supervision and administration?
4. How can supervisors help teachers and workers be more resourceful and take the initiative in their work?
5. How can supervisors help church workers formulate a sound educational philosophy?
6. How can the supervisor become the coordinating and unifying force in the church school?
7. Discuss the evidences of creative supervision.
8. What kind of supervisory program can be planned in a small church?
9. Develop a Christian philosophy of leadership.
10. Study factors which affect leadership.
11. Discuss the personality traits of a good supervisor.

Questions for Local Church Use

1. Discuss the results one expects to receive from supervision. Do not focus on matters like cooperation or participation, but rather upon people and conditions involved in teaching and learning.
2. What are the supervisory functions of the pastor, general superintendent, and department superintendent?

3. In what ways can supervisors help church teachers feel more secure and confident in their work?
4. Discuss a plan for discovering the needs of workers and teachers.
5. Make a list of instructional problems in your church.
6. Study to what extent supervision goes on in the church school and possible ways to improve it.
7. Create a job analysis or description for a Director of Christian Education.
8. What qualities are you looking for in a Director of Christian Education?

Notes for Chapter Two

1. McKibben, Frank M., *Guiding Workers in Christian Education* (Nashville, Abingdon, 1953), p. 12.
2. Gangel, Kenneth D., *Leadership for Church Education* (Chicago, Moody, 1970), pp. 297–98.
3. Ibid., p. 299.
4. Kraft, Vernon R., *The Director of Christian Education* (Chicago, Moody, 1957).
5. Byrne, H. W., *Christian Education for the Local Church,* rev. ed. (Grand Rapids, Zondervan, 1963), Chapter 4.

Outline for Chapter Three

The Leadership for a Program of Improvement and Supervision in Church Education

A. The Supervisor as Person

1. The Definition of a Supervisor
2. The Role of a Supervisor
3. The Duties of a Supervisor
4. The Philosophy of a Supervisor
5. The Personnel of Supervision
6. The Positions of Supervision
7. The Levels of Supervision
8. Relationships of Supervision
9. Qualifications of the Supervisor
10. Selection and Preparation of Supervisors

B. The Supervisor as Educational Leader

1. Definition of Educational Leadership
2. Importance of Educational Leadership
3. The Context of Educational Leadership
4. The Christian Concept of Leadership
5. Qualities and Skills of Leadership
6. Functions and Types of Christian Leadership
7. Factors Affecting Leadership
8. Developing Adequate Leadership

Questions for Class Discussion

Questions for Local Church Use

Notes for Chapter Three

CHAPTER THREE

The Leadership for a Program of Improvement and Supervision in the Local Church

A. The Supervisor as Person

1. *Definition of the Supervisor.* The supervisor actually is an in-service teacher of teachers, whose function is to assist them in improving their efforts. In the church this concept has been broadened to include the supervisor as teacher of all workers to deepen the quality and effectiveness of the total program.

2. *The Role of the Supervisor.* The role of the supervisor can be seen in terms of the functions of supervision as part of the administrative program of the school.

Expectancies for supervisors seem to fall into four categories: (1) they provide inspiration, (2) they help develop programs of in-service education, (3) they facilitate group work, and (4) they help create a climate for growth. All of these are directed by democratic principles.

Drawing heavily also on principles of leadership, the role of the supervisor in general and public education is that of being a supervisory statesman, leaning heavily on the inspirational and decision-making elements. Such a role is based, not on skills of human relations primarily, but rather on the character of good education and a good school. In this concept of his role the supervisor will provide assistance in the formulation of aims and goals and in motivating the school personnel with a sense of mission.

This latter concept should be acceptable to church workers. Not only are supervisors here concerned with the specifics and mechanics involved in the program of supervision in the church, but they should constantly be motivating people to accept, understand, and work by the principles of good Christianity and quality Christian education. The goals of accomplishing the will of God as revealed in the Word of God thus become dynamically relevant.

The concept of the supervisor's role as master teacher and leader is held very widely in church circles today. The progress of specialization, which as a trend is now in the church, has not developed sufficiently to change substantially the traditional concept of the supervisor as one person with master teacher abilities. Perhaps the size of the church and economic factors have served to inhibit this development in the church. One could hope that the concept of the supervisor as educational statesman would soon be realized in the church.

A parallel development in the church may be seen which led to the need for a professional worker known as Director of Christian Education who would do the work of the supervisor in the local church school. As churches and Sunday schools grew larger, and as the departmentalized system took hold, churches began to see the need for a new worker in the church school. The pastor and general superintendent found themselves working more and more at the operational level of administration and less with the improvement of teaching. Thus, the Director of Christian Education fills an important role as a member of the staff of ministers responsible for the work of the church.

3. *The Duties of the Supervisor.* Actually, previous discussion on the functions of supervision and the role of the

supervisor have indicated categories of responsibility for this worker.

Lucio and McNeil have indicated at least six kinds of duties for the supervisor.

1. Planning—individually and in groups; he helps to develop policies and programs in his field
2. Administration—he makes decisions, coordinates the work of others and issues necessary directions
3. Supervision—through conferences and consultations, he seeks to improve the quality of instruction
4. Curriculum development—he participates directly in the formulation of objectives, selection of school experiences, preparation of teaching guides, and selection of instructional aids
5. Demonstration teaching—he gives and arranges for classroom demonstrations of teaching methods, use of aids, and other *direct* help to classroom teaching
6. Research—through systematic surveys, experiments, and studies, he explores current conditions and recommends changes in practice.[1]

In the church the Director of Christian Education as supervisor would definitely be expected to be, in addition to the above matters and in keeping with the principle of Christian fellowship, (1) a spiritual counselor, and (2) a friend.

Among evangelicals, in pamphlet No. 101 entitled "Guidelines—The Church and the Director of Christian Education," the National Association of Directors of Christian Education suggest eight duties of the supervisor:

1. He will help the church develop an educational viewpoint in all its work

2. He will provide executive leadership to the board or committee of Christian education
3. He will assist the pastor by relieving him of administrative responsibilities relative to the education program
4. He will bring into focus the educational objectives of the church program
5. He will unify the educational thrust of the church
6. He will train lay leadership to serve the program
7. He will introduce and develop new ideas and ministry with the church
8. He will explore and interpret trends in the field of Christian Education.

4. *The Philosophy of the Supervisor.* No one can be helped to any large extent by a supervisor unless he has a philosophy of education and supervision to guide him. He must set his ultimate goals and methodologies by this philosophy. Due to the extreme spiritual nature of the church, supervisors in the church school would be expected to follow the ethical, moral, biblical, and spiritual values of the constituency he expects to serve. His is an important position because he is involved in decisions which govern lives. He is in a position of power and responsibility. The particular thrust of the supervisor's spiritual values will be determined more or less by his theological stance—liberal or conservative, and shades of difference in between.

The philosophy of the supervisor embraces the way he goes about his work. The nature and functions of supervision plus the stated duties above denote the proper approach to his work. His philosophy of leadership has direct bearing here. Democratic processes when evoked stress teamwork, sharing, and freedom in serving Christ and the church. A dictatorial attitude will command by spoken and written directions in the spirit of personal authority.

The supervisor needs patience in making attempts to change attitudes and practices. He needs to be sympathetic, serving as a "listening post" and counselor to workers with problems and hang-ups. He seeks ideally to promote harmony and unity as a philosophy of workmanship. He should have deep appreciation for people and faith in their ability to learn and develop.

It will be wise perhaps for the supervisor to assume leadership initially in areas of least controversy. Once he demonstrates his competence here, he builds up confidence in others in his ability to lead in more controversial issues. Teachers are notoriously hard to change and without such confidence the supervisor cannot succeed as well.

In addition to the moral, ethical, spiritual, and psychological aspects of the supervisor's philosophy, there is also his concept of the educative process. Different philosophies will favor different ideas about supervision.

The experimentalist will approach his task with a tentative frame of mind, stressing research to find best answers, whereas the absolute philosopher will stress answers by means of personal authority.

Different psychologies advocate various approaches to supervision. Analytical psychologies will stress individual differences and measurement in supervision, whereas wholistic psychologies will emphasize teacher growth based upon democratic principles of cooperation and problem solving.

Likewise, one's theological position affects his supervisory practices. Liberal views tend to adjust themselves to a more open-ended procedure and life-view, whereas conservative and evangelicals views advocate and stress the centrality and authority of Christ and his Word.

5. *The Personnel of Supervision.* In a school system one will find many people at various levels involved in the work of supervision. There are those in the local school itself as well as those at administrative levels outside the individual school.

When one studies the availability of supervisors in the church, he finds, at least potentially, more than one might expect:

Supervisors Outside the Local Church

International Agencies
  World Christian Education Association
National Agencies, such as
  National Council of Churches of Christ
  National Association of Evangelicals
Denominational Agencies
  Field Secretaries
  National Departments of Sunday School
  Regional Department of Christian Education
  State Directors
  District Directors
Inter-denominational Agencies, such as
  National Sunday School Association

Supervisors Inside the Local Church

Official Board
Board of Christian Education
Pastor
Associate Pastor
Minister of Education
Director of Christian Education
Sunday School Superintendent
Divisional Superintendents
Department Superintendents
Helping Teachers
Volunteer Supervisors
Advisors (from public schools or other agencies)
Parents
Friends

- State Sunday School Associations
- Community Sunday School Associations
- Community Church Councils

Professional Organizations
Publishing Houses

6. *The Positions of Supervision.* Obviously, space in this work devoted to the description of positions of supervision in public education must be limited. It is not our purpose to discuss such work, nor is it our purpose to discuss supervisory services available to the local church from outside agencies. Following is a short discussion of key positions in the church and church school where supervision is relevant and dynamic. The position is named and then suggestions on supervisory practices for the position are indicated:

Pastor and Associates

1. Overseer
2. Evaluation
3. Inspection
4. Resource
5. Example
6. Worker training
7. Enthusiasm
8. Spiritual depth
9. Coordinator
10. Integrator
11. Mediator

Minister of Education and *Director of Christian Education*

1. Philosophy
2. Resources
3. Objectives
4. Unity
5. Coordination
6. Integration
7. Training
8. Surveys
9. Evaluation
10. New ideas

12. Counselor
13. Advisor
14. Motivator
15. Problem-solver
16. Standards
17. Leadership selections
18. Spiritual objectives
19. Building morals

Superintendents
(General and Department)

1. Stress standards
2. Stress good organization
3. Call for reports
4. Good communications
5. Teachers' meetings
6. Workers' conferences
7. Classroom visitation
8. Consultation
9. Committee work
10. Personal opinion
11. Praise or censure
12. Special studies on method
13. Special studies on curriculum
14. Recognition of achievement
15. Check facilities
16. Check resources
17. Morale
18. Help individual teachers
19. Stress training.

11. Trends
12. Diagnosis
13. Problem-solving
14. Needs
15. Planning
16. Promotion
17. Counselor
18. Organization
19. Communication
20. Team-work
21. Policies
22. Innovator
23. Diagnostician
24. Personal conferences
25. Classroom visitation
26. Placement
27. Good records

Specialists

1. Speeches
2. Demonstrations
3. Surveys
4. Resources
5. Consultation
6. Advisor
7. Motivations
8. Exhibits
9. Observation
10. Counseling

A study of the positions of supervision shows that official responsibilities have been scattered among many people on the church staff. Some work at the policy-making level, while others work more closely to the level of teaching. Thus, supervision from this standpoint is a distributive function and a common dimension in the expected role of church and church school leaders. Perhaps the following figure will illustrate this:

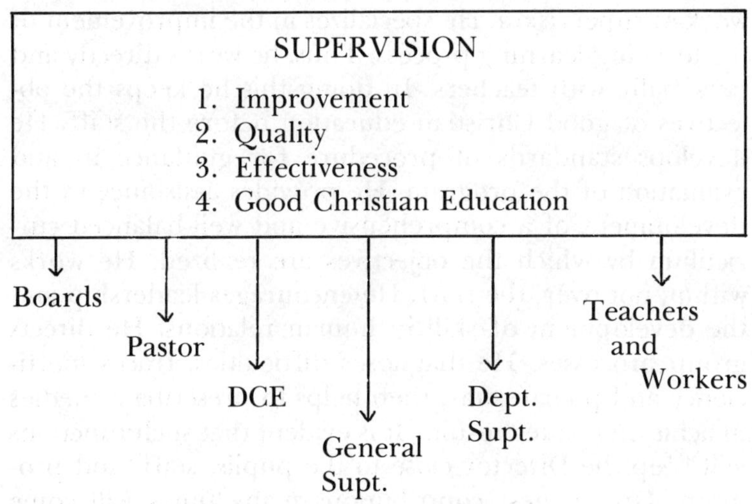

While the distributive function of supervision is recognized, as above, the work of supervision really centers most especially in the professional person known as the Director of Christian Education. While some other church officers and workers do supervisory work, the Director is a specialist. He has delegated responsibility from the governing boards of the church and the pastor to do his work. He works with the pastor and superintendents in a team relationship. The genius of his work lies in providing assistance fulltime to the lay workers in the church, integrating, correlating, coordinating the workers in an effort to deepen and improve the quality of their work.

In most churches the Director is called upon for general leadership and helpfulness, leadership training, some administration, teaching and shepherding workers, and is expected to promote the cause of Christian education in the church. His greatest opportunity, however, lies in his work of supervision. He specializes in the improvement of the teaching-learning process. Thus, he works directly and personally with teachers. In doing this he keeps the objectives of good Christian education before the staff. He develops standards of procedure for guidance in and evaluation of the program. He provides assistance in the development of a comprehensive and well-balanced curriculum by which the objectives are realized. He works within, not over, the staff. He encourages leadership and the development of skill in human relations. He directs group processes. He diagnoses difficulties, traces inefficiency and poor results, then helps to prescribe remedies in achieving better results. It is evident that such functions will keep the Director close to the pupils, staff, and program. His greatest contributions many times will come through working with people. It is obvious also that he must know the educational essentials of a good program and staff before good supervision can take place.

Divisional and departmental superintendents are supervisors. Age-group specialization calls for specialized knowledge and procedures in dealing with the various age groups. In the list of responsibilities for superintendents listed above, one finds many of their duties. Such duties, however, are graded to the level of the people dealt with. Such workers should be encouraged to secure formal training for their work where possible. Without this, constant reading, experimentation and observation prove helpful. When these workers sponsor studies on improvement better results are achieved.

Beyond, and perhaps above, individuals in the church program who have supervisory responsibilities and opportunities lies certain responsible administrative boards. Two important ones include the Official Board (governing body of the church) and the Board of Christian Education. Such boards may exercise supervisory responsibilities through cooperative planning, good administration, well-structured organizations, and policies which call for efficient, well-trained workers, good facilities, adequate financial support and sufficient resources for a total church program of education. Calling for reports of progress places emphasis on results.

Some assistance can be secured by calling in professors in Christian education from Christian schools, colleges and seminaries. Such people can provide evaluational, inspirational, and training services.

Some supervisory assistance is available from people who work in church councils, Sunday school associations, and professional organizations in church work. Denominational field officers often send staff out into local churches for such work. Selected publishing houses make available, often free of charge, administrative and curricular specialists who visit the local church for workshop and consultative services.

At the local church level, where we give primary attention, in addition to administrative leaders who supervise, some churches utilize special teachers or helping teachers, volunteers, and advisors. Such people may be educational assistants. Public school teachers with special sensitivity and qualifications for church work are helpful. Students in

Christian education are used at times for supervisory work. Churches with limited means look to such people. Care needs to be taken that such people are qualified, as far as possible, for the work.

Not to be overlooked in the list of people who at least affect supervision are individuals and parents. They express opinion on such matters as purposes and curriculum. They protest when the school does not measure up to their values. Parents teach teachers about their children. They are in a good position to interpret to the teacher an understanding of child needs, health, attitudes, and achievements. Even the children themselves contribute to good supervision by making teachers and workers aware of their needs, desires, successes and failures. In many ways, however, these and perhaps others contribute to school supervision, but we are not directly concerned with these at great length in this work.

7. *The Levels of Supervision.* At least four levels or areas can be identified at which the work of supervision takes place.

1. National level
2. Regional or state level
3. Community level
4. Local church level

The national level supervisory services are exercised by a national, denominational or interdenominational agency. The same is true at the state or regional level. In some towns councils of religious education supply supervisory services to local churches of the community. The local church, however, is where the greatest emphasis needs to be placed. In this work primary emphasis is laid at this level.

8. *Relationships of Supervision.* At least three categories of relationships of the supervisor can be identified:

1. Relations with administrators
2. Relations with teachers
3. Relations with the constituency

The first two of these categories focus on the local school situation, whereas the third centers in people outside the school situation. In public education the supervisor's relation with administration includes the Board of Education, Superintendents, Principals, Department Heads and Educational Specialists. In the church at this level, the supervisor, as Director of Christian Education, will be related to the Official Board, the Board of Christian Education, the Pastor, Associate Pastor, the General Superintendent, Divisional and Departmental Superintendents, and Educational. Specialists. Administrators are concerned with policies and organization, operating and supporting the school system. Supervision is concerned with depth, quality, and improvement, particularly of the teaching-learning process.

The only solid basis upon which all human relations can be firmly built is mutual respect for personalities. Dictatorial administration lacks the integrity of respecting each personality and thus will fail to build an adequate educational program. To this the church would add Christian love and fellowship as a basis of relationship and action.

Clearly the only sound basis for developing a program of supervision is democratic theory and action, the exemplification of attitudes of interest, respect, fairness, etc., in building cooperative relationships between people, the demonstration of a willingness to help people grow on the job, and the development of the ability to coordinate the work of the supervisor.

While administrators are called upon far more frequently to deal directly with the public, supervisors are occasionally called upon to work with individuals, groups, and agencies in the community, most certainly the home.

In the church the supervisor can be properly related to his constituency—the home and other publics to be served. Here two-way cooperation is also needed. The supervisor should review such contacts, not as incidental, but as special opportunities to advance the church and cause of Christian education.

In general, ways of dealing with the public should follow the highest standards of Christian ethics and principles of public relations. Some of the more specific ways a supervisor in the church can work with the various publics in the church include:

1. Open house
2. News bulletins
3. News letters
4. Committee work
5. Special events highlighting the teaching program
6. Parent-teacher organization (PTA in public school)
7. Visit homes
8. Adult Education program in the church
9. Worker participation in community life

It is in the third category stressing his relationship to teachers that the supervisor perhaps will do his best work. Here his professional abilities and skills in human relations are put to greatest use.

All teachers need supervision, not just the poor and weak ones. In stimulating growth both personal and professional the supervisor helps all teachers. In the face of higher standards and constant changes in the culture and educational system all teachers need assistance.

Teachers' needs vary widely according to preparation, experience, and teaching competence. Supervisors must step in wherever gaps appear and needs are made known.

New and inexperienced teachers will need special attention, particularly in getting adjusted to their colleagues, the educational environment and duties. The supervisor should be sensitive about these matters, ready to assess both strengths and weaknesses. Later on special attention will be given to ways and means of helping teachers with problems. Beyond these, however, is the need for continuous growth and in this the supervisor can help.

9. *Qualifications of the Supervisor.* Many studies have been made of personality factors among public educators. In the main they have been divided into two primary categories—personal and professional. Following is a list of the more common ones expected of the supervisor. The lists are intended to be used as guides.

Personal Qualities	*Professional Qualities*
Ability to win respect and confidence	Broad, general education
Empathy and sensitivity	Good Christian education
Enthusiasm	Adequate professional education
Feeling of adequacy	Teaching skill
Originality	Knowledge of the teaching-learning process
Sense of humor	Leadership skill
Sincerity	Knowledge of curriculum
Imagination	Ability to evaluate teaching and learning
Resourcefulness	
Openmindedness	

Objectivity
Creativity
Approachability
Perceptiveness
Aspiration, vision, faith
Spiritual life
Spiritual growth
Fruit of the Spirit
Sense of divine call to the work

Proficiency in experimentation and research
Growth
Knowledge of people
Knowledge of human relations
Philosophy of education
Counseling skills
Principles of supervision
Motivate improvement
Make effective decisions
Communicate policies

10. *Selection and Preparation of Supervisors.* Ideally, broad and inclusive training is needed for supervisors in church education. To effect improvement demands exacting work. Formal training for the work of a Director of Christian Education would include basic studies in Bible, theology, church history, philosophy of religion, philosophy of education, educational psychology, educational methodology, the teaching-learning process, personality development, curriculum construction, organization and administration of the program, counseling, group dynamics, and supervisory leadership. Such training may be obtained in professional schools and seminaries under church auspices.

Volunteer workers in supervision may secure training in the educational institutions mentioned above, in leadership training courses in the local church, through reading, workshop attendance, and conventions. Part-time supervisors in the local church program may be trained in the leadership training program of the church.

Supervisors are selected for church work by ministers, personnel committees, and the Board of Christian Education. Directors of Christian Education are selected by means of the personal interview. Personal, spiritual and professional qualifications are used for guidance purposes in these interviews. Helpful literature on the work of this officer can be secured from the National Association of Directors of Christian Education (NADCE), Wheaton, Illinois.

Professional growth of church supervisors should be emphasized. Experiences here can be gained through additional formal education, through reading, experimenting, and attendance at workshops, conventions, and laboratories.

B. The Supervisor as Educational Leader

1. *Definition of Educational Leadership.* Supervisors work with people to effect changes in attitude, understanding and behavior in order to realize the results of improvement. This takes educational leadership. Good's *Dictionary of Education* defines leadership as "the ability and readiness to inspire, guide, direct, and manage others."

In general, such a definition is workable within the context of church work, but Christian leadership has its own specific aspects. The Apostle Paul said, "Follow me as I follow Christ" (I Cor. 11:1). Essentially, therefore, Christian leadership is following Christ; it is accepting the leadership of Christ as pattern and guide; it is the seeking and doing of the will of Christ. A Christian leader, therefore, will guide his followers in coming to know, to love and to serve Christ. The will of God, through the life, teachings, death, and resurrection of Christ and the Bible, becomes the guiding factor in the educational leadership of the supervisor in church education.

Essentially, Christian leadership possesses all the good

qualities of secular leadership plus Christian elements which make a difference in its basic nature. The principle of a goal-centered approach is workable for the Christian if his goals are based on divine revelation, not on humanistic experimentalism.

Leadership within the church does not concern itself with power or status, or even with personality traits. Instead, it has to do with the dedicated use of Christian talents in God's service (Eph. 4:11–13).

Actually, *followship* precedes leadership. A good leader must first be a good follower. Christian leadership is only relative. Christ is the only leader—the rest are humble followers.

Christian leadership is *servantship*. A Christian leader should think of himself as a servant. This was Christ's attitude when he declared that the "Son of man came not to be ministered unto, but to minister, and to give his life a ransom for many" (Mark 10:45). So likewise, the Christian leader will be identified among his people. Christ said, "Whosoever will be chief among you, let him be your servant" (Matt. 29:27).

2. *Importance of Educational Leadership.* Effective group work depends on leadership. Despite the quality of teachers and administrators, they need the guidance of leadership in the establishment of goals, in direction, in cooperation, in stimulation and encouragement. Without leadership it is difficult for school personnel to keep the proper perspective, to avoid the danger of specialization, and lose interest in improvement and growth. In relation to individuals the leader motivates and guides; in relation to groups he serves as the catalyst to the combination of individual talents in effective common action.

Many people share the responsibilities of leadership in the church school, but it remains for the supervisor in large measure to supply the leadership for the teaching-learning process. Indeed, the best supervision is achieved when the supervisor as leader fosters and develops in individual teachers and workers a sense of and talent for leadership.

The importance of educational leadership is seen in the efforts of the supervisor to create an attitude of *educational* concern. This includes an emphasis on improvement of teaching and learning, the creation of a wholesome human environment, and the establishment of a spiritual atmosphere as the context of activity. These are no small tasks.

3. *Context of Educational Leadership.* Educational leadership in public education today draws primarily from the principles of democracy and group dynamics. The leader is to function within the framework of group relationships, and he seeks to provide assistance to the group in decision making. Christian leadership may draw from and learn much from secular writings on educational leadership. Here again, however, a plus factor is present. Christian leadership works within the context of the will of God revealed in the Word of God and within the framework of the church as the body of Christ. Furthermore, there are dynamics present in Christian educational leadership not to be found in other leadership.

4. *The Christian Concept of Leadership.* Not a great deal of literature is available on Christian concepts of leadership. One may find practical treatments however.

The concept of Christian leadership begins in one's concept of Jesus Christ and the church. A good definition was expressed by Crossland.

> Leadership, then, in the local church is the noble art of cooperatively planning and unitedly achieving the goals God has set for mankind in the life and teachings of Jesus

> Christ. In the life of the church leadership is far more than methods of machinery or techniques or holding an office. In essence, a leader is a Christlike personality, whose wisdom, self-sacrifice, and labor cooperate with others in finding the will of God.[2]

To the evangelical Christian the authority for Christian leadership is based on the revelation of God's divine will as found in the Bible, the written Word of God. This distinguishes it from secular education which is basically naturalistic and humanistic.

The quality and provision for Christian living are sufficient to provide some distinctives for Christian leadership which contrast it with secular leadership. While Christian leadership may embrace acceptable elements of leadership from secular sources, it remains for certain spiritual dynamics to give it a special quality not present in secular leadership. The work of the Holy Spirit in the heart and life of the leader brings another dimension into the work of leadership, giving Christian leadership the character of a cooperative enterprise between God and the leader. The depth of the Christian leader's devotional life, a sense of divine call to his work, the claims of Christian discipleship, and following in the footsteps of the Savior, all serve to distinguish the quality of Christian leadership and add new dimensions to its character and practice.

Kenneth Gangel has stated this very well when he says

> When translated from a set of principles to a more formal definition, Christian leadership may be considered the exercise by a Christian member of the group of certain qualities and abilities given by the Spirit of God and based in Christian character, which at any given time, acting upon

> the call of God and the authority of his word, he will offer in loving service to the group for the sake of Christ, in order to facilitate the change of group behavior in the direction of Christlikeness and toward the achieving of the eternal goals of his church.[3]

From the tenets of the above discussion perhaps it is possible to summarize the concept of Christian leadership into a set of principles, as follows:

1. The authority for Christian leadership is Bible-revealed.
2. The context of Christian leadership is church-oriented.
3. The responsibility of Christian leadership is Christ-centered.
4. The dynamic of Christian leadership is Spirit-controlled.
5. The application of Christian leadership is people-related.
6. The ethic of Christian leadership is love-directed.[4]

5. *The Qualities and Skills of Leadership.* The trend in secular education is to depreciate the trait approach to leadership. Instead, the supervisor as a member of the group, leading in group decisions, is most popular now. Human relations factors stand out in this view. In Christian leadership the supervisor will incorporate all of the acceptable qualities of the secular leader, but to these he will strive to add qualities implied in Christlike character and action. Who Jesus was, what and how he served, provide clues for the Christian leader. Certainly the marks of other biblical leaders are most worthy of emulation as well.

Clues for Christian leadership are to be found in the example of Christ both in His *being* and *doing.* Following are some qualities of Christlike character and service.

Personal Qualities

1. Saintliness
2. Humility
3. Sincerity
4. Faith
5. Prayer
6. Sacrifice
7. Love
8. Clear thinking
9. Patience
10. Joy
11. Discipline
12. Strong convictions
13. Vision
14. High ideals
15. Unselfishness
16. Sense of call
17. Consecration

Professional Qualities

1. Knowledge of will of God
2. Knowledge of Word of God
3. Knowledge of people
4. Knowledge of teaching
5. Knowledge of methods
6. Has definite goals
7. Makes adjustments
8. Adequate preparation
9. Well-read in Scripture
10. Positive and practical
11. Freshness
12. Practiced His teachings

Leadership Qualities

1. Strong example
2. Clear instructions

3. Planned operations
4. Strong motivation
5. Pure motives
6. Accountability
7. Cooperation
8. Respect for personality
9. Thoroughly prepared
10. Practiced democratic principles
11. Excellence
12. Freshness
13. Secured results

In addition to the general qualities and skills noted above perhaps it is possible to summarize the skills of the supervisor as leader by the following categories:

1. Human relations
2. Communications
3. Group work
4. Delegation

Some factors to be considered are listed under each of the four categories, as follows:

Human Relations

1. Practice Christian love
2. Avoid use of force where possible
3. Stress consideration
4. Emphasize cooperation
5. Observe rights and privileges of others
6. Study morale factors
7. Meet worker needs
8. Be open-minded
9. Know individuals
10. Be a good listener

11. Visit workers, develop feeling of belonging
12. Study reasons for actions
13. Personalize the work
14. Eliminate personal traits that offend
15. Give honest praise
16. Be sympathetic, courteous, cheerful
17. Provide in-service training

Communication

1. Issue clear directions
2. Keep people informed
3. Use commonly understood language
4. Visualize as much as possible
5. Listen
6. Test feedback for proper interpretation
7. Use written methods for contact
8. Plan meetings carefully
9. Speak plainly
10. Know names
11. Use variety
12. Give honest praise
13. Explain carefully
14. Let people talk
15. Get the facts before action
16. Make decisions known

Delegation

1. Make clear assignments
2. Provide job descriptions
3. Trust people to perform
4. Call for reports
5. Give workers freedom to act
6. Practice accountability
7. Give honest praise
8. Give credit
9. Publicize achievements

Group Work

1. Understand group behavior
2. Have free discussion
3. Develop good morale and a group conscience
4. Use high standards
5. Set definite goals
6. Call for progress reports
7. Evaluate progress
8. Seek the leadership of the Holy Spirit
9. Allow full participation
10. Plan group activities
11. Be fair
12. Crystallize discussion
13. Publicize and recognize results
14. Respect individual worth
15. Relate work to God and the church
16. Set ground rules for working together
17. Set deadlines for action
18. Work on problems considered to be important by the workers.

6. *Functions and Types of Christian Leadership.* Certain people in the church have been designated to work in particular ways to help equip members and leaders to engage in ministry and witness, to effect responsible churchmanship and faithful Christian witnessing in all of life. While this general function is recognized, the work in the church also requires "designated leadership," focusing on selecting and equipping certain persons to carry out designated tasks or functions in such a way that individuals and groups can do their work, to relate to other persons and groups, and with them to move toward the accomplishment of the unifying purposes for which they all exist,

namely, discipleship or ministry to the world in the name of Christ and the church.

One basic idea in Christian leadership is guidance. This involves skill in guiding a person or group to accomplish goals sought for. It is steering the energy and ability of people into church activities which lead to the achievement of commonly agreed upon goals, to the accomplishment of the mission of the church in the world. This mission, not only preserves the way of living taught by Christ, it propagates Christ's truth from generation to generation, and helps people to put the principles of Christian living into everyday practice. To do this leadership is to function in the following suggested ways:

1. It assures united activity
2. It gives direction to united activity
3. It assures wise planning
4. It assists workers in achieving worthwhile goals
5. It serves
6. It inspires, motivates and guides
7. It helps to evaluate results

Leadership in the church finds its expression in many ways and through varied places of service. Leaders may lead as *administrators* in guiding people in management, as *organizers* in providing assistance in structuring the work and exercising executive duties. *Chairmen* will preside over business sessions and correlate the work of planning, scheduling, appointing and reporting. *Counselors* will help individuals and groups solve problems. *Supervisors* will guide in deepening the quality of service rendered. *Teachers* will be concerned, not only with the impartation of truth, but also with the training and guiding of people in the process of "learning to do by doing."

There is always a price to pay for this kind of leadership. The leader must be completely consecrated to God. Self-renunciation and self-dedication are the price of triumphant leadership. At its heart lies self-sacrifice also (Mark 10:21; 8:35). It costs also in the hard work demanded. It may require the endurance of loneliness and pain. It may result in being unappreciated, unassisted, and pushing to new frontiers alone. But joy and happiness, the rewards of success, will be great!

While the principles and concepts of the best kind of leadership in the church are clear, it is not often that one finds complete adherence to such standards. In fact one may find a wide variety in types of leadership to be found in church work. Following are some representative types to be found.

1. The Autocrat
   I define a problem, consider the alternatives, choose the action, and then tell the group what we are going to do. I do not consult the group.
2. The Persuader
   I too identify the problem and make the decision without involving the group. The difference is that I try to persuade the group that the decision is best for them and for the organization.
3. The Benevolent Autocrat
   I have the members of my group at heart and always know what is best for them. I oversee what they do and what happens to them and solicitously care for them. Some people say I am an autocratic leader, but my personal intentions are benevolent.
4. Laisez-faire
   I like for the group to do what it pleases. I try to reflect what I think the members think, and I try to keep the

group united. Sometimes I am called "a do-nothing" leader.

5. The Consultant

I like to come to a group with tentative plans, but from the beginning the group has a chance to influence my decision. Sometimes I simply provide the problem and some background for it and ask for possible solutions. Though the final decision is mine, I have the increased number of possibilities for a workable plan.

6. The Democrat

I encourage individuals within the group to participate in the group and react to decisions before us. I feel that my role is not to wield power, but to stimulate. I use persuasion and conciliation rather than force in order to move the group. My relation to group members is as a friend and not in a distant relationship. My main function is serving as a catalyst.

7. The Delegator

As a leader I sometimes leave the final decision for others to make by delegating responsibility. I define the problems and set the boundaries—then leave it to the delegation to come up with the solution. Whatever they decide I accept as long as it falls within the defined limits.

7. *Factors Affecting Leadership.* Leaders and supervisors are conditioned by a large number of situational factors. Specific situations largely determine what leaders can or cannot do. Already considered are such factors as the concept of leadership, the role of the supervisor, the levels at which the work takes place, relationships with other leaders and workers, qualifications, experience, types or style of operation, goal-setting, and human relations.

Human relations, as we have seen, refers to the psychological climate for interpersonal relations, patterns of participation, attitudes and communication. It remains for us to consider two more important factors: (1) individual differences, and (2) organization.

Individual differences among church workers are great. Teachers and workers differ widely in motivation, abilities, skills, understandings, needs, attitudes, temperament, work pace, emotional stability, gregariousness, and disposition to accept and benefit from criticism. These differences, and others perhaps, cause varying degrees of successful operation. Leadership is more effective when these matters are considered in job placement and work adjustments. Such differences, however, cannot be dealt with intelligently unless recognized, analyzed, and understood. This is difficult.

Problems to be considered here include (1) motivation for work, (2) conception of roles, (3) feeling tone, (4) perception, and (5) discovery of abilities and needs. Supervisors should give particular attention to the solution of these problems.

Two types of organization affect leadership: (1) formal organization, and (2) informal organization. Pastors and Boards should cooperate with teachers and workers in goal setting and problem solving. Conflicts between the formal organization and workers at the classroom level should be resolved and strong support given. It should be clear to workers at the classroom level how much freedom of choice and action they have. Boards and general church officers, involved in administrative responsibility and practice, should see that rulings, laws, and regulations, even well-established customs, do not impose unnecessary restraints on workers at the departmental level. At the same time, however, limits must also be clear.

Informal organization refers to small groups within the context of church work. Dangers here involve the undue use of influence, position, power, money or prestige in forcing adoption of policies and programs. Illustrations of this in the church would be an influential and wealthy individual member or an independent adult class. Such groups may also work from the standpoint of prejudice, jealousy, or tradition. Such groups may develop undue rivalry within the ranks. On the other hand if such groups foster cooperation, increase personal satisfactions, and improve morale, they are highly desirable.

Often times informal groups are formed as a reaction to ineffective official leadership, or where worker needs are not met. Kept within bounds these groups can provide a good forum for discussion of problems and issues and can contribute to better communication and mutual understanding. Otherwise, general policy should be formulated to control such situations.

There is another particular kind of organizational factor which affects leadership. A current and interesting assessment of organizational life was pictured in a very unique book, *The Peter Principle,* by Dr. Lawrence J. Peter and Raymond Hull (William Morrow and Co., 1969). The principle, briefly stated, is, "In a hierarchy every employee tends to rise to his level of incompetence." This generalization described what might be termed the "pathology of success" that tends to move people along the ladder until they find a spot where they are stretched beyond their real ability or competence. It is at this point in their experience that others recognize they are not fully adequate in their work and therefore are not good candidates for promotion. They have reached their level of incompetence. This can be seen in management where people, who were successful at lower levels of work and even along the way, suddenly become incompetent at the so-called top.

There is a measure of truth in this for Christian leadership. Many church workers have been successful at teaching or committee work, for example, but when moved to an administrative office or chairmanship cannot produce.

Supervisors must be sensitive to this possibility in leadership. Do not think of church work in terms of a heirarchy. There are no more important positions in the church "higher up" than that of teaching or worker assistant in the church school organization. Teachers and workers are just as important where they are as in other positions involving perhaps administration or supervision. This is practicing the "graded principle" in leadership. People should serve where they operate best, where they have high interest, genuine ability and growing competence. Training experiences and rich resources should be provided to support and maximize this competence. Furthermore, job descriptions should define the competence that is needed in church school service situations. This will make improvement and evaluation more certain.

8. *Developing Adequate Leadership.* The supervisor should seek to develop strong and effective leaders for the local church. Constant study of plans to this end needs to be made, determining how best to release, guide, train, and supervise human resources for a program of church education. Peter G. White has suggested a supervisor's responsibility list to help produce and develop adequate leadership.

1. Make the facts about leadership needs and resources known to the present teaching staff.
2. Make these facts known to the congregation.
3. Assess the maturity of the staff as a whole to determine whether or not heavy responsibilities are falling on younger, less experienced persons, or possibly on older persons who find change difficult.
4. Discover by questionnaire who would be willing to teach in pairs to increase effectiveness.
5. Make lists of persons in the congregation who should be offered training for specific teaching tasks.
6. Assess present leadership training opportunities within the local church in the light of available budget and expand them if needed.
7. Assess denominational and interdenominational training opportunities and budget available and arrange for teachers to attend.
8. Plan ways for delegates who attend training events to share benefits with others on the staff.
9. Develop a visiting team to meet prospective leaders in their own homes.
10. Discuss leadership needs with youth and adult groups, since leaders of these age groups should be chosen, by, or with the help of, the groups themselves.
11. Select those persons who have talent for "supervision," i.e., those who can help others review the effectiveness of their work, those who can bring a change and growth in others.
12. Encourage teachers to find good resource books (in addition to their teacher's guides) and have them added to the church library. A teacher chosen library is likely to be used.
13. Make a list of all people in the congregation who have special skills and abilities which could be made available to the teaching staff: carpenters, musicians, doctors,

professional teachers, amateur photographers, electricians, play directors, social workers.

14. Make a supplementary list of community personnel (such as librarians, recreational directors and agency leaders) who might be approached for advice and help on occasion.
15. Discover what other congregations are doing to develop leaders. Exchange plans, have observations visits, with evaluation sessions following.
16. Plan special attention to the informing of adult groups in the congregation about Christian education.
17. Assign a special detail to make plans for family involvement, since parents are the basic "teachers" of their children.
18. Set up records.
19. Consider the special gifts of the minister.[5]

Questions for Classroom Use

1. Why is status leadership a part of the role of the supervisor?
2. How does the role as "group leader" differ from that of "status leader"?
3. How can the supervisor share his authority and leadership?
4. How can the program of supervision be planned to meet needs which teachers have in common? To meet individual needs?
5. What does the supervisor do if he sees that workers and teachers fail to recognize problems?
6. Formulate a set of principles for supervision.
7. What are common mistakes that supervisors make in their relations with teachers and workers?
8. Develop a complete strategy for orienting new teachers and workers.
9. Compare various philosophies of education with that of church education.

10. Work out a set of general and age group objectives for church education.
11. Create a complete set of Christian education standards for evaluating the total church education program.

Questions for Local Church Use

1. What are the basic elements of true group leadership?
2. How can the "we" spirit be developed in our church school?
3. Make a list of job satisfactions which teachers want.
4. How can teachers be sensitized to instructional problems?
5. How are problems selected for study? What are problem-solving steps?
6. Discuss problems of the Sunday school with parents and others outside the church and see what you can learn from them.
7. Outline some of the characteristics of effective educational leaders.
8. Create a job description booklet for your workers.

Notes for Chapter Three

1. Lucio, William H. and John D. McNeil, *Supervision* (New York, McGraw-Hill, 1962), p. 26.
2. Crossland, Weldon T., *Better Leaders for Your Church* (Nashville, Abingdon, 1955), p. 9.
3. Gangel, Kenneth, *Leadership for Church Education* (Chicago, Moody, 1970), p. 176.
4. Refer to Kenneth Gangel, ibid., Chapter 15, for a full discussion of a biblical philosophy of Christian leadership. The set of principles listed by the writer avoids the proliferation of "centers, " in the Gangel list.
5. Peter G. White, "How to Develop Adequate Leadership," in *International Journal of Religious Education* (September 1964), p. 15.

Outline for Chapter Four

Evaluation in a Program of Improvement and Supervision for Church Education

A. The Evaluation Process

1. The Nature and Importance of Evaluation
2. The Function of Evaluation
3. The Process of Evaluation
4. The Scope and Purpose of Evaluation
5. The Pattern of Evaluation
6. Principles of Evaluation
7. Methods of Evaluation
8. Use of Results of Evaluation
9. Evaluation and Supervision.

B. Evaluation According to Concepts of Education

1. Good Education—Basic Premise
2. Educational Foundations
3. Representative Philosophies of Life
4. Representative Educational Philosophies
5. Implications for Church Education
6. Representative Religious Viewpoints
7. Representative Church Education Philosophies
8. The Evangelical Concept of Church Education
9. The Supervisor and Educational Concepts

C. Evaluation According to Objectives of Education

1. Definition of Objectives
2. Source of Objectives
3. Function and Use of Objectives
4. Principles and Objectives
5. The Content of Objectives
6. Objectives and the Supervisor.

D. Evaluation According to Standards of Education

1. Definition of a Standard
2. Needs for a Standard
3. Uses and Purposes of Standards
4. Types of Standards
5. Sources of Standards
6. Standards and the Supervisor

E. Implementation of Change as a Result of Evaluation

1. The Need for Change
2. Motivation for Change
3. The Process of Change
4. Guiding Principles for Change
5. Reactions to Change
6. The Supervisor and the Strategy for Change

Questions for Class Discussion

Questions for Local Church Use

Notes for Chapter Four

CHAPTER FOUR

Evaluation in a Program of Improvement and Supervision for Church Education

A. The Evaluation Process

1. *The Nature and Importance of Evaluation.* Evaluation means to find the value of, to determine the worth of, to appraise, to test and measure. Evaluation is concerned with the ascertaining and establishment of quality in education. It involves the determination of the present state and status of the educational system. It concerns the measurement of success or failure. It lays the groundwork for making changes necessary to the achievement of improvement. It concerns the identification of needs, problems, clear objectives, efficient processes, adequate resources, and sufficient outcomes. In some respects it is rather subjective in character. This whole matter is securely based on scriptural foundations (I Thess. 5:21; I Cor. 11:28; II Cor. 13:5; Gal. 6:1–5; I Tim. 3:10; Matt. 7:20; Jas. 2:14–17).

Two other terms are (1) testing and (2) measurement. Both of these terms focus on more objective attempts to evaluate. Some kind of examination, scale, or standard is used to gather data by which comparison can be made and conclusions drawn. Thus, where evaluation is concerned with qualitative analysis, testing and measurement are concerned with quantitative data.

Continuous efforts need to be made in evaluation if improvement is to have any permanency. Appraisal and revision should be conceived as integral parts of a good supervisory program.

The church should feel the importance of evaluation. We are working with immortal souls of infinite worth. What is happening to these people, why and how? Yet church work is often characterized by carelessness and superficiality. There is great need in the church to discover what kind of evaluation can and should be done, to shed light on what aspects need appraisal, and to guide and coordinate the work of evaluation systematically.

2. *The Function of Evaluation.* If supervision is to effect improvement, it must result in the revision of existing educational principles and practices. The function of evaluation, therefore, is to discover and identify strengths and weaknesses upon which effective changes can be made. The process of evaluation thus contributes a factual basis for cooperatively determining the policies and practices that should be developed and improved or discontinued. The functioning process would eventuate in the following steps:

1. To determine the need.
2. To measure progress and achievement.
3. To evaluate the effectiveness of the educative process, materials and equipment.
4. To help lay out a plan for improvement.

3. *The Process of Evaluation.* Fundamentally, evaluation involves making changes. Efforts, therefore, should be threefold: (1) examine the situation and get the facts, (2) pass judgment on them cooperatively, and (3) make plans for revisions. The principles of the problem-solving

approach are helpful in this. Value judgments on the status and growth of the program and personnel are made in the light of the concepts, values, standards, and goals accepted. Every effort should be made to be as objective as possible. Progress is measured not only in terms of present status but also in terms of growth in Christlike character, numbers, and resources.

4. *The Scope and Purpose of Evaluation.* Evaluation is concerned with the scope and quality of the goals, purposes, functions, and program of the total church educational program and the extent to which needs are being met in keeping with one's philosophy of church education.

The appraisal of all elements in the total church program of education would include the evaluation of the following elements:

1. Pattern (Structure)—Provision
   The organization of the school
   The administration of the school
   The physical facilities of the school
2. Process—Method
   The goals
   The curriculum
   The teaching-learning process
   The materials, equipment and facilities of teaching and learning
3. Product—change
   Christian character development—evangelism and growth
   Behavioral change
   Quality of Christian fellowship
   Participation in service activity

Purposes to be recognized would include:

1. To guide teaching and learning processes
2. To appraise personal growth and development
3. To clarify objectives and concepts
4. To test effectiveness of methods
5. To validate hypotheses
6. To appraise adequacy of facilities and resources
7. To assist supervisors in selecting supervisory techniques
8. To aid in planning
9. To help develop higher standards
10. To determine the spiritual needs and problems of individuals and groups.

5. *The Pattern of Evaluation.* It is not an easy task to evaluate, test and measure any educational system. The whole process is both dynamic and complex. There is perhaps no set pattern for the use of data supplied by evaluation, but hopefully the following pattern will prove valuable in the evaluation of church education:

1. Evaluate the program according to the concept of education that designs and controls it. This involves one's philosophy of education. It yields principles which guide the application of the philosophy.
2. Evaluate according to objectives
3. Evaluate according to standards
4. Evaluate according to the program principles and elements
5. Evaluate according to program coverage
6. Evaluate according to teaching-learning practices
7. Evaluate according to individual growth and development
8. Evaluate according to increase in numbers
9. Evaluate according to service activities

Each of the above steps will be taken up respectively in that which follows.

6. *Principles of Evaluation.* To effectively operate a system of educational evaluation certain principles must be recognized and practiced. Suggested ones are included in the following:

1. Evaluation should be comprehensive in scope and method
2. Evaluation should be consistent with one's educational philosophy in the church
3. Evaluation should be a cooperative enterprise
4. Evaluation should be a continuous enterprise
5. Evaluation should emphasize quality, depth, and growth
6. Evaluation should be as economical as possible
7. Evaluation should give special attention to teachers and learners
8. Evaluation should specialize in the identification of proper outcomes in teaching, learning, and behavior
9. Evaluation should identify problems with clarity
10. Evaluation should identify data required to solve problems
11. Evaluation should clarify good objectives
12. Evaluation should be as accurate, precise, and relevant as possible.

7. *Methods of Evaluation.* Church educators have been slow to develop methods of evaluation, measurement, and testing. In the past individual testimony and observation were used to determine worthiness of a person for admission to baptism. The catechism was used to determine the worthiness of an individual for the rite of confirmation. An early book was written by Goodwin Watson in 1927

and entitled *Experimentation and Measurement in Religious Education.* During the 1920's and 1930's paper and pencil tests were tried. Among these were the Laycock Biblical Information Test, Northwestern University Tests of Religious Education. A later book was produced by Arthur L. Miller entitled *Tests and Measurements in Lutheran Education* (Lutheran Education Association, 1957).

Some local churches and denominational agencies have sought to produce a few tests to be used in connection with Sunday school lessons. A few publishers have produced simple paper and pencil tests for curriculum materials. Departments of research are also being developed by some publishers and denominational Christian education agencies. Likewise evaluation of curriculum materials is being sponsored by such people. A very few local churches are sponsoring research projects in teaching and learning.

In the area of character Hartshorne and May produced a three volume work on *Studies in the Nature of Character* (New York, Macmillan, 1928, 1929, 1930). They attempted to show that such qualities as honesty, helpfulness and self-control could be measured. Ernest Chave made some attempts along this line in his work *Measure Religion* (University of Chicago). The most extensive work in character education, however, has been that of Ernest M. Ligon, director of the Character Research Project, Union College, Schenectady, New York.

Efforts at evaluation is seen in the work of the Bureau of Research of the National Council of Churches of Christ in the U.S.A. In 1959 they sponsored an institute on evaluation at Drew University. A book entitled *Evaluation in Christian Education* was published. Another workshop was conducted on curriculum evaluation at Cornell University in 1961. The Religious Education Association sponsored a workshop on research design at Cornell, 1961. In 1962 D. Campbell Wyckoff produced *How to Evaluate Your Christian Education Program* (Westminster, 1962). A second book was made available by the Presbyterians, *Evaluate Your Christian Education Program,* Board of Christian Education, United Presbyterian Church U.S.A. A recent book is *Make Your Sunday School Grow Through Evaluation* by Harold J. Westing (Scripture Press, 1976).

8. *Use of Results of Evaluation.* After measurement takes place some kind of synthesis should be made which reveals the total picture. Then comparisons are made of this picture with one's concept of expected outcomes, and with one's philosophy of church education, then some judgments can be made regarding the quality of the work and the progress made in terms of adequacy of the product. Outcomes would possibly include the following steps:

1. Help clarify objectives and state them in measurable form
2. Help determine the effectiveness of procedures—the achievements
3. Help validate hypotheses on which programs are built
4. Help provide encouragement and instruction for workers

Some of the following methods could be considered for use in this process.

Methods of evaluation for

Structure	*Process*
1. Self studies	1. Questionnaires
2. Questionnaires	2. Clinics
3. Clinics	3. Standards

4. Professional consultation
5. Rating scales
6. Standards
7. Records
8. Principles compared with results
9. Objectives
10. Checklists

4. Observations
5. Records
6. Check lists
7. Principles
8. Written tests
9. Rating scales
10. Objectives
11. Activity records
12. Anecdotal records
13. Follow-up studies

Product

1. Paper and pencil test
2. Character tests
3. Bible tests
4. Questionnaires
5. Clinics
6. Standards
7. Records
8. Interest finders
9. Case studies
10. Oral examinations
11. Objectives
12. Testimony
13. Check lists
14. Activity records
15. Interviews

9. *Evaluation and Supervision.* Through their directive functions supervisors help teachers increase the effectiveness of teaching and assist administrators in deepening the quality of their work, so that all may come closer to the realization of the aims and goals of the church and good Christian education.

Supervisors can help church workers develop a philosophy of education that can be practiced. They can then evaluate that philosophy. Supervisors can assist teachers with problems involved with the curriculum and the teaching-learning process, trying to discover problems and the means of improvement through evaluation. They can help teachers with self-appraisal and the determination of teaching and learning goals. More will be said about this matter in the following chapter.

The total program can be placed under scrutiny to determine effectiveness, balance, and comprehensiveness. Are the needs of people being met? Meetings with individuals and groups can be called to cooperatively and prayerfully consider the resources, means, and proposed outcomes of supervision.

B. Evaluation According to Concepts of Education

1. *Good Education—Basic Premise.* One's concept of good education determines directly his ability to evaluate that education. Testing, measurement, and evaluation imply a set of standards and principles by which one compares what is with what ought to be. Such evaluation will depend upon the clarity with which one conceives his educational theory and practice. Both theory and practice are based on philosophical foundations. It becomes necessary, therefore, to determine the nature and quality of education by identifying the philosophy from which it is drawn.

From the philosophy, theory and practice developed one can identify the necessary essentials and standards by which evaluation of the total system can be made. Therefore, the frame of reference within which a particular educational system operates determines its character, content, and practice.

The improvement and proper supervision of church education is based directly upon the discovery of the elements which are most productive of the desired results. An understanding of these matters yields illumination on how to proceed in the whole matter of evaluation.

2. *Educational Foundations.* Educational supervision and improvement is a means to the end of achieving better education. This is true of all kinds of education, inside or outside the chruch. The supervisory process is the means of stimulating, accomplishing and evaluating the purposes and practices of education. Unless the supervisor himself is imbued with a philosophy of education which directs and influences his efforts, his supervision is likely to be superficial and mechanical. He will not have a clear concept of the ends of education. Thus, the concept of education and the broad functions of the school are concerns of supervision. Philosophical concepts are directly related to the immediate tasks facing the supervisor in planning, organizing, and evaluating a supervisory program.

A philosophy of education is actually a philosophy of life. The educational process is invariably an implementation of a philosophy of education. So what is done by the supervisor is inevitably linked to the philosophy which he holds.

One of the first needs in the evaluation process is to show workers the importance of formulating a clear philosophy out of which proper goals are abstracted, goals which are both sound and attainable. Then supervisors and teachers must be convinced that their major efforts should be directed toward the attainment of these goals rather than being concerned with the refinement of the technical details of instruction.

In church education a philosophy of education rests upon one's concept of God and His kingdom, reflecting a code of values by which the Christian lives. His concept of the Good Life, therefore, is different from that of public or secular education, because it is based, not on social or humanistic bases, but rather on the revelation of the character, the will and the word of God. From this source the Christian builds his philosophy of education to include definition, purpose, function, process, practice, and goal. It is by this concept that he is able to evaluate the characteristics of his educational system.

3. *Representative Philosophies of Life.* Philosophies of life determine philosophies of education. This is the reason supervisors should understand backgrounds of educational philosophy and why they should develop their own philosophy of education based on their life-views.

There are only three starting points or presuppositions upon which philosophies of life are built: (1) nature, (2) man, and (3) God. Five major or mother philosophies have been developed on these premises.

Naturalism may be defined as that view of the world, and of man's relation to it, in which only the operation of natural laws and forces is assumed. All events in the cosmos are a part of the inclusiveness of nature. The core teaching is to be found in the orderliness of nature; nature can be depended upon.

Naturalism works on the assumption that truth is obtained only by the inductive method or the scientific method of the physical sciences. The basic weakness of this method to the Christian is that it denies the reality of the spiritual and supernatural.

Of particular significance to education is the philosophy of *pragmatism,* an outgrowth of the philosophy of naturalism. This is a philosophy which judges events in the light of their practical consequences. It is maintained that an idea is good if it works. The core teaching of this philosophy is that experience (one aspect of natural reality) is the test of all things. Where pure naturalism places its confidence in consistent nature, pragmatism emphasizes one element of nature—experience.

Realism is a child of naturalism. Most of its theories of reality and epistemology are similar to that of basic naturalism. Its distinctives lie in the emphasis it gives to the senses and the nervous system as the mediums of knowledge and action.

Idealism, a second mother philosophy, is antithetical to that of naturalism and probably a reaction against it. Idealism is the theory that reality is the same as the observer's consciousness of it. Reality is mental in character and can be demonstrated by coherence. Thus, mind or spirit is the essence of reality. The core teaching is that ultimate reality is spiritual. Of course, what this spiritual reality is becomes a matter of opinion to some.

In its theory of reality the totality of the universe in its essence is mind or spirit. This essence is personal in quality to some and has the nature of selfhood. At its very least the universe is mental stuff of some sort. Ultimate reality may be one self, a community of selves, or a Universal Self within whom are many individual selves. The emphasis on Person to some places this view within the context of Christianity so that we have what is called Personal Idealism or Idealistic Christianity. God is the Absolute Self, mental and conscious.

To the Christian the idealistic emphasis on absolutes, the

reality of the spiritual, its emphasis on moral laws, its belief in freedom and the existence of God, are commendable. But its denial of the reality of evil, its finite God, its hazy conception of God, and its elevation of abstract concepts to the ultimate level above God all serve to weaken its position from the Christian theistic standpoint.

Humanism is a philosophy which is man-centered. It also has strong naturalistic tendencies. Reason is at the heart of this view and the method becomes one of developing it. The accomplishments of the past provide content for study. Human values are central in this view. Emphasis is placed on the classics with intellectual development as a direct corrolary. Humanists believe that the combination of the acquisition of one's cultural heritage and modern scientific genius results in the right kind of knowledge and leadership.

This philosophy, too, has had marked effect on both secular and religious education. In the church this influence is reflected in the view of religious humanism.

Rationalism as a philosophy is classified here because of its humanistic tendencies. Others would place it under the category of the naturalistic. Its emphasis on mind, however, places it here. Rationalism assumes that a world view can be formulated through the use of pure reason. Such a position is no longer tenable, for pure reason is only a fragment of experience. Then, too, it is built upon arbitrary assumptions.

Christian Theism is a third mother philosophy, set over against those of naturalism and idealism. It is that view of the world and universe which postulates the existence of a personal God, such as the Bible sets forth, who maintains a personal relation to all of reality.

No less than others the Christian begins with an assumption. He has a conviction that the supernatural world is just as real as the natural world. God does exist there and has chosen to bridge the gap between the two worlds by a process of Self-revelation. Such revelation is transcendent; it comes from God Himself. The Christian world view is built upon the assumption that reality is supernatural as well as natural, divine as well as human, that there is revealed knowledge as well as natural knowledge. This is the point of disagreement with all other views. No claim is made that written Revelation covers the whole gamut of truth, however, it does provide a means whereby all truth is measured.

Direct implications for education of all kinds can be seen from the Christian view. Education must become a reinterpretation of God's revelation. It is seeing things as God sees them; it is thinking God's thoughts after him. Christian education centers in Christ who is the personal Self-relation of God. All other avenues of knowledge also stem from God and are interpreted in the light of Christ's nature and works.

The purpose of education is to show God revealed. The goal of education is to qualify man to reveal God in his total being and total environment. The ultimate objective is the Kingdom of God to come. All education, in and out of the church, thus becomes God-centered and God-revealing. All curricula content is related to God. Thus, the revelation of God becomes the heart of the educational curriculum.

4. *Representative Educational Philosophies.* The various philosophies of life considered above have been responsible for the development of educational philosophies. The following summary compares several representative philosophies of education.

Secular Educational Philosophies Compared with Christian Theism

Philosophy	Definition of Education	Function of Education	Knowledge	Method
Naturalism	Social and Vocational	Adjustment to and Improvement of Environment; human excellence	Natural phenomena Propositional	Inductive and scientific
Humanism	Acquisition of knowledge and mental discipline	Development of reason, knowledge and culture	Classical learning Propositional	Reason Inductive
Pragmatism	Reconstruction of experience	Personal and social efficiency; growth	Social and natural phenomena Propositional	Problem-solving Inductive

continued

Secular Educational Philosophies Compared with Christian Theism

Idealism	Individual and mental development	Personality integration and development; adjustment to God	Social science and Religion Propositional and Personal	Reason Inductive and deductive
Realism	Conditioning of the nervous system	Harmonization with the laws of nature	Natural phenomena Propositional	Reason Inductive
Christian Theism	Reinterpretation of God's Revelation	Revelation; accomplishing the will of God; redemption; Christlikeness; Kingdom of God	Divine Revelation; spiritual phenomena, then social and natural Propositional and personal	Revelation plus reason Deductive and Inductive

5. *Implications for Church Education.* At this point we may summarize the views of secular education. In these views man is but a body-soul being, only a living body, reacting to external stimuli. Learning, therefore, is reacting to environment; it is experience. Education thus becomes the reconstruction of experience through experience. Sense perception is the only method of studying human reactions. This is made scientific by experimental conditions. Method, therefore, is experimentation; revelation has no place, instead man discovers everything.

Man is a social animal, so his education is pupil-centered. His highest qualification in life thus becomes social efficiency. Personal qualifications and values have significance only in their social context. The aim of education, therefore, is social efficiency—as a citizen, as a worker. Civic and occupational efficiency become paramount. Hence conduct is defined in terms of pragmatic philosophy.

Views based on Christian theism may be summarized also. Education is God-centered. Man was created by God as a living soul. Other creatures were created lower than man after their kind.

Man learns through revelation and experience. To learn is essentially to listen to the will of God. Knowledge is derived from the Scriptures and nature. General and Special Revelation provide the content. The Word of God is the fullest revelation of God and therefore is the most precious knowledge. Reason must have the support of faith and revelation to guide it. Therefore, God must be in the center of man's mental development. In the process of learning the teacher becomes an essential guide and master.

Man is also a social being but he is essentially an individual who must live with his neighbor. Individual responsibility therefore becomes just as important as socialization of the mind.

Man's highest qualification in life is perfection (maturity) and holiness before God and other men. Personal qualifications always stand in relation to man's eternal calling to live to the glory of God. Education, therefore, may be defined as the thorough furnishing of the man of God unto all good works, so that he may be perfect (mature) (2 Tim. 3:17).

Human conduct is defined in terms of man's eternal calling to know, to love, and to serve God to his glory. His conduct is prescribed and determined by the law of God.

In practice for the Christian, the school is not pupil-centered but Christ-centered. It is Christ's world in a love environment. Pupils live in a holy community of Christian believers, looking to Jesus Christ for salvation. Everyone esteems everybody else better than himself. His needs, interests, aptitudes, and abilities are not developed for self-expression but spent rather in the service of God and man.

6. *Representative Religious Viewpoints.* Religious viewpoints have felt the impact of the great mother secular philosophies. Idealism, for example, gave birth to two points of view in the church: (1) *absolute idealism,* and (2) *personal idealism.* In the first view the Great Idea of Plato is elevated to the "doctrine of the Absolute, who is held to be all-perfect, immutable, and all-inclusive." The basic premise is that reality is personal, self-conscious, self-directive, creative intelligence which is both source and ground of all reality.

Pragmatism motivated a theory in the church known as *Religious Pragmatism.* On the educational side the views of

John Dewey were most influential, while on the religious side the views of William James bore great weight. In the writings of George A. Coe one will find a virtual adoption of Dewey's educational pragmatism in the church. Coe thought of the church as a religious democracy. Other influences of this view can be seen in the use of pupil-centered lesson materials, social projects, and problem-solving methods of teaching. The Bible is thought of as instrumental, a resource book, rather than an authoritative norm.

The influence of naturalism is seen in the theories of *Theistic Naturalism.* Here attempts were made to make philosophical application of the theory of biological evolution to religious philosophy. It goes on under a variety of names including theistic naturalism, naturalistic theism, cosmic theism, and even religious realism.

Religious Humanism was an outgrowth of classical humanism. Knowledge is confined to natural phenomena and the sense world, so there is no place for the objectivity of religion. Reason supplants revelation as the method of knowledge. Religion is to be used to better the human situation rather than relating man to the divine situation.

Religious Psychologism focuses on the question of subjectivity in religion. Revelation originates in man's feeling of dependence produced by existence in the universe, not a divine self-disclosure. Religion is a result of wishful thinking. God was created out of a sense of need. Conversion is only self-reformation. God works only in natural ways and is divinely immanent in all things. The supernatural and objective aspects are derivations.

Other influences of psychology can be seen in the effects of developmental psychology on the use and application of teaching materials and methods. Personality theories have influenced objectives and curriculum theory also.

Religious Existentialism is a mixture of orthodox and liberal views. The classical understanding of God, the creation, the fall, the incarnation, redemption, and second coming of Christ, as held by orthodox evangelicals, are unacceptable to existentialists. They stress God as wholly other, completely transcendant, so he cannot be understood. But he does reveal himself, not in the literal words of the Bible, but through "the Word spoken in Christ." Myths and paradoxes explain these things. Man, as a sinner, is guilty and full of anxiety and loneliness.

This philosophy has influenced religious education. Buber's "I-Thou" emphasis has greatly influenced the attitude toward teacher-pupil relationships. Learning takes place best through relationships with God and men. Knowledge becomes personal, and not merely propositional.

7. *Representative Church Education Philosophies.* Church education philosophies have been developed largely in some circles from a twofold source: (1) from the influence of secular views and secular educational philosophies, and (2) from the influence of religious views. It is important for the supervisor to recognize the sources of the views faced in church education literature and to choose his own source from which he develops a personal philosophy of church education. On the following pages is a summary of representative church educational philosophies based on their respective religious foundations.

8. *The Evangelical Concept of Church Education.* From the evangelical standpoint, church education develops its concept from general Christian education. In terms of its view of reality, its concepts of value, purpose, and goal,

School	Aim	Goal	Philosophical Rootage	Basic Theological Rootage
Naturalistic Liberalism	Personal creativity	Social adjustment	Naturalism, Humanism Realism Naturalistic idealism	Immanence; anthropocentric
Social Liberalism	Spiritual growth	Democracy of God Self-realization	Naturalism Humanism Pragmatism Realism	Immanence, anthropocentric
Neo-liberalism	Growth in grace	Faith relationship Social reconstruction	Humanism Realism Christian Theism	Immanence; anthropocentric
Neo-Orthodox	Conversion growth in grace; nurture	Christian Discipleship	Christian Theism Humanism Realism	Transcendental Theocentric

continued

School	Aim	Goal	Philosophical Rootage	Basic Theological Rootage
Psychological School	Nurture Encounter	Acceptance Changes in self	Christian Theism Pragmatism Humanism	Transcendental Theocentric
Church Emphasis	Transmission of culture and spiritual heritage Growth in grace	Realize the authority of fellowship in the church	Christian Theism Realism	Transcendental Theocentric
Evangelicalism	Revelation Conversion Growth in grace	Christlikeness The Church The Kingdom of God	Christian Theism Christian Realism	Transcendental Theocentric

church education is the same as that of general Christian education. However, church education specializes in the work of the church. It functions within the framework of personal truth. This is truth concerning the Lord Jesus Christ, the Bible, Christian experience, and the responsibilities of the church. The thrust of the curriculum for church education concerns the implications of redemption as seen in the revelation of the Written Word and salvation provided through the redeeming work of the Living Word—the Son. The curriculum is Christ-centered through the work of the Holy Spirit, Bible-based, pupil-related, and socially applied. The curriculum is operated within the framework of the manifestations of the work of the Holy Spirit in love, faith, hope and obedience—in the fellowship of the saints, the church as the body of Christ.

The need for teaching comes out of the obligations of the church to teach. People need discipling. Beyond a knowledge of facts, church members need care, concern, discipline and obedience. Two terms characterize the early ministry of the church: (1) *kerygma* and (2) *didache.* Kerygma means proclamation. The term actually involves two meanings: (1) the act of preaching, and (2) the content of preaching (I Cor. 1:21). It refers to the acts and facts of the Gospel. It is a body of knowledge based on what Jesus said and did. It forms the very heart of our work—the Gospel.

Didache (teaching) is a much broader term than *kerygma.* It includes the *kerygma,* but also indicates a way of life. It was to be taught and interpreted; it was to be absorbed, learned. It elaborates on the *kerygma,* answering objections to it. It appeals to decision, corrects, instructs, even rebukes.

More than words is needed to be a Christian. There

must be follow up to see true Christian changes in lives. It is not enough to say, "Jesus Christ died for our sins." Disciples need orientation and explanation to make this key truth clear.

Three other words are related to the *didache.* There is *katecheo* (catechism) which stresses facts. *Paideuo* (child training) concerns the instruction and discipline of children. *Matheteuo* (make disciples) stresses learning, but not memory reproduction (Eph. 4:11–13).

Thus, the *didache* stresses depth, thoroughness, and breadth of knowledge and living. This involves Christian teaching as a ministry with the teacher as an oracle of God. The church, therefore, becomes a teaching church.

The church has a teaching ministry the function of which is to communicate the Word of God and assist in accomplishing the work of God in the world. This means a total church concept of the teaching ministry. A total church program of Christian education consists of all the activities, materials, resources, physical facilities, and personnel involved in carrying forward the full range of ministries of the church to its total constituency. All the activities which produce the kind of experiences needed to transform the life into that which God intended for the individual must be taken into account when planning a total church program of Christian education. Some of the implications of this concept follow:

1. Christian education is the church at work teaching and learning
2. The tasks and objectives of the church and Christian education are the same
3. The church finds a major place in the context of Christian education
4. Christian education serves as a feeder and builder of the church

5. The spiritual atmosphere of the church directly affects the effectiveness of Christian education
6. Christian belief in large measure determines the nature of Christian education in the church
7. All Christian ministry has been given to the church
8. Since the purposes, tasks and goals of Christian education and the church are the same, there must be church control
9. Christian education is in, of and for the church
10. The church has a teaching ministry.

9. *The Supervisor and Concepts of Education.* Supervisors can help church workers clarify and state a philosophy of Christian education built on an understood philosophy of life. Individual and group study guided by Biblical and educational principles should be helpful at this point. The supervisor will help to evaluate an already established statement of philosophy also. Most certainly he will be able to point out the various schools of thought within church education, making such distinctions as orthodoxy, conservatism, liberalism and evangelicalism. Group studies regarding the theological position of the church will prove helpful in both teaching and evaluation. This has a direct bearing also on curriculum materials. In the final analysis some kind of general agreement must be achieved between supervisors and church workers so that cooperation and evaluation are made possible.

C. Evaluation According to Objectives of Education

1. *Definition of Objectives.* Several terms are used to identify the character of objectives. *Aim* or *purpose* is used to set direction, intent, or desire. The term *goal* or *objective* focuses on outcomes, the changes which should take place

in the program and pupils. Some educators use the terms *immediate* objectives and *ultimate* objectives to make these distinctions. In the educative process the purpose or aim is to teach but the goal or objective is to learn. In the church the purpose is to provide a church school but the objective is to produce disciples and to glorify God and help build his Kingdom.

2. *Source of Objectives.* One's philosophy of life, setting his value-system, and his philosophy of education, describing his concept of education, determines the source of his objectives.

The Christian draws his objectives from the philosophy of the Christian world view based on divine revelation. Christian theology, Christian philosophy and Bible furnish primary sources. In church education these sources are used and added to one's concept of the church. Thus, objectives in church education provide a very practical basis for church action.

Theological evaluations are important in church education. Theology is the source of the curriculum. It serves to test doctrine and practices that exist, testing them by the Word of God. Our goals concerning *what* to learn, *how* people behave, and relationships to God and man are determined by our theology. All psychological and socialized practices are illustrated and used by means of theological insights. Thus, it is important to ascertain if what is happening in church education is connected with Christian truth. In the final analysis all of our evaluation will be conducted in terms of our theological position. The achievement of our objectives will be tested by our concept of theological outcomes. The test of individual growth and development rests directly on our theological concept of redemption and personal experience through grace and faith.

3. *Function and Use of Objectives.* In general the function of objectives is to provide the direction for the whole educational process. More specifically, objectives guide, motivate and inspire teachers with worthwhile endeavor, a sense of purposefulness, and destiny. Guidelines are provided for the selection of materials and methods. Objectives serve pupils by motivating pupil response, laying a better basis for cooperation and learning, all resulting in meeting their needs, greater interest, concentration, and effort. The whole curriculum is integrated by objectives, and relationships of truth are revealed. Proper sequence is given to all educational activities. Objectives also set the pattern for leadership training and the production of curriculum materials.

Ultimately, aims and goals provide a basis and method of evaluation. If the objectives are clear and followed, the status and gain can be ascertained. Thus, both the quantitative and qualitative aspects of education can be appraised, tested, and measured. On this basis changes can be made which lead to improvement.

4. *Principles and Objectives.* Certain general principles should guide in the use of objectives.

1. They should point toward the ultimate goal of Christianity
2. They should cover all elements in good Christian education
3. They should be practical and tangible
4. They should reflect the needs of pupils
5. They should be graded to pupil ability
6. They should be stated in meaningful terms
7. They should emphasize action as well as knowledge
8. They should be revised periodically

5. *The Content of Objectives.* The purpose and goals of Christian educators vary widely, directly dependent on

their philosophy of Christianity. Among naturalistic liberals goals center in making a religious adjustment to one's environment. Social liberals would emphasize the "democracy of God" and pragmatic influences. A divine-human democracy is a final social ideal. Neo-orthodox advocates would stress right relationships to God through the church. Catholics emphasize the role of the church also in Christian growth.

All such views above can be summarized perhaps in the following statement produced by sixteen Protestant denominations:

> The objective of Christian education is that all persons be aware of God through his self-disclosure, especially his redeeming love as revealed in Jesus Christ, and that they respond in faith and love—to the end that they may know who they are and what their human situation means, grow as sons of God rooted in the Christian community, live in the spirit of God in every relationship, fulfill their common discipleship in the world, and abide in the Christian hope.[2]

Among evangelicals objectives are derived from divine revelation. Christian education here becomes a reinterpretation of God's revelation. Its purpose is to show God revealed and to assist man in revealing God in his total life and environment. In outline form the objectives may be summarized as follows:

1. Individual objective—Christlike character (Matt. 5:48; 15:4) and spiritual maturity (Eph. 4:1; 2:10; 5:16)
2. Social objective—the production of the church and preparation for the Kingdom of God
3. Prophetic objective—Second Coming of Christ and establishment of the Kingdom of God.

6. *Objectives and the Supervisor.* The supervisor will examine general and specific objectives and compare them with a statement on philosophy. Revision should be made from time to time. He will help workers clarify objectives and state them clearly, particularly at the level of the teaching-learning process. He will apply objectives to the total church program to test its total impact and effectiveness. He will help workers interpret the results of evaluation.

Frequently, objectives are stated at the departmental level in church school work. The supervisor will help evaluate or restate these in terms of meeting needs and in terms of the ability of the workers to handle them.

Some efforts ought to be made to determine if the teaching purposes have resulted in the outcomes desired. The determination of specific goals at this level, however, is not very common.

Supervisors should be sensitive regarding the matter of achieving good balance in a statement of objectives. Evangelism should be at the heart of the work, but development and knowledge should not be overlooked. Service activities are important as well. Meetings with individuals and groups will be necessary to achieve this. (See Appendix No. 1).

Specific objectives become very important. These have to do with pupil needs, problems and specific learning outcomes. Such matters as attendance, punctuality, soul winning, giving, service projects, and many others should have specific goals and plans related to them.

Objectives regarding the practice of evangelism and development of spiritual life are most important. Here the supervisor in Christian education must be particularly sensitive in the use of Biblical standards and guidelines.

D. Evaluation According to Standards of Education

1. *Definitions of a Standard.* Webster defines a standard as an approved model, a grade or level of excellence. A Christian education standard is an established rule in measuring, guiding, and judging the total Christian education program in its organization, administration, curriculum, leadership, methods, and spirituality. A standard has been likened to a map for a traveler, a footrule for the carpenter, a chart for the pilot, a pattern for a dressmaker, and a blueprint for a builder. Essentially, standards become the means whereby one's philosophy of church education and the goals set up are realized, practiced, and measured.

2. *Need for a Standard.* The prophet Isaiah challenged the people when he said, "Lift up a standard for the people" (Isa. 62:10). So often Christian education workers are satisfied with a low level of efficiency but a standard will help overcome this. Standards help provide a basis for improvement, help overcome a lack of vision and cooperation, and provide a basis for evaluation. Many churches seem unaware that there are better ways to operate the program of church education. Standards help point the way toward improvement.

In order to have good church education, workers must know what good church education is, make plans to achieve it, and carry out the specific requirements to accomplish the ideals and goals set up. Standards help lay the basis for such action.

3. *Uses and Purposes of Standards.* Evidences of the use of standards are seen in daily life. The footrule and yardstick are standards of physical measurement. For spiritual measurement we are admonished to be like

Christ, to walk in the things of the Holy Spirit. Paul compared individual Christians to Christ, he compared other Christians with himself, and one church with another. Standards thus become the means whereby one can compare what is with what ought to be. The standard provides the answer to the question, "How do you know whether or not you have a good program of Christian education?"

Purposes and functions of standards are many. Chief among these are:

1. Standards lay the basis for planning
2. Standards reveal the essentials of good Church education
3. Standards provide the incentives for action
4. Standards reveal the basis of good balance in the program
5. Standards help achieve unity and uniformity of thought and action
6. Standards provide a practical basis for evaluation

On the other hand, standards are no panaceas. They are limited by the understanding, application, and determination of the workers in using them. In the final analysis improvement will result not only in vision but in the quality and effort of the workers in accomplishing the essentials of good church education.

In a study of eight churches of various denominations in Richmond, Ky., in 1970, it was found that the higher the percentage of score on a church education standard was, the larger was the number of professions of faith. It appears, therefore, that the use of a standard will result in better quality of work and a larger evangelistic harvest.

4. *Types of Standards.* Spiritual standards refer to the

basic character and ethical principles of Christian life and behavior. Administrative standards guide in the organization, operation and supervision of the total program. Educational standards refer to the technical qualities and activities involved in teaching and learning. Professional standards refer to convictions and procedures regarding one's preparation and service. Social standards refer to social graces and ethical conduct. Personal standards deal with appearance, attitudes, personality and spiritual life. Evangelistic standards focus on soul winning. Standards of relationship indicate means whereby Christian love is translated into person-to-person daily contacts. Overall, therefore, standards become the basis for testing, measuring, and evaluating results.

5. *Sources of Standards.* The Christian looks to the Bible as his source of authority for his standards, to the very nature and function of the church. Standards derived from these sources indicate what the character and program of church education should be. Some of these standards would include the following:

1. The church school is the school of the church (Eph. 4:11–13)
2. The church school is a seeking school (Luke 19:10)
3. The church school is an evangelistic school (Luke 19:10)
4. The church school is a missionary-minded school (Matt. 28:18–20)
5. The church school is a concerned school (Col. 2:6,7)
6. The church school is a studious school (2 Pet. 3:18; 2 Tim. 2:15)
7. The church school is a spiritually-maturing school (Acts 1:8; 15;8,9)

8. The church school is a well-trained school (Rom. 12:1,2)
9. The church school is a competent school (2 Tim. 2:15)
10. The church school is a well-organized school (1 Cor. 14:40).

On the basis of these essential elements the standards would be organized in writing under the following categories. Standards for

1. Organization
2. Administration
3. Supervision
4. Curriculum
5. Leadership Qualifications and training
6. Evangelism
7. Missions
8. Attendance
9. Outreach
10. Facilities
11. Teaching and learning
12. Home-church relationships

Standards may be constructed and prepared in written form for local church use by the application of educational philosophy, theory, and objectives. Ready-made standards may be secured from denominational and other sources, evaluated, modified, and adopted. Illustration of the use of standards in program and leadership improvement will be given in Chapter Five. Samples are included in the Appendixes.

6. *Standards and the Supervisor.* Where the value of a church education standard is recognized, the supervisor will find in the use of it a means for carrying out his work, for evaluation of status and results in the program, and a means for the motivation of his workers toward improvement. The supervisor, therefore, should move, as early as possible and as tactfully as possible, in getting the workers

in the local church program of Christian education to adopt and use standards. Illustrations and sources are included in the Appendixes (No. 2–6).

E. Implementation of Change as a Result of Evaluation

1. *The Need for Change.* If improvements are to be made, change must take place. Such changes will not only better the quality of the work, but will also help to solve any problems of the staff and meet needs. The generally low level of Sunday school teaching is cited as one of these needs. No supervisor will prove to be effective unless qualitative changes are made, therefore a strategy for change based on evidences gathered from evaluation is needed.

As churches face the rapidly changing world of this century "holding power" is not sufficient. If there is no planning for change to meet the demands of the time, if successful, purposeful change is not effected, the unlimited opportunities anticipated in the new day may leave some churches working on "survival plans" rather than "battle plans."

2. *Motivation for Change.* If changes are to take place, workers must make them. They will not make changes unless they see the reasons for and values in them. This demands both information and motivation. If proposed changes make sense and help to meet basic needs, if they contribute to improvement generally acceptable to the workers, then cooperation in implementing changes will be secured.

Supervisors should emphasize the will and Word of God in seeking motivation. Based on these sources, good Christian education becomes a strong motivating power to effect changes. It is not a matter of personal opinion or desire, but what will glorify God, accomplish his will, and advance the cause of the church. People will very likely change attitudes toward acceptance of change if it can be shown that such changes will result in better teaching and learning and in reaching more people for Christ. Changes must, therefore, contribute to the achievement of the objectives of the church and church school.

3. *The Process of Change.* Changes cannot be simply announced. Instead, everyone involved must be drawn, as far as possible, into the decision-making processes.

Certain questions need to be asked in implementing change, such as

1. What is to be accomplished?
2. Why is it necessary to make a change?
3. What methods will be used to effect change?
4. What precisely will be changed?

The techniques to be employed would include (1) identifying the problems, (2) getting the facts, (3) passing group judgment upon them, (4) laying plans for improvement, and (5) implementing the plans and reporting results.

Decision making is relevant to communication and change. Good decisions are often lacking due to bad communication, misunderstanding, prejudice, fear, or lack of adequate information. The application of good principles connected with the approach to problem solving will contribute to improving the techniques of decision making.

4. *Guiding Principles for Change.* When changes are proposed and attempts made to implement them, varying reactions are to be expected from the workers. Such reac-

tions will vary from outright opposition to enthusiastic approval.

Where resistance to change is present, sometimes people have very valid reasons for their objections. These should be considered but at the same time efforts should be made to meet them adequately. Some people resist because of a feeling of guilt about not living up to the best in Christian education. Since change involves possible turbulence, others are afraid to face the situation. Anxieties, fear, and tension result, causing a hesitancy to move. Threats to status and position perceived in change cause opposition. Failure to understand the process of change and lack of resources for effecting the change are other reasons for resistance.

6. *The Supervisor and Strategy for Change.* Supervisory activities should influence the direction, rate, and quality of change. While it may be true that change will occur without supervision, the supervisor should develop a strategy for producing the best changes. His role, however, is not one of creating change but rather one of facilitating a change process. The task is to (1) analyze where the program and workers are in relation to needed or proposed changes, (2) remove roadblocks, and (3) develop strategies whereby change is achieved. Following are some general suggestions regarding strategy.

1. Create an awareness of need
2. Create an interest in the needed change through evaluation of possibilities
3. Demonstrate the nature of the proposed change
4. Explore possible implementations of the change
5. Build convictions about the value of the change
6. Illustrate the change through trial and evaluation of outcomes
7. If outcomes are positive, adopt the change

The supervisor is able to change people by motivating them with the concepts and principles of Scriptural Christianity, a biblical philosophy of Christian education, and practicing the best principles for change. To these he will add plans for introducing innovations, restructuring the teaching-learning situation and up-grading the teaching-learning practices.

There are two additional factors for creating the climate for change in a local congregation. One is the support of the pastor and administrative boards. Strong administrative instruction and/or support for change is helpful, if not necessary. Support for change can be most readily secured from those who share a concern for a common problem and participate in the search for viable solutions.

This leads to a second factor. Change can be secured more often when participation in the process is widespread. It is helpful and necessary for those who are most likely to be affected by change to participate in its planning. Supervisors should seek these ends.

Questions for Class Discussion

1. How may the program of supervision provide for continuous evaluation?
2. Compare various non-Christian philosophies of education with that of a Christian philosophy of education.
3. Study various philosophies of church education and compare them with an evangelical view.
4. Study the place and function of objectives in church education.
5. What is the philosophy of evaluation to be used in church education?
6. What and how are educational standards adopted by a church?

7. What evaluation instruments are suitable for church education?
8. Design a list of questions which cover a total church program of education.
9. Evaluate a unit of study in Sunday school lessons to discover objectives. How can they be improved?
10. What kinds of evidence can be gathered to determine the extent to which educational purposes are being achieved?
11. What difficulties are there in interpreting results of appraisal programs?
12. Develop a complete philosophy of church education.

Questions for Local Church Use

1. Make a study of the theological position of the church. What effect does theology have on the church school?
2. Formulate a set of age-group objectives for children, youth and adults.
3. Study the denominational standards advocated for your church school.
4. How can we evaluate our total church program of education?
5. Prepare simple questionnaires asking for pupils, parents, and members to tell what they like or dislike about the church school.
6. How should results of evaluation procedures be made known to pupils, workers, parents, and the church?
7. What is good church education? How can this be determined in our church?
8. What concept of education prevails in our local church?
9. How can resistance to change be solved in our church?
10. Is the process of evaluation understood in our church?
11. What steps should be taken in our church to evaluate (1) the total program, and (2) specific areas in the program?
12. What are the changes we need to face?

Notes for Chapter Four

1. The reader is referred to the author's previous work *A Christian Approach to Education,* rev. ed. (Mott Media, 1977), for a fuller treatment of this subject.
2. Cooperative Curriculum Project, *The Church's Educational Ministry: A Curriculum Plan* (Bethany, 1965), p. 8.
3. Dean, Kenneth M., "Principles for Guiding Successful Change," *The Sunday School Builder* (May, 1970), p. 17.
4. Gangel, Kenneth O., *Leadership for Church Education* (Chicago, Moody Press, 1970), pp. 316–319.

Outline for Chapter Five

The Evaluation and Improvement of a Total Church Program of Church Education

A. The Total Church Program Concept

1. Definition and Responsibility
2. Church Educational Agencies

B. Evaluation of the Total Church Program

1. Scope and Means of the Evaluation
2. Evaluation of Church Education Philosophy
3. Evaluation of Church Education Objectives
4. Evaluation of Administrative Practices in Church Education

C. Improving and Supervising the Total Church Program

1. Planning Where to Begin in Improvement
2. Planning Procedures for Improvement
3. Organizing Procedures in Improvement
4. Motivating Procedures for Improvement
5. Developing the Program of Improvement and Supervision
6. Research

D. Improvement and Supervision of Program Elements

1. Improving Curricula Practices
2. Improving Facilities, Equipment, and Resources
3. Improving Evangelistic Practices
4. Improving Instruction
5. Improving Worship Activities
6. Improving Social Life and Recreation
7. Improving Human Relations and Fellowship
8. Improving Service Training Activities
9. Improving Age Group Work and Agencies

Questions for Class Discussion

Questions for Local Church Use

Notes for Chapter Five

CHAPTER FIVE

The Evaluation and Improvement of a Total Church Program of Church Education

A. The Total Church Program Concept

1. *Definition and Responsibility.* Church education is Christian education at the level of the local church. It is based squarely on the responsibility for a ministry of teaching which is derived from the nature of the church itself and according to the revelation of standards of New Testament Christianity. Since the church teaches it must have a school and the school which results is most properly called the *church school.*

The function of the church school is to carry out the demands of the *didache* (teaching ministry), in not only proclaiming the *kerygma* (gospel), but also in helping the church to do the work of the church. Church education, therefore, is something which does two primary things: (1) it provides a Bible-teaching ministry, and (2) it supports, penetrates, and integrates the work of the total church without at the same time interfering with any of the distinctives and functions of the church. Instruction, therefore, permeates, guides, and deepens all the work of the church. On the basis of its total function then, church education is expressed in the total program of the church, and therefore from this function derives its name as the total church program of church education. Church leaders and officials are directly responsible for both the operation and improvement of the total program. The local church Board of Christian Education guides and coordinates this. The pastor and Director of Christian Education take strong parts, particularly the latter, in formulating policies, developing the means, and carrying out the processes involved in evaluating and improving the total program. Most certainly all workers should cooperate and participate in the efforts involved.

2. *Church Educational Agencies.* For *general* Christian education there are at least three channels through which the ministry of teaching can be expressed: (1) the home, (2) the Christian school, and (3) the church. Here we are concerned only with the agencies for instruction in the local church.

Church education is characterized by the possibility of the presence of several schools within its program. Such possibilities include:

1. The Sunday School
2. Vacation Bible School
3. The School of Missions
4. The School of Evangelism
5. The School of Prayer
6. School for Leadership Training
7. Mission School
8. Extension schools

Not only is the instructional process expressed through formal schools but also through program elements and church activities. Possibilities would include such channels as

1. The music program
2. Children's work
3. Youth work
4. Adult work
5. Stewardship
6. Social action
7. Bible study
8. Christian ethics
9. Church history
10. Worship

11. Christian homemaking
12. Christian citizenship
13. Christian culture
14. Church membership and Christian life classes
15. Special days
16. Recreation and fellowship
17. Children's church
18. Weekday activities
19. Community activities
20. Christian literature
21. Denominational program
22. Special groups

Evaluation and improvement are concerned, not only with the number of agencies, but primarily with the quality of work that goes on in the agencies that are present.[1]

B. Evaluation of the Total Church Program

1. *Scope and Means of the Evaluation.* A broad, comprehensive, and thorough plan of evaluation is needed to properly appraise the total educational program of a local church. Included in this plan would be schedules for evaluating the following aspects of the total program:

1. Evaluation of the Philosophy
2. Evaluation of the Objectives
3. Evaluation of the Structure
   Includes organization, administration, supervision, facilities, and resources
4. Evaluation of the Processes
   Includes curriculum and methods of teaching and learning
5. Evaluation of the Product
   Includes leadership, pupil development, and supervisory results

Questions to be asked would include:

1. Are we reaching our objectives?
2. How effective is the program?
3. Are our methods the best?
4. How can we test and measure progress?

Such questions would indicate somewhat the function of the evaluative process in the total program which is

1. To determine what the needs are
2. To measure progress and achievement
3. To evaluate the effectiveness of the educative process, materials, and equipment
4. To help formulate plans for improvement.

Evaluations are made by applying the philosophy, objectives, and principles in the forms of standards of excellence to the total program. In this way a comparison of what *is* with what *ought to be* is made possible.

2. *Evaluation of Church Education Philosophy.* Out of the foundations of church education, based solidly in the presuppositions of the Christian faith and divine revelation, comes the philosophy and objectives of church education. One's concept of what good Christian education is provides a basis for comparison. Discussion on this question was given in the previous chapter along with several representative philosophies.

In making an evaluation of philosophy, church workers would have to identify the distinctives of each philosophy and compare them with their own or some other philosophy. Among evangelicals this process is one of comparing ideas on definitions and purposes of church education with those derived from Scripture and conservative reasoning. Each of the several elements of philosophy would be compared. These include: (1) definition and function, (2) view of reality (metaphysics), epistemology (knowledge), logic, and axiology (values). Such matters as concepts of man, truth, values, curriculum, teaching, learning, and adminstration would be considered. In church circles, schools of thought have a bearing on these matters: (1) what does the liberal say? Neo-orthodox, naturalistic, etc., (2) compare with evangelical views.

To illustrate this process briefly, the following twelve principles are listed for purposes of comparing the evangelical view with that of others. Church education is

1. God-centered in its concept of reality
2. Christ-centered in its goals
3. Spirit-controlled in its program and leadership
4. Revelation-revealed in its concept of Truth
5. Bible-based in its psychology
6. Pupil-related in its psychology
7. Spiritually-derived in its value-system
8. Pupil-focused in its methods
9. Love-directed in its discipline
10. Church-managed in its program
11. Growth-conscious in its evaluation
12. God-glorifying in its total process.[2]

Most philosophies, when applied to education, issue in some kind of statement on *educational theory*. Principles are derived from the philosophy and form the basis for practice. Many statements of church education principles can be found in the literature. Comparisons can be made of these principles with those practiced in a particular local church.

For sake of illustration and comparison, following is

found a statement of the most commonly accepted program principles among evangelical church educators:

1. Church education is the church at work educating
2. The objectives of church education and the local church are the same
3. The tasks of church education and the church are the same
4. Church control is required (through Official Board)
5. A centralized planning agency is needed (Board of Education)
6. The program should be based on Scripture
7. The program should be practical (useful)
8. The program should be comprehensive (all ages included)
9. The program should be integrated (one unified program)
10. The program should be graded (age-adaptations)
11. The program should be simple (easily followed)
12. The program should be flexible (allow for changes)
13. The program should be democratic (freedom)
14. The program should be clear (easily understood)
15. The program should be functional (duties clear)
16. The program should be well-organized
17. The program should be efficiently administered
18. The program should be effectively supervised
19. The program should be periodically evaluated
20. The program should be expanded when needed.[3]

The whole program should be Christ-controlled through the work of the Holy Spirit, Bible based, pupil-related, and socially-applied.

The *questionnaire* is a helpful instrument to guide in the evaluation of philosophy in the church. The following list of questions is suggestive:

1. Has a philosophy of church education been developed by the Boards and leaders of the church in cooperation with officers and teachers?
2. Is the philosophy published and available to all personnel?
3. Is there constant reviewing, revision, and revitalizing of the philosophy?
4. Does the philosophy make provision for a statement on educational practice among the age-groups?

3. *Evaluation of Church Education Objectives.* Objectives are practical formulations which serve as guides for the educative process and are derived from one's philosophy of life and philosophy of education. Discussion of their nature, function and use was given in Chapter IV.

Evaluation of the objectives, purposes, aims, and goals of church education for any particular local church can be made in several ways. Find a statement of objectives from a source which can be counted on and compare your own set with this. Perhaps it will be found that no such statement exists in the local church. Or it may be found that the current statement is inadequate and needs revision. A test of one's statement of objectives may be made by investigating the source, functions and use of objectives in the local church program. The written statement needs evaluation in the light of the principles of good objectives (see previous chapter). The content of the objectives should be examined to see if all facets are covered—individual, social, and prophetic.

Statements of objectives should be formulated for each level of the educational process, as follows:

General or Ultimate Objectives—come out of the purpose of the church and Scripture

Specific Objectives
Individual and personal—Christian maturity
Social—development of the church
Prophetic—Kingdom of God
Age-group Objectives
Curriculum Objectives—courses and units
Classroom Objectives—teaching and learning

Statements of objectives have been made by Christian educators, publishing houses, schools of thought in Christian Education, writers, denominational Christian education headquarters, and local churches. Some of the sources of such objectives may be examined by making reference to Appendix No. 1.

Statements on specific objectives can be found in general church literature, denominational, and interdenominational curriculum materials, and elsewhere.

General objectives can be illustrated by reference to the following list of general objectives for the church as a whole.

1. Investigation	—	Find them—Luke 19:10 (seek)
2. Evangelization	—	Win them—Luke 19:10 (save)
3. Identification	—	Hold them—Col. 2:6,7
4. Information	—	Build them—2 Pet. 3:18
5. Sanctification	—	Empower them—Acts 1:18
6. Consecration	—	Use them—Rom. 12:1,2
7. Supervision	—	Improve them—2 Tim. 2:15
8. Perfection	—	Mature them—2 Tim. 3:174

Pastors, superintendents, and supervisors would find it wise, helpful, and very useful to call for a statement of age-group objectives annually. Three of these would be required, as follows:

1. What we seek to do among children this year.
2. What we seek to do among youth this year
3. What we seek to do among adults this year

Certain key questions could be asked:

1. Has a set of general objectives for the total church program been formulated, published and made available to all workers?
2. Does the curriculum have aims and objectives that fit the needs of the individual pupil?
3. Do these objectives fit the needs of the church community?

Help on the formulation of written statements of objectives can be secured by referring to the volume entitled *Preparing Instructional Objectives* by Robert F. Mager (Belmont, California, Fearon Publishers, 1962).

4. *Evaluation of Administrative Practices in Church Education.* One of the *structural* elements to be involved in evaluation is that of the administrative practices which prevail in any given local church. Such practices involve the organizational framework, administrative procedures, facilities, equipment, and resources. Several approaches to the evaluation of such practices have been developed to include questionnaires, rating scales, surveys, clinics, administrative standards, professional consultation services, among others.

One of the most common forms of administrative evaluation is through use of the *questionnaire.* Questions in written form are asked about each facet of the educational program from purposes to product. Kenneth Gangel has suggested this approach for a church. Following is a list of categories to be covered. For more details see the Appendices (No. 2–6).

Evaluating the Organizational Structure
Evaluation of Curriculum and Instructional Procedures
Evaluation of Records, Evangelism and Outreach
Evaluation of Personnel Recruitment and Training
Evaluation of Church-Home Relationships
Evaluation of Facilities and Equipment[5]

There are certain *administrative devices* that can be used for total program evaluation. As an illustration, for many years the *Sunday School Superintendent's Problem Finder* supplied in the Leadership Education Audio Visual Kit of the National Council of Churches of Christ has been helpful. This device can be examined by referring to Appendix No. 4.

Other illustrations of administrative devices include *surveys* of program emphases and *age-group programs.* An illustration of this kind of evaluation is provided in what is called a "Correlation Pattern for Christian Education in the Local Church," published by Harvest Publications (Appendix No. 7).[6]

There are a few published surveys for use, such as *How to Improve My Church's School* by Guy P. Leavitt.[7] The survey is made in four sections: (1) My Job and I, (2) My Purpose, (3) My School's Organization, and (4) Administering the Affairs of My School, with twenty questions in each section. An Improvement Grading Chart gives the score. On the basis of the data gathered a church will find it possible to decide what improvement is needed, how improvement is to be made, and plans developed to implement the desired changes.

Two other publications provide suggestions for a complete system of evaluation for church education. The United Presbyterian Church U.S.A. through their Board of Christian Education published a volume entitled *How to Evaluate Your Christian Education Program.*[8] This is a denominational publication but has many fine suggestions adaptable to any local church. Questions directed at evaluating the total program are given.

The second published volume was that produced by D. Campbell Wyckoff on *How to Evaluate Your Christian Education Program.*[9] This work was prepared at the request of the Division of Christian Education of the National Council of Churches of Christ as a standard for use in local church evaluation of the total program. A set of evaluation forms is included.

Another excellent work produced by evangelicals is *The Key to Sunday School Achievement,* edited by Lawrence O. Richards, for the Greater Chicago Sunday School Association (Moody, 1965). Sets of detailed standards on the total program along with a scoring guide are provided.

Administrators and supervisors have also found that the application of an *administrative standard* helps to evaluate a total program. Illustrations of these can be found in Appendix No. 5. A discussion of the nature, substance, and function of standards was provided in the previous chapter. Administrative standards are based squarely on the nature and work of the church. The essentials of the standard, therefore, are derived from the nature and work of the church. The process of doing this will look like the following by using the Sunday school as an example:

Church Purposes			*Sunday School Essentials*
1. Spiritual life	—	Being	1. Church School—Eph. 4:11-13
2. Investigation	—	Finding	2. A Seeking School—Luke 19:10
3. Evangelization	—	Winning	3. An Evangelistic School—John 4:35
4. Identification	—	Holding	4. A Concerned School—Col. 2:6,7
5. Information	—	Building	5. A Studious School—2 Pet. 3:18
6. Sanctification	—	Maturing	6. A Spiritually Maturing School—Acts 1:8, 15:8,9
7. Consecration	—	Using	7. A Well-trained School—Rom. 12:1,2
8. Competency	—	Improving	8. A Competent School—2 Tim. 2:15
9. Efficiency	—	Producing	9. A Well-organized School—I Cor. 14:40
10. Perfection	—	Growing	10. A Growing School—2 Tim. 3:17

Based on these principles it is possible for a church to formulate a written statement on administrative standards which covers the entire gamut of activities and age-levels where instruction takes place.

For use in small churches the author developed an evaluation device, using standards as its basis. The total program is covered. See Appendix No. 8 for this.

Still another technique for evaluating the total church program is use of *Church School Clinic* procedures. These efforts are guided generally by outside Christian education consultants or denominational field representatives.

Procedures involve both church workers and consultants in a direct and personally involved study of the actual situation which exists in the local church. A professionally developed set of evaluation questions and guidelines, based on Christian education standards, is used in gathering data for evaluation. Then plans are laid after analysis for improvement. The Board of Christian Education and the Presbyterian Church, U.S. has sponsored evaluation clinics of this nature. The work is described in a publication entitled *The Church School Clinic* by Sara Little.[10] An exceedingly thorough analysis of a church education program is made by using the procedures of a clinic. It is possible that such service may be secured through contacts made by local churches with their respective denominational headquarters.

C. Improving and Supervising the Total Church Program

1. *Planning Where to Begin in Improvement.* If improvement and supervision are to take place, the data derived from the efforts of evaluation must be put to use. Action must follow evaluation. This requires planning, and supervisory plans are put into action through the medium of the program of supervision.

Supervision is not a matter of personal opinion. It concerns the glorifying of God and the quality of the educational program. These have priority and become highly motivating factors leading to program evaluation and work which issues in improvement.

Asking certain key questions may help supervisors and church education leaders set a priority system for the use of data gathered through evaluation.

1. Ask teachers and workers what they consider to be the present and urgent needs, by using conversation, interviews, questionnaires, etc.
2. What can one find in church education literature on the needs of leaders and workers in church education?
3. What surveys can we use to get information on our needs?
4. What are the needs in other churches and Sunday schools?
5. What are the needs of beginning teachers and other workers?
6. Are we satisfied with present results?

If the supervisor wants to avoid over-dependence upon his own work, then it would be wise for him to rely on the initiative and resourcefulness of the educational workers, and particularly the teachers. A program which is based on the needs, problems, interests, and concerns of the workers will probably get further along the road toward improvement. Supervisors, therefore, should make a real effort to show how evaluated data relate to such matters. When recognition of needs among workers is absent, then the supervisor should stimulate the workers to become aware of their needs. This he can do, not only through pointing out the negative things revealed in the evaluated data, but primarily by showing what possibilities and potentialities are present for improvement.

2. *Planning Procedures for Improvement.* At the heart of improvement and supervision are the principles of problem-solving. Much has been said in the literature about the procedures involved in the handling of data, leading to the solution of problems. The problem itself emerges, objectives are set up, means and procedures are worked out for the gathering of data bearing on the prob-

lem, cooperative efforts are then made to solve the problem, followed by any modifications and adjustments deemed necessary, Democratic techniques are also involved in these procedures, making provision for common, free and cooperative study, sharing, discussion, and meeting of minds in solving the problem.

A wide variety of types of planning is available to supervisors and church workers. Short-range planning refers to daily or annual planning. Long-range planning involves a much longer time span, usually two or three years or more. Improvement of administrative and teaching-learning processes would involve short-range planning. Improvement of philosophy, objectives, curriculum, and facilities would require more long-range planning.

At times special planning becomes necessary. Planning for improvement of special days, use of music, art, and teacher problems might be classified here. A fourth type of planning involves working with individuals and groups for a particular purpose in a specific situation, department or class. Group planning is very popular in educational circles at present. How to work with individuals and groups will be dealt with further on. Some people would include research as still another kind of planning procedure. However, not too much of this is done in church work.

In all types of planning room should be left for freedom and flexibility. This needs to be made available, however, by tactful guidance on the part of supervisors who help individuals and groups work out their own problems.

3. *Organizing Procedures in Improvement.* In the public school system provisions are made for supervisory services in the administrative organization of the system. Most churches, however, have no such formal system. In its ab-

sence reliance must be placed on individuals and boards for supervisory services. In the local church, where sensitivity exists for providing a supervisory program, either formal plans are made to organize a program of supervision with a Director of Christian Education to handle it, or supervision is laid on the shoulders of committees and officers to get the work done. Such committees may be made a permanent part of the Official Board or Board of Christian Education. The duties of such committees would be to create policies and plans for evaluating and supervising the total educational efforts of the church. In this latter plan responsibilities for supervision are shared widely by the entire educational staff.

4. *Motivating Procedures for Improvement.* Since the development of a supervisory program leading to educational improvement is a collective task, motivation is demanded if maximum results are to be achieved. Educational changes cannot be successfully made without careful preparation for this. To do this it becomes necessary to create a mood or mind-set on the part of the workers—even pupils and members—so that they will be receptive to new developments.

Teachers, for example, need to be made psychologically ready, made to understand fully the proposals for supervision and improvement and asked to give substantial approval and support. Educational reform should not be forced, if promise of success is achieved. Accordingly, it is wise to stimulate discussion, invite criticism, and meet objections squarely. The positive advantages of supervisory plans must be made clear and acceptable. Workers do not like to run risks of having their inadequacies and weaknesses exposed, so it becomes necessary to show how supervision and improvement will fit in without threatening the status of the workers. Rather, it should be pointed out how each teacher and worker is capable of making a contribution through cooperation with improvement efforts, thereby strengthening the sense of security among all workers. It would be wise also to seek the understanding support of parents, pupils, and church members.

5. *Developing the Program of Improvement and Supervision.* Whether formal or informal in organizational structure, improvement and supervision take time. No supervisory program of any scope should be conceived as a mere addition to other activities in the total church program. Time for planning and development must be found somewhere and somehow for effective results. If the work is communicated as important then priority can be given to it.

If development takes place the supervisor must have time to meditate, consider and plan for improvement. Once headway is gained patience is needed to secure results. Obstacles must be expected and accepted as normal. Persistence is needed to achieve the goals. The supervisor should be available at all times to workers to give assistance when needed and called for. If the program has been well-planned and skillfully started, its development should take place in an orderly and cooperative fashion.

The supervisor will serve as a catalyst in motivating, coordinating, removing difficulties, maintaining high standards, and providing resources. He must be quick to act when difficulties arise. Attempts should be made to receive varying points of view, to reduce tension, conflicting and irritating factors in the interest of working smoothly and cooperatively. People often have to learn how to work together. "By his own persistent, tactful and skillful activity the supervisor can do much to promote the program's development in a cooperative, democratic manner."

6. *Research.* Research has had a place and function in general education for a long time. Not too much, however, has been done in research in the field of church education. As far as supervision goes educational research would center more or less in the problems of teaching and learning and experimentation. In the church school perhaps the supervisor could assist teachers who might be interested in carrying on simple research projects.

A few publishing houses maintain departments of research. Among evangelical Christian educators this is illustrated by Gospel Light and Scripture Press. The latter has recently introduced to local churches a new program entitled "Church Evaluations Research Service." Sets of questionnaires administered to youth and adults help the local church evaluate such matters as pupil attitudes toward and responses to the teaching-learning ministry in the church. Indications where help is desired on the part of pupils are also supplied. Through use of computerized processes statistical data on these issues are organized and analyzed and conclusions drawn from which the local church can derive evaluation information pursuant to program improvement.

Various denominational publishers do some research of their own. In the field of character education the work of Ernest M. Ligon at Union College has been significant. Certain Christian schools have done research but much of their work is left unpublished.

There may be efforts at research off the record in local churches but this is unknown. On record reference is made to research and evaluation in a Presbyterian Church in Dallas, Texas, where efforts were made to evaluate knowledge, ethics, and doctrine.[11] Reference was also made to research projects sponsored by the Department of Christian Education of the Episcopal Church in curriculum development research and evaluation of published materials.

Rightly used research can be emphasized by the supervisor as a method of learning. Research efforts provide vision and vital information on improving teaching-learning processes. The reader is referred to Appendix No. 9 for a suggested list of possible formal and informal research projects.

D. Improvement and Supervision of Program Elements

1. *Improving Curricula Practices.* Improvement of curriculum is based directly upon one's concept of curriculum and his ability to evaluate the curriculum. In its narrow sense of meaning curriculum refers to the subject matter to be taught. In its widest meaning it refers to the entire program, to all elements which have a bearing on teaching and learning.

Any evaluation of curriculum should begin with its philosophy, theory, and objectives. These should be studied carefully. In secular education various curriculum theories stress knowledge, mental discipline, social and creative skills. For the Christian divine revelation forms the basis for developing purposes and objectives by which authority is guided. Thus, in the Christian concept, the curriculum is Christ-centered through the work of the Holy Spirit, Bible-integrated or Bible-based, pupil-related and socially applied. The setting and atmosphere in which Christian teaching and learning goes on is characterized by Christian love, faith, hope and obedience, all the outcomes of the presence and work of the Holy Spirit who provides the divine element in the educational process.

Many principles underlie good curriculum theory and practice. Perhaps the following list will suggest means of evaluating a curriculum in the local church:

1. The curriculum should be Christ-controlled through his Spirit
2. The curriculum should be Bible-based; the Bible is the textbook
3. The curriculum should be pupil-related, graded to the needs of the pupil and psychological laws applied
4. The curriculum should be socially-applied, providing suggestions and opportunities for practicing the Gospel and recognizing the obligations of the church to the community, to society as a whole, and to the home
5. The curriculum should seek to develop personality in its fullest—physically, mentally, socially, spiritually
6. The curriculum should be unified in purpose, content, and scope
7. The curriculum should be comprehensive, including subject matter, skills, the total Christian heritage, and all ages
8. The curriculum should be evangelistic, seeking to bring all ages to a knowledge of Jesus Christ as Savior and Lord
9. The curriculum should build the church of tomorrow, evoking convictions, service, and leadership
10. The curriculum should be missionary, appealing to all ages, all groups, and all nations
11. The curriculum should be flexible, making room for changes in scope, content, and methods

12. The curriculum will provide for balance, giving adequate time for comprehensive treatment
13. The curriculum should be well-organized so that sequence will provide for themes, seasonal interests, units of study and cumulative learnings
14. The curriculum should provide attractive and practical materials of high quality

Factors to be considered in the curriculum would also include objectives, place of the teacher, pupil and Bible, teaching and learning practices, and subject matter and teaching-learning materials. In the liberal view the Bible serves as a resource guide, an illustration of Christian character and conduct, as one source in solving personal and social problems. To the evangelical, the Bible is the inspired Word of God, his source of authority, the primary source of truth-content for teaching and learning, and the means whereby the presence of truth is tested and measured. Various types of curriculum materials have been developed to handle Christian truth and biblical content. Major types include uniform lessons, closely graded lessons, departmental lessons, graded elective materials, weekday materials, and Vacation Bible School materials. Special materials for special groups are also available.

Those responsible for choosing the curriculum for a particular church should study the entire organization and purpose of each curriculum and then make the decision as to which of the planned curricula best fits the local situation and comes closest to the ideal for the particular school in mind. Most publishers have written statements of curriculum philosophy and practice available and these should be carefully studied. A curriculum chart will reveal the curriculum pattern and control over a period of years.

Where possible, the mixing of materials in a single program should be avoided. An exception to this might be adults and older youth where electives are common. Otherwise efforts should be made to adopt one curriculum system at least through the high school age.

In addition to Bible content, so-called collateral activities in the curriculum should be carefully reviewed. These include such matters as music, art, visual aids, memory work, handwork, stewardship and service activities.

Control and evaluation of curriculum materials should be placed in the hands of responsible people or a good Curriculum Committee. Superintendents and other officers can be helpful to teachers and departmental workers in the selection and use of curriculum materials. Individual teachers, classes and departments may share in the selection of materials but final approval should be given by the Board of Christian Education or its equivalent. Selections should be made on the basis of Scriptural principles, age-group needs, the total church program, and the long-range plans of the publisher. Other factors to consider include cost, denominational emphasis, size of school and classes, pupil backgrounds, past experience of workers, time available for class with classroom space and equipment, and teaching methods. Some of the principles involved in selection would include:

1. Are materials in harmony with the Bible?
2. Are materials in harmony with objectives?
3. Are materials graded to meet pupil needs?
4. Are materials practical for teacher use?
5. Are materials attractive and of high quality?
6. Are materials adaptable to the local situation?
7. Are extra-biblical materials true to the Bible?

8. Are materials provided for expressional activities which are in line with the will of God revealed in the Bible?
9. Are materials comprehensive, rich, and spiritual enough in content?
10. Are materials in harmony with good educational principles?

In the use of such principles as listed above evaluations should be made according to a threefold analysis: (1) are materials theologically and philosophically accurate? (2) are they educationally sound? and (3) are they psychologically adequate? An evaluation tool which might prove helpful at this point was developed by the Greater Chicago Sunday School Association.[12] In Chapter Four standards were provided to evaluate Sunday school materials with regard to theology, pedagogy, pupil-relatedness,and teachability. Various types of curriculum materials were also described in this work. A rating scale was provided with an evaluation guide and point system useful in comparing several curriculum systems.

Another evaluation device was compiled by Professor Margaret M. Swaim, Alderson-Broadus College. Categories to be evaluated included objectives, content, educational factors, methods, units, evaluation, literary quality, teachers, the home, and mechanics. The reader is referred to Appendix No. 6 for an examination of this work.

The application of *Administrative Standards* to curriculum materials and processes is also helpful in curriculum evaluation and improvement. These standards ask key questions and suggest guiding factors for using the curriculum. The reader may refer to a discussion of standards previously given.

Not to be overlooked in curriculum procedures is the matter of integrating the curricula of the various church educational agencies. Proper integration will help to ensure good balance and will assist workers in avoiding overlapping and outright omission of important curriculum elements. Five program elements have been developed to guide in the construction of the curriculum as a whole. They are (1) evangelism, (2) instruction, (3) worship, (4) fellowship, all issuing in (5) service (Acts 2: 41–47). Each church should study and evaluate its curricula offerings in terms of these five elements. Suggested factors involved in a comprehensive program might include the following:

Evangelism

1. Soul winning
2. Enrollment and Attendance
3. Follow-up of absentees
4. Religious census
5. Outpost and mission schools
6. Instruction in evangelistic techniques
7. Missions
8. Church membership and Christian life classes
9. Special days
10. Visitation

Worship

1. Atmosphere and setting
2. Scriptures
3. Prayer
4. Devotional arts, such as pictures, stories, etc.
5. Offering
6. Liturgy
7. Leadership
8. Training
9. Act of worship itself

Instruction

1. Bible study
2. Christian doctrine
3. Christian ethics

Fellowship

1. Burden bearing
2. Recreation
3. Use of leisure time

4. Church history, organization, polity
5. Missions
6. Teacher training
7. Leadership education and development
8. Stewardship
9. Social action
10. Techniques of evangelism
11. Worship
12. Fellowship and recreation
13. Prayer
14. Christian home making
15. Christian citizenship
16. Christian culture
17. Service training

4. Christian ethics
5. Christian athletics
6. Social etiquette
7. Christian culture
8. Leadership development
9. Personality development; morale building
10. Correlation and integration with other instructional items
11. Cultivation of the Christian spirit

Service

1. Home missions
2. Foreign missions
3. Class projects
4. Home department
5. Group projects
6. Gospel teams; witnessing teams
7. Ministering to human need

The program as outlined above will have certain *characteristics:*

1. It should be *graded,* to provide for individual differences and to meet the needs of the various age levels
2. It should be *varied,* to engage and hold the interest, to motivate the best interest, and to retain permanent aspects
3. It should have *unity,* to show the individual that he is a part of the whole, to avoid duplication and omissions, to

provide for concerted and strong action, and to give balance

4. It should be *comprehensive,* to give depth as well as breadth to the program, to provide content and quality to the offerings, and to avoid being fragmentary
5. It should be *spiritual,* to avoid professionalism and formalism, to be honored of the Holy Spirit, and to reach the spiritual objectives.

Program coverage for the separate age groups is important. Study and analysis should be made of this factor as well. Previous reference was made on the use of standards in this regard but perhaps the following possibilities would also prove helpful.

CURRICULUM POSSIBILITIES FOR CHILDRENS' WORK

Sunday School Classes
Expanded or Extended Sessions
Childrens' Church (May be Beginner, Primary, Junior)
Sunday evening Sessions
School of Missions
Weekday Religious Education
Weekday clubs
Weekday Nursery School
Vacation Bible School
Day Camping
Child evangelism
Supervised recreation
Christian Life, Church Membership class
Children's choirs
Ushers
Accolytes
Story Hours
Summer Program (camping, special activities)
Drama Groups
Hobby Clubs
Extended VBS
Scouting
Denominational program
Christian Day School
Child Care Center
Kindergarten Program

Variation of Above Programs

Extended session of SS on weekdays
Weekdays free Kindergarten for Poor
Six week study group on Sunday evening
Four week study group on missions with bus tours included
After school story, activity time-weekly
After school supervised play
SS extended to Wednesdays for children 3:30–5:30—paid teacher—small tuition fee
Thursday or Saturday church school
Winter day camping
Saturday afternoon Stamp Group
Musical enrichment sessions—listen, sing, study
Choir and study sessions
Choir and church membership session (weekday)
Choir and activities (arts and crafts)
Junior Fellowship (Grades 4,5,6)—meets twice month—1⅓ hours each
Once a month movie and recreation day

Special Groups

Good News Club
Bible Memory Club
Arts and Crafts Club
Scouting
Pioneer Girls
Christian Service Brigade
Sky Pilots
Child Evangelism Fellowship
Children's Bible Mission
Rural Bible Mission
Youth Gospel Crusade
Children for Christ
Challenger Club
Youth for Christ
Christian Endeavor
Special Schools for the Retarded, Blind, Deaf, etc.

Saturday morning adventures—activities, trips
Neighborhood playmate program—club ideas
VBS in a Basket
Junior Club Program
- Fall—school of missions
- Winter—hobby and craft groups
- Spring—study groups; pastor's class

CURRICULUM POSSIBILITIES FOR YOUTH

Christian Endeavor, YF, etc.
Sunday School
Youth Choir
Missions Club
Ushers
Youth Week
Membership Training
Help with Worship Services
Librarians
Drama
Visitation
Recreation and athletics
Visual aid helpers
Musicians
Song Leaders
VBS students or workers
Church officers
Church offices
Projects
Day camping
Resident camping
Special music (uke bands, etc.)
Denominational program
Inter-denominational programs
Youth revival
Youth prayer groups
Service groups—jails, rest homes, etc.
Youth for Christ
Bible memorization
Scouting
YMCA, YWCA
Retreats
College campus ministry
Conventions
Weekday religious education
Weekday education groups

Debate teams
Pastor's classes
Counseling and guidance
Special interest groups—music, art, etc.

CURRICULUM POSSIBILITIES FOR ADULTS

Sunday

Morning worship
Sunday school
Evening study sessions
Evening worship
Choir
Ushers
Host and hostesses
Sermon seminar
Visitation
Drama
Musical groups
Special services
Buzz sessions
Forum, lectures, discussion groups
School in Christian training
Home Department
Extension Department

Weekday

Midweek prayer and praise
Membership training
Bible-study
Organizational meetings
Christian Family instruction
Board meetings
Pastor's hour-parsonage discussion groups
Retreats
Bible conferences
Family camps
Literature league
Social events
Evangelistic meetings
Surveys-census
Athletics and recreation
Child-parent activities—PTO
Mission school
Workshops
Special clubs
Men's Brotherhood & women's society
Mother's club
Special groups—hobby, crafts, etc.

Obviously, no local church will make provision for all of these curriculum suggestions, but selections can be considered in the interest of enlargement and deepening of the quality of the work done. Not to be overlooked, however, is also the possibility that a church might be doing too much.

Clifford Anderson developed a device for evaluating program *coverage* for the age groups. (See Appendix No. 10).

Evaluation of curriculum may also be approached by studying reasons for *drop-outs* and use of *opinion polls.* The follow up of drop-outs will possibly give clues as to what to change in the curriculum. Polls of opinion among pupils, parents, leaders and teachers may possibly supply some guidance.

To summarize, the curriculum will be judged to be good or bad in the degree to which it contributes to the effectiveness of learning, to growth and achievement as a Christian. In an early effort at evaluation of curriculum Frank McKibben offered an outline of questions to be used to analyze and evaluate courses of study, textbooks, course outlines, series of projects, and the collection and use of pupils experiences. (See Appendix No. 11).

2. *Improving Facilities, Equipment, and Resources.* If a total program of church education is to work effectively, provision must be made for the availability and proper use of facilities. Improvements made will depend directly on how well the church school is meeting departmental space and equipment requirements, how efficient is the use of the space, and what plans are laid for remodeling and/or expansion.

It is unfortunate when a church fails to have a Master Plan for its property as a whole. The educational facilities need to be part of these plans. Multiple purpose buildings and rooms provide flexibility in use at less cost.

Few churches are able to afford "ideal" facilities, but all schools need to make the most of what they have. By placing pupils of relatively the same characteristics and ages together the basis for departmentalization is established. To do this requires facilities, equipment and resources which "fit" the respective age groups. Space should be assigned to groups only in the light of the *total* program and *total* needs of the school. Space quantity and space type will vary according to the age groups. In general, smaller children need more space than older ones. This is why the needs of children should be considered first. An annual survey of space and equipment needs will prove beneficial. *Questionnaires* are used in some instances to make such surveys.

It is a gross waste of valuable resources to hinder teachers by forcing them to work in outdated buildings and with obsolete materials. There are many who will argue that the creative teacher will be able to do a good job in almost any type of building. There is some truth in this argument, but we must remember that improvement is in the forefront, not simply a good job.

If the pastor and educational workers lack information on facilities and equipment, seek expert counsel. Such counsel is available at denominational headquarters, outside sources, and church architects. They can provide information on trends and use of facilities.

Supervisors should be alert, not only to standards of good usage, but also to conditions which present problems to educational workers. A classroom is bad for children when

1. Walls are dark and drably furnished
2. When furniture and wood work are dark
3. When sunlight and other light is glaring

4. When chalkboards are of adult size
5. When furniture is permanently fixed to the floor
6. When glossy surfaces on equipment are glaring
7. When plants shut out air and light through the windows
8. When light fixtures are unshielded
9. When there is not enough light on dark days
10. When physical discomforts are present

When church workers become aware of how much physical surroundings affect learning, perhaps the basis is laid for improvement. It does not take a great deal of money to keep things clean and attractive. Surplus materials placed in storage saves time, space, and money. Checks on heating and ventilation may prove to improve attendance and decrease absenteeism.

Standards for church buildings are currently available. Many denominations set up their own standards for buildings, remodeling, and use of space and equipment. Local churches should consult these sources first. Certain independent sources are available as well. C. Harry Atkinson produced *Building and Equipping for Christian Education* for the National Council of Churches of Christ.[13] This work provides standards, principles, plans, space requirements and guidelines for use of facilities for both large and small churches. A recent publication of the same type is *Focus: Building for Christian Education.*[14]

Occasionally, churches have found *rating scales* useful in studying space and facility needs. Such factors as classroom comfort, including seating, lighting, heating, decorations, equipment arrangement, and audio-visuals are rated.

A very helpful publication for small churches was produced by Adams and McCort, *How to Make Church School Equipment.*[15] Excellent suggestions were made in this work for adapting to the space a church already has and making equipment for local use. Multiple use of space and equipment in small churches effects economy.

Whether large or small, church schools should strive to meet standard classroom requirements. Set up the ideal and then strive to meet it, even over a long period of time. Studies should be made, not only of space requirements and use, and equipment, but also of the *upkeep* of facilities. Lack of cleanliness, orderliness, and comfort can interfere with the teaching-learning processes. The proper administrative procedure to be used, therefore, is an *annual survey* of space and equipment needs and the meeting of requests of workers and teachers for materials promptly.

Not to be overlooked is the matter of future plans. Are long-range plans being made for the anticipation of the needs for physical plant based on growth statistics?

3. *Improving Evangelistic Practices.* Evangelism is a responsibility of supervisors along with all other curricula elements. Improvement is needed in soul winning responsibilities, enrollment and attendance, visitation practices, and missions. Perhaps the place for improvement to begin in the church school is in examining the church's philosophy of educational evangelism.

Evangelism is the good news of salvation in Christ; it is in the deliverance of this message that evangelism is realized. It is the work of church education to evangelize as well as to teach Bible. Evangelism is the heart and life of church education. Without it there can be no real Christian education. Thus, every Christian worker must bring his own service within the perspective of evangelism. Each of them must have Christ as a personal Savior. Each of them should know how to present Christ and explain the way of salvation. If you feel that workers cannot do this, here is the place to begin the work of improvement. Every opportunity should be taken to present the Gospel. Every worker should rely heavily and personally on the Holy Spirit and pray much.

Emphasis on evangelism can be given in many ways. Following is a list of suggested activities:

1. Study lesson materials to discover evangelistic emphasis
2. Are the elements of the Gospel message clearly presented?
3. Are the needs of pupils revealed and stressed?
4. Stress the conversion of people of all ages
5. Be careful about emotional appeals
6. Be sure to follow up all converts
7. Stimulate teachers to do the work of an evangelist
8. Train leaders and workers in presenting the Gospel
9. Plan special programs geared to evangelism
10. Stress the reaching and winning of parents
11. Make available evangelistic materials for use in the work
12. Locate, enroll and win new prospects
13. Hold departmental meetings and workers' conferences to plan evangelistic programs
14. Set goals for soul winning and prayer
15. Study the use of the record system for evangelistic implications
16. Promote the spiritual life of the school
17. Maintain a responsibility list which includes home members, irregular members, and prospective members

A second phase of the evangelistic program is *enrollment, attendance,* and *outreach.* Growth is important but consistent attendance is also necessary. For years the percentage of attendance to enrollment has been set at about 80 percent. If the school drops below this, an unhealthy situation prevails.

A strong visitation program helps both attendance and growth. The first step toward growth is to locate prospects, then call on them. Each church school should adopt a pattern of visitation for its work. Continuous and consistent visitation is best in the long run over special short-range periods of emphasis.

Perhaps improvements can begin by checking the church membership roll to determine who are going to Sunday school among church members. Check the visitation records of departments and classes and stir them to new action. Strong Cradle Roll, Home and Extension Departments reach, enroll, and win many. The Cradle Roll stresses a home ministry while the Home and Extension Departments stress reaching the shut-ins and the shut-outs. Other efforts to promote the interests of the school should be made through use of newspapers, bulletins, and other mass media. Use of other devices such as special days, contests, special programs, community canvass, and outreach emphases likewise help. Careful attention should be given to the absentee follow-up system. It is more important to hold those we already have than to try to plug the holes of those who drop out. Maintain a warm-hearted atmosphere of friendliness, cheerfulness, and fellowship.

A third phase of evangelism is *missionary education.* The Great Commission is at the heart of church education. The causes of missions should be promoted in the church school. A knowledge of missionary needs, personnel, and program is imperative. Both staff and pupils should be kept missions-conscious. Definite plans for missionary emphasis and projects will contribute to the improvement of missionary emphasis. Following is a suggestive list of possibilities:

1. Distribute missionary literature
2. Feature missions in departments, classes, and workers' conferences
3. Help teachers emphasize missions
4. Hold missionary conferences and schools of missions
5. Use missionary speakers and special days
6. Use missionary visual aids
7. Sponsor displays, exhibits, and curios
8. Plan home and foreign missionary projects
9. Support foreign missionaries
10. Fix responsibility for promoting missions
11. Set financial and prayer goals for missions
12. Emphasize the service motive in all age groups
13. Highlight missionary needs through lessons, prayer, and music

4. *Improving Instruction.* Classroom instruction is at the very heart of the program. If improvement is to be made at all, here is where it should take place. The work and ministry of teaching is the life's blood of Christian education. While we recognize this as a part of the program, the importance of this subject is so great that discussion of it is reserved for special attention in the next chapter.

5. *Improving Worship Activities.* Because the life principle is so important in church education, worship is brought into central focus. The improvement of worship activities by the supervisor will affect all that goes on in the school, because the practice of good worship leads to a recognition of the presence of God through the Holy Spirit in the teaching-learning process and fellowship of the people. It becomes, therefore, the responsibility of the

supervisor, in improving worship activities, to improve both the concept and practices of worship.

The supervisor needs to develop a clear and common understanding of the nature of true worship. Worship is more than an "opening exercise," it is realizing and practicing the presence of God, to commune and fellowship with Him. Whenever worship is genuine, the following elements are present:

1. Adoration
2. Praise
3. Thanksgiving
4. Message-truth
5. Offering-giving
6. Confession and penitence
7. Humility and dependence
8. Sincerity
9. Prayer
10. Atmosphere—rooms and attitudes

The purposes of a worship program are twofold: (1) to provide for worship itself (the act), and (2) to provide training for worship participation for both workers and pupils.

Improvement in worship will very likely begin with the concept of worship. Do workers and pupils understand true worship? Do our departmental worship sessions reflect this? Are worship sessions well-planned? Are they properly graded to the age-groups? Are the worship elements (listed above) recognized and practiced?

The supervisor's plan for worship improvement would include at least the following aspects:

1. Locate and diagnose weaknesses and defects
2. Design objectives for improvement, to include
    a. Deepening of the sensitivity to the nature of true worship
    b. Improve present practices
    c. Train the leadership

d. Promoting a worship training program
e. Correlation of all worship activities in the church

An evaluation should be made to determine needs and present status of the worship program. *Questionnaires* are useful in this regard. For example, one church distributed a questionnaire to the church school membership devoted to two topics: (1) what do you like about our worship program?, and (2) what do you not like about it, and what do you suggest for its improvement? Pupils might be asked to react to and evaluate particular worship services.

Standards and *check lists* are useful in guiding worship as well as in locating weaknesses. By applying them it becomes possible to compare what is with what ought to be and thereby chart future courses of action. Sample Standards and Check Lists are included in Appendix No. 11.

Efforts to improve practices might center in the following possibilities:

1. Can the "spirit" of worship be improved? Reverence?
2. Are announcements, greetings, business matters and social emphases taking too much time?
3. Is the time adequate?
4. Are physical conditions just right?
5. Are programs well-planned?
6. Are programs well-handled?
7. Are leadership training opportunities in worship available?
8. Are departmental worship program adequate?
9. Is there a sufficient number of worship-workers to help leaders?
10. What is the situation regarding class worship activities?
11. Are occasional periods of worship teaching provided for pupils?

12. Is the pastor involved in church school worship activities?
13. How much correlation is employed between church school and other worship activities in the church?
14. How often and in what ways is cooperative study of worship problems realized?
15. Is there a worship committee to help plan worship activities?
16. Are worship materials readily available to workers and pupils?
17. Is the order of worship services changed periodically?
18. How much pupil participation in planning and conducting services of worship is evident?
19. What emphasis is placed on personal devotions? Home worship?
20. Are worship sources available in the church library?

6. *Improving Social Life and Recreation.* This area of emphasis not only finds a place in the life and development of the Christian as an individual and as a group but is also an important part of the curriculum of church education. Leisure time activities are also encompassed by this curriculum element. Supervisors will need to know the real significance of this area so proper interpretation can be given, adequate provision in the program made, and thorough evaluation achieved. Fellowship is part of the relationship in being and acting Christian. A rich spirit of fellowship should pervade all relationships and activities in the church school. Wholesome social activities are needed in all age groups, geared to the needs and interests of the pupils. Suggestions for use of leisure time as a Christian are helpful. An emphasis on burden bearing is greatly neglected in the average church. Caught up in all of this is a sense of God's presence, the development of right attitudes, ideals, and habits.

Any evaluation of this curriculum area will require answers to certain key questions, such as

1. Is the need felt for real emphasis in this area?
2. Has a philosophy of social life, recreation, and fellowship been worked out in the church, to form the basis for action and to show relationships to spiritual living?
3. Have policies and plans been formulated for the various church education agencies in the church for this area?
4. Is there a year-round calendar of well-balanced activities provided for the whole church?
5. What is the relation of the church social program to available opportunities provided in the community?
6. Is there a need for one leader to direct the work in this area?
7. What training is provided for workers and pupils?

Standards for use in evaluating and directing the program in this area are useful. The author has discussed this matter in a previous work.[16] A good book to consult for guidance is *Recreation and the Local Church,* edited by Frances Clemens and others.[17]

An evaluation of the program and activities in this area would include

1. Setting up of objectives
2. A survey of the present program provisions
3. Measuring results of what is done

McKibben has suggested a *survey schedule* for use in evaluation of the program. (See Appendix No. 12). Such matters as general provision, objectives, scope, quality of activities, pupil participation and leadership, leadership and supervision, and physical equipment were covered by this measuring instrument.

Measuring results is difficult. Outcomes in this, as well as other areas, are very subjective. Actually no measuring instrument is adequate, but critical analysis and judgment must take place. Some expected outcomes might include evidences of the deepening of appreciation for one another, spirit of good fellowship, deepening of appreciation for and loyalty to the church, good sportsmanship, fair play, honesty and excellence of spirit, clean speech, choice of pure recreational activities outside the church, and evidences of greater initiative and assumption of responsibility.

7. *Improving Human Relations and Fellowship.* Fellowship and human relations among Christians is based on the quality of Christian love (Matt. 22:34–40; 25:31–46). Good works toward our fellowmen prove our Christian love (I John 4:20). Fellowship is developed and deepened by worshiping together, studying together, and serving together. Organized Sunday school classes help to realize and foster these goals. To improve this program element other concerns should be emphasized, such as genuine burden bearing, the proper use of leisure time, Christian ethics, social etiquette, morale, and Christian culture.

Voluminous literature is available on human relations and group dynamics. Improvements in human relations can be improved by observing and practicing, among others, the following principles derived from this literature.

1. There should be faith in the ability and value of each staff member
2. Consideration should be given to the wishes and feelings of individuals involved in a decision or action
3. Decisions should not be made arbitrarily but in terms of their effects upon others

4. Decisions should, as far as possible, be based on principle rather than on personal opinion
5. Be cheerful and friendly; overlook faults
6. Do extra things for workers and pupils
7. Be courteous, kind, and thoughtful
8. Be prompt in keeping appointments and agreements
9. Ask, do not order that things be done
10. Be sure to give credit where it is due; be willing to share credit
11. Be available for counseling in behalf of both spiritual and other problems
12. Use the technique of group decisions as often as possible
13. Air differences as a step toward progress
14. Do not allow differences to become personal matters
15. Harness criticism to win appreciation
16. Criticize in private, with a smile; give praise first; appeal to self-interest, in a constructive way
17. Pray much

8. *Improving Service-Training Activities.* All that has been said previously leads up to the question of service—to God and fellowman. Jesus said that he came not to be ministered to but to minister even to the point of death. Service, therefore, should be the natural outcome of Christian experience, study, training, and prayer.

The first step toward improvement is prayer and vision. "Where there is no vision the people perish" (Prov. 29:18). "We are saved to serve." How much service activity is actually going on among members of the church school, both on the part of individuals and in the organized educational program? This is a paramount question. Motivation to this end must be given by the supervisor.

Achievement of vision depends directly upon one's philosophy of service. This in turn is developed from two sources: (1) one's concept of stewardship, and (2) Scriptural teachings about ministry. The Christian concept of stewardship is based completely on the teachings and example of Jesus Christ and demands the giving of one's time, money, talents, and complete self to the service of God and fellowman. The Bible reveals at least three types of ministry to be engaged in by laymen besides those types of ministry engaged in by church leaders.

1. The Ministry of Reconciliation—2 Cor. 5:19,20
2. The Ministry of Restoration—Gal. 6:1,2
3. The Ministry of Service—Gal. 6:10; Matt. 25:31–46

It is at the Sunday school class level where perhaps the greatest improvement in service activities is needed. These classes can go into action to serve God and help meet human need. Practical projects should be planned for achieving this. Following is a suggested list of such activities.

1. Organize an Extension Department—reach shut-ins and shut-outs
2. Organize a Home Department—reach aged and home bound
3. Organize a Cradle Roll Department—reach parents and infants
4. Stress Home and Foreign Mission Projects
5. Work with community agencies in social service activities and projects
6. Study lesson materials for suggested activities and projects
7. Start a furniture warehouse
8. Plan a clothing and food room

9. Visit jails, hospitals, retirement homes, and other institutions to help meet needs
10. Reach special people and groups, such as retarded children, crippled, blind, deaf and dumb
11. Be sensitive to the needs of the homeless, lonely, and jobless people
12. Bear a burden for the diseased, immoral, and outcasts of society
13. Relate the interests of church members to unchurched people, i.e., early morning golf group, hot-rod club, etc.
14. Start Nursery Schools, kindergartens, Christian day schools, supervised play periods, etc.
15. Use telephone, radio, and TV to make services available to people in times of need and emergency
16. Conduct work camps at home and abroad to assist underprivileged people
17. Work in inner city and slum areas
18. Get interested in the problems of society, such as drugs, alcohol, war, poverty, etc.
19. Harness the time, talents, and energies of youth in these projects and others
20. Organize gospel teams for witnessing, visitation, and music
21. Conduct training classes to equip people for service

Evaluation of service activities can be made by the use of standards, rating scales, and questionnaires. Frank McKibben provided an Observation Outline for evaluating these areas of the curriculum (See Appendix No. 13). It covers such matters as definition of service, quality of service activity, pupil participation, giving, adult supervision, and training outcomes. Suggested measures for possible improvement would center on the creation of objectives for service, training program, correlation of all service activities in the church and church school, making available service materials and suggestions, and reporting progress.

9. *Improving Age Group Work and Agencies.* Age-group work refers to the educational program outside the Sunday school for children, youth, and adults. The scope of the work for the age groups was dealt with in Section B. of this chapter. Beyond the scope, however, lies the quality of work that goes on in the respective age groups. Space prohibits the full discussion of this matter at this point, but supervisors should be concerned with the internal progress of each age group. Some concerns would include

1. Are there committees to plan each of the programs for the age groups?
2. Are objectives established and reported for each group?
3. Are materials and equipment and facilities adequate?
4. Is the work of each group correlated with that of the Sunday school and church work?
5. Are the teaching-learning processes at a quality level?
6. Are regular reports of work of these groups given to the church?

Agencies concern organizations inside and outside the church constituency related to the educational program. The home has first place among such agencies. Do teachers visit in the home? Is there a Home Department? Is there a plan for promoting family worship? What about Christian Family Education? Are there special classes for parents? Special days? These and other key questions need to be asked.

Agencies outside the church would include denominational, interdenominational and community relationships, even international ones. While these are important they do not fall within the province of this particular work for discussion.

Questions for Class Discussion

1. Discuss the philosophy of a total church program of education.
2. How is supervision related to the problem of selecting and developing curriculum materials?
3. What criteria should be used to evaluate curriculum materials?
4. How is a group conference conducted to analyze units of teaching and learning?
5. How does one determine what is important to teach?
6. Outline in some detail a plan that one might use in making a study and evaluation of the curriculum as a whole or in some particular area of learning (worship, recreation, etc.)
7. How does a church improve its worship programs?
8. How does a church determine the effectiveness of its service training program?
9. Develop a Christian philosophy of fellowship, social life and recreation.
10. Develop a complete set of criteria for evaluating a total church program of education.

Questions for Local Church Use

1. Define a total church program of education for the local church. What goes into it?
2. How does the church school determine how good its lesson materials are?
3. How is a good filing system for curriculum materials set up?
4. What criteria should be used in evaluating the curriculum?
5. What are the criteria to be used in evaluating the facilities?
6. What theological factors are important in curriculum adoption?
7. How can Sunday school lessons be related to other curriculum aspects more effectively, such as worship, service, recreation and evangelism?

8. What are the objectives for worship in the Sunday school?
9. What are the objectives for service in the Sunday school?
10. What are the objectives for fellowship, social life and recreation?
11. What are the objectives for evangelism?
12. What kinds of research should be used in our church?
13. How are the age-groups agencies integrated with the Sunday school?

Notes for Chapter Five

1. For a more extended discussion of church educational agencies readers are referred to one of the author's previous publications, *Christian Education for the Local Church,* rev. ed. (Zondervan, 1963).

2. For a more extended discussion of the philosophy of Christian education readers are referred to one of the author's previous publications, *A Christian Approach to Education,* Mott Media, 1977. Reference is also made to Kenneth Gangel, *Leadership for Church Education* (Moody, 1970), Chapter Two. The list of principles included, here, however, avoids the pitfalls of too many "centers" as offered in the Gangel list.

3. See Byrne, *Local Church,* Chapter One, for detailed discussion.

4. See Byrne, *Christian Approach,* Chapter One, for detailed discussion.

5. See Gangel, *Leadership,* Chapter Five, for discussion of this question.

6. Used by permission of the publisher.

7. Standard Publishing Co., Cincinnati, 1953.

8. *How to Evaluate Your Program of Christian Education,* Board of Christian Education, United Presbyterian Church U.S.A., Witherspoon Building, Philadelphia, Pa., n.d.

9. Westminster Press, 1962.

10. Board of Christian Education, Presbyterian Church, U.S., Richmond, Va., 1953.
11. Consult *Evaluation and Christian Education,* National Council of Church of Christ, p. 63 and 75.
12. Consult *The Key to Sunday School Achievement,* edited by Lawrence O. Richards (Moody, 1965).
13. Atkinson, C. Harry, *Building and Equipping for Christian Education,* New York, National Council of Churches of Christ, 1956.
14. Widber, Mildred C. and Scott T. Ritenour, *Focus: Building for Christian Education* (Pilgrim, 1969).
15. Westminster, 1955.
16. Consult Byrne, *Local Church,* Chapter 8.
17. Brethren Press, Elgin, Illinois, 1965.

Outline for Chapter Six

The Improvement and Supervision of the Teaching-Learning Process in Church Education

A. Improving and Supervising the Teaching-Learning Process

1. Definitions
2. The Concept of Learning
3. The Improvement of Learning
4. The Concept of Teaching
5. The Evaluation of Teaching
6. The Improvement of Teaching

B. Improving and Supervising Individual Workers

1. Concepts of Supervisory Services
2. The Supervisory Approach
3. Supervising Personnel Administration
4. Working with Personality Factors
5. The Supervisor and Problems of Teaching
6. Methods of Assisting Individual Workers
7. The Supervisor and Problem Teachers

C. Group Methods for Improvement and Supervision

1. Morale Factors
2. Human Relations Factors
3. Working Together
4. Group Methods of Improvement and Supervision
5. Leadership Education

D. The Evaluation and Improvement of Individual Growth and Development

1. Priority of Individual Development
2. The Approach to Evaluation of Individual Growth
3. Criteria for Evaluating Individual Growth
4. Means and Methods of Evaluating Individual Growth
5. Assistance in the Evaluation of Individual Growth
6. Diagnosing Learning Difficulties
7. A Testing Program

E. The Evaluation of Supervision

1. Evidences Among Workers and the Program
2. Self-evaluation

Questions for Class Discussion

Questions for Local Church Use

Notes for Chapter Six

CHAPTER SIX

The Improvement and Supervision of the Teaching-Learning Process in Church Education

A. Improving and Supervising the Teaching-Learning Process

1. *Definitions.* The teaching-learning process is also known as the educative process. It focuses on instruction. It involves both teaching and learning. In one sense it is one process, with teaching and learning two facets, parts of the same process. It is also a manifold process, involving objectives, teacher-pupil relationships, content (curriculum), methods, and other related factors, such as environment, personality, and the power of God.

Actually, very little is known about learning itself. We do know, however, that learning involves motives, attitudes, desires, perceptions, comprehension, and other factors.

Teaching involves attitudes, aims, materials, methods, preparation, and presentation. The task of the teacher is to recognize and work with the dynamic and manifold nature of teaching and learning. In this whole process he works with the Spirit of God in integrating these varied factors to focus them on the learner in an attempt to realize the great goals of Christian teaching. Thus, the Christian teacher is to work with God in bringing the pupil to Godlikeness and kinship (I Cor. 3:9; II Cor. 6:1). This is the very essence of Christian Education.

2. *The Concept of Learning.* There are many definitions of learning. Perhaps they can be summarized in an over-simplification by saying that learning is change—in mind, in heart, in habits, in experience, and in behavior. More important than definition, however, is what happens when learning takes place. No one knows exactly. Whatever takes place in the nervous system is still largely a matter of conjecture. There is rather general agreement, however, on conditions most conducive to learning. It *is* known that where learning takes place changes take place in thinking, feeling and doing, brought about through perceptual, intellectual, emotional and motor activity.

Learning is dynamic, multiple, and quite individualistic. There are dynamic relationships between thinking, feeling, and doing. All learning is quite unique to each individual. Teachers should be aware of this dynamic and individualistic quality in learning.

Secular educational psychologists have done much to reveal the laws and principles of learning, as follows:

A. The Principle of Pupil-activity (Self-activity)
   1. Learning comes from the pupil's own responses to stimuli
   2. Repetition—the more often something is repeated, the better we remember, the deeper our self-activity.

B. The Principle of Motivation (Interest)
   1. The intensity of the learning response depends upon interest
   2. Effect—we remember and want to repeat pleasant experiences while trying to forget and avoid unpleasant ones.
   3. Use—the use of knowledge and practice of what we know tends to make truth more easily remembered and understood.

4. Recency—the more recently we've studied something, the better we remember it.

C. The Principle of Apperception (Preparation and Mental Set)
   1. The nature of the learning response depends upon past experience and present frame of mind.
   2. Readiness—there are special times when a pupil's mind is unusually open to certain kinds of learning; age and maturity also enter in here.

D. The Principle of Individualization—learning responses are determined and limited by individual differences in ability

E. The Principle of Socialization
   1. Every response has its social implications—"No one lives unto himself alone."
   2. By-product learnings—all truths are accompanied by many by-product learnings; sometimes these concomitant learnings are more important and valuable than the central facts being considered, for as the pupil learns he is forming vital attitudes.

While there might not be a Christian concept of learning as such, there is a Scriptural point of view on this subject. The Christian is not truly educated until he experiences God. Learning to the Christian is not narrowly conceived in intellectual terms, change, or adjustment, but it embraces all of these and much more—regeneration by the Spirit of God.

The Christian can go along with many of the findings of scientific psychology on the physiological basis of learning. He will insist, however, that beyond the physical nervous system lies the soul or spirit which is responsible for conscious responses.

Because the Christian point of view is the whole-person-in-life, learning is not confined merely to "mental" processes. Instead, other factors are present. These include purpose, maturation, emotions, motivation, understanding, apperception, and the pupil's attitudes. Certain external factors also affect learning directly, such as class spirit, class size, building and equipment, and others. These factors are descriptive of an integral phase of learning termed "Concomitant learning."

Then, too, the Christian insists on the importance of certain spiritual factors in the learning process. These include the capacities of the regenerated heart-life of pupils, the person and work of the Holy Spirit who is the Spirit of Truth, the power of the Word of God, and the spiritual affinities of the nature of man to respond to the wooings of the Spirit and divine truth. Also, faith provides a way for truth and personality to meet most effectively.

Donald Joy advocates what he calls meaningful learning.[1] Learning goes beyond perception and mere memory to the place where the learner can organize meaningfully the information he has for permanent use. The teacher seeks to determine the concepts that pupils need to know and relates them to needs, all of which issues in life-changing ideas. Motivation becomes necessary to arouse the curiosity of the pupil to gain the information necessary for building the big ideas. The function of the teacher in this view is to offer temporary ways of organizing information for meaning with the hope that the pupil will soon do his own organizing of ideas into concepts. This theory Dr. Joy has called "conceptual learning" and it is offered within an evangelical context.

At least four steps to learning have been identified:

1. Motivation—learner must *want* something
2. Stimulation—learner must *notice* something
3. Participation—learner must *do* something
4. Reward—learner must *get* something

Perhaps these steps will be found suggestive in evaluating the learning process.

3. *Improvement of Learning.* Implications of learning for the supervisor in effecting improvement are many. As far as possible all distractions and interferences should be removed. Careful attention in achieving this should be given by supervisors and administrators resulting in the protection of the teacher and class time. Learning is enhanced when cooperative planning in teaching and learning is experienced in the classroom. Wherever possible pupils should be involved in decision making and free discussion of procedures. Stimulation of pupils on the part of the teacher in the selection of materials of instruction has the tendency to create more interest in what is being taught. It is helpful also to invite pupils to evaluate progress because everyone wants to know, "How am I doing?"

It is generally known that learning takes place best in an environment characterized by beauty, comfort, and pleasantness. Emotional satisfactions in this regard contribute directly to better learning. Here is a matter often neglected in church education. Learning is a result of experiences which are good and related to one's environment. This is environment that is both social and physical. The climate of learning is set by attitudes of acceptance or rejection and by inter-personal relationships. Since learning takes place largely in groups, then group life becomes of great importance. The sense of "belonging" becomes paramount and conducive to better learning.

Teachers can do much to effect a better physical environment for learning by making things bright, pretty, clean, and attractive. The teacher's own personal impact is of importance here also, because teaching is largely the teacher himself. Supervisors, therefore, should help teachers in self-analysis because the ideals, attitudes, goals, and communication methods directly affect learning. This is particularly true for a Christian teacher.

Since physical facilities affect learning, every effort should be made to provide the best. Supervisors, therefore, can assist administrators in planning and remodeling buildings, can assist teachers and workers in the selection of equipment, and in the psychological groupings of pupils for the learning situation.

Certain factors when present seem to contribute to better learning. Supervisors should be sensitive about these factors, call attention to them, and guide leaders and teachers and workers in the use of them.

Psychological Factors

1. Purposes and goals must be clear
2. Good emotional climate
3. Freedom
4. Understanding and comprehension
5. Good pupil attitudes

Spiritual Factors

1. Capacities of the regenerated self—new eyes of the Spirit
2. Power of the Word of God—John 6:63
3. Person and work of the Holy Spirit
4. Influence of Christian personality on pupils

External Factors

1. Good teacher attitudes
2. Class size and spirit
3. Buildings and equipment-location

4. *The Concept of Teaching.* In church education Christian teaching is considered ideally as a ministry, a high calling of God. Christlike character and thorough preparation are characteristics of his background. As a Christian the Christian teacher is called to be a witness, to reveal God, to manifest the fruit of the Spirit. As an educator he carries out God's mandate to teach (I Pet. 4:10, 11) and therefore functions as an *oracle* of God (John 7:16–18).

Negatively considered, Christian teaching is not religious teaching. The latter presents religious ideas and ideas, but Christian teaching presents Christ. It is not merely the transmission of ideas; it is not molding passive, docile subjects. Learners are self-active. They select from the perceptual field and identify with it. It is not the teacher's job to get the pupil *under* the Word but *into* the Word. Teaching is not dishing out adult organized subject matter to children and youth. They perceive somewhat differently than adults do. There must be a point of contact for them.

Looking at teaching more positively, it is the teacher's responsibility to inspire the pupil, so that the pupil is motivated. Pupils need to be directed toward goals which are Christian. They should create unrest, curiosity, attention and interest on the part of the student.

The teacher instructs but the learner explores. The teacher organizes and presents a learning situation. The learner selects from this presentation the things which meet his needs and enable him to reach the goals set up.

These things are the materials of self-activity, the external resources which the learner makes internal.

The teacher disciplines and the pupil obeys. The teacher should support the learner in his efforts to reach the goal; he must provide supplementary incentives to provide this support. At times some firmness may be necessary.

Generally speaking, in church education the teaching process must follow the pattern of the learning process. The psychological laws mentioned above most certainly will help the teacher in his task.

The teacher will also evaluate student achievement. He will help students judge their own progress and will encourage constant self-evaluation of both status and progress.

Christian teaching has a great many things in common with other types of teaching. Some things, however, are quite distinctive. Christian teaching has the advantage of the presence and work of the Holy Spirit. This provides a divine element to teaching not enjoyed by secular teachers. Christian teachers, therefore, should learn to depend upon the Holy Spirit in the teaching-learning process.

Christian teaching deals with divine revelation. Revelation does not consist of a group of ideas or facts placed alongside of others, but is God making Himself known through Self-revelation. Here again is a new dimension in learning. A very fine discussion of this fact is given along with a comparison of several types of teaching with that of Gospel teaching by Wayne R. Rood.[2] He lists five forms or types of teaching as (1) transmissive, (2) debate, (3) discussion, and (4) encounter. He advocates (5) Gospel Teaching as a superior form of teaching, providing a divine element and a new dimension.

Practical assistance in the teaching process can be provided to the teachers by the supervisor who stresses the importance of the *written* lesson plan. Many teachers do not use lesson plans, others write notes to themselves along the margins of their Bibles or quarterlies. The written lesson plan is superior because it provides a blueprint for teaching. By its use the teacher thinks through his teaching materials, methods, and class procedures in advance. Plans are made for introducing, developing and closing lessons, planning for carry-over values, and assignments for coming lessons. An example of a written lesson is provided in Appendix No. 14.

5. *The Evaluation of Teaching.* To begin with it may be helpful at this point to think about some reasons why Christian teachers fail. Many possible reasons could be cited. Following is a list of possible and common ones.

1. They fail to manifest Christlike qualities
2. They fail to pray and have faith
3. They do not understand the goals of Christian education and cannot translate them
4. They do not understand their pupils and cannot deal with them
5. They do not use proper techniques and methods and thus do not communicate thoroughly
6. They cannot select and use curriculum materials
7. They cannot plan and teach lessons adequately
8. They lack professional and personal judgment and discretion
9. They do not get along with people
10. They do not know their Bible
11. They do not understand the teaching-learning process
12. They do not know how to evaluate teaching outcomes
13. They do not know or perform duties outside of class
14. They fail to visit and evangelize
15. They do not feel a divine call to the work
16. They are lazy and indifferent

Because of the grave importance of teaching and learning, supervisors should make every effort to *get the facts.* This requires a careful and thorough study of the instructional processes and situations. Judgment about these facts must be passed on, followed by the use of remedial devices and improvement plans.

Symptoms of teaching problems may show up in pupil life and performance, sometimes in teacher behavior, and sometimes in the teaching-learning situation itself. Possible evidences of problems might be seen in

1. Disorderly conduct and discipline problems of pupils
2. Low level of interest
3. Absenteeism and decrease in attendance
4. Poor personal relationships
5. Poor lesson planning and preparation
6. Inadequate learning
7. Emotional instability of both teacher and pupils
8. Limited participation
9. Poor cooperation
10. Disinterest
11. Inactivity in service responsibilities
12. Lack of guidance by supervisors and administrators
13. Lack of philosophy of church education and teaching
14. Lack of good curriculum materials
15. Low morale
16. Poor organization and class groupings
17. Limited and unsuitable facilities and equipment
18. Budget shortage
19. Lack of support of the workers
20. Discouragement
21. Lack of training; incompetence

At least four methods for studying and evaluating instructional practices can be identified:

1. Analysis of learning outcomes in pupil character and behavior
2. Direct observation of teaching practices
3. Analysis of reports from officers, workers and pupils
4. Examination of the record system

Evaluation of individual growth and development will be dealt with in a section of this chapter to follow. Suffice at this point to say that such evaluation often leads to evidences directly connected with teaching.

Many approaches have been designed to observe the complexity of teaching practices. Supervisors must not only be skilled in the use of observational techniques but should also be aware of their limitations and applications in any given situation. The choice of any particular method depends on the purpose and appropriateness of the technique chosen. Observation of instructional practices might include some of the following techniques:

Aspect of Teaching	*Analysis Procedure*
1. To check objectives	1. Checklists; reports; observations
2. To analyze concept of learning	2. Checklists; observations; tests; interviews
3. Organization of curriculum	3. Analysis of Sunday and weekday programs
4. Organization of class	4. Checklists; records; reports; groupings
5. Principles of learning	5. Checklists; records; reports
6. Participation	6. Time studies; diagrams of activities
7. Provision for individual differences	7. Checklist of methods; reports; and observations

8. Personal and group relations	8. Sociogram
9. Needs and difficulties	9. Reports; interviews; observations

Other general methods to be employed would possibly include recording behavior through use of diaries and anecdotal records, use of sound recordings in the classroom, and closed circuit television.

Where direct observation is not possible, the supervisor may choose the method of analyzing any reports of work available. Very likely he will have to depend upon others to get this information. It may come from the minister, workers' conference programs, check lists, analysis of written lesson plans, interviews, self-evaluation, self-rating scales, questionnaires or others. Occasionally, teachers may be asked to list their needs, problems, and difficulites. Cooperative study by the entire teaching faculty often reveals needs and problems. Questions regarding use of curriculum materials often bring to light teaching difficulties.

The record system is often revealing and becomes a good source for the evaluation of workers. Records often reveal ways and means of selection, guidance, and replacement of workers. Achievement records for workers and pupils are often quite revealing. Statistics often teach a story.

Data-gathering devices have at least three purposes for use: (1) to describe the program, (2) rate teachers and workers, and (3) secure information on worker background and qualifications. Curriculum guides and program elements previously described help in describing the program in operation. Rating of workers is illustrated by the use of Self-rating Scales. (See Appendix No. 15 for examples.) Such scales rate qualities and operational techniques on a sliding scale of numerical values based on an arbitrary standard of achievement. Applying the principles of good teaching and effective learning are other ways of evaluating processes.

Rating of teachers is often achieved by the use of observational schedules in assessing the details of teaching and learning. Frank M. McKibben has listed and described a wide variety of such devices. They are illustrated in the Appendices No. 16–24 and cover the following aspects of teaching and learning:

1. Observation of Questioning (Method of Teaching, No. 16)
2. Directed Discussion and Problem-solving (No. 17)
3. Observation of Story-telling (No. 18)
4. Observing Drill Memorization Procedures (No. 19)
5. Observation of Dramatization (No. 20)
6. Observing Supervised Study and Activity (No. 21)
7. Observing Lesson Assignment Practices (No. 22)
8. Check List on Class Management (No. 23)
9. Observation of Pupil Activity (No. 24)

Ernest Chave has also suggested observational schedules for use in assessing classroom practice. (See Appendices No. 25–29). Areas covered include:

1. Schedule on Teaching Method (No. 25)
2. Pupil Response (No. 26)
3. Analysis of Routine and Environmental Conditions (No. 27)
4. Observing Discipline and Classroom Management (No. 28)
5. General Observation of Class Visitation (No. 29)

In a later work Frank McKibben suggested another general observation guide for analyzing the teaching-learning situation as a whole. (See Appendix No. 30).

Gathering data on workers' qualifications and background should be a part of the record system. Again, Frank McKibben has provided an illustration of this procedure. (See Appendix No. 31). Each worker should have a personal file on these matters and information should be cumulative through the years.

Of special note for church school workers in the matter of the evaluation of teaching is a special program recently developed to evaluate the effectiveness of teaching in the church school. It is called INSTROTEACH—an *Instr*ument for the *O*bservation of *Tea*ching Activities in the *Ch*urch. The instrument itself is a series of twenty-seven five-point scales, stating teacher behavior in items ranging downward from the optimum to considerably below standard. Each scale is accompanied by a description giving the rationale for the item. This instrument is described in a twenty-six page booklet entitled *Five Areas of Church Teacher Competence,* The Instroteach Board, and available through Westminster Book Stores. The five areas defined are (1) director of learning, (2) guide and counselor, (3) mediator and interpreter of the Christian faith, (4) link with the community, and (5) participant in the church's teaching ministry. The measuring instrument is an adaptation of IOTA (Instrument for Observation of Teaching Activities) developed as a public school in-service training program for teachers and administrators, Arizona State University.

Not to be overlooked in the ma‚ter of the evaluation of teaching is *self-evaluation* on the part of teachers themselves. The important thing here is the teacher's purpose to evaluate self in order that learning might be made more effective. Criteria for doing this should be agreed upon and the teachers themselves should have a large place in establishing such criteria. Methods vary widely for encouraging self-evaluation. Mention has already been made of the use of self-rating scales, illustrated in Appendix No. 15. Other methods of encouragement and motivation would possibly include

1. The use of outside speakers to challenge and interest teachers in self-improvement
2. Secure pupil response to the teaching process
3. Put emphasis on learning improvement rather than on the person of the teacher
4. Have staff create a self-evaluation check list
5. Visit other classes
6. Video-tape analysis of teaching situations

6. *The Improvement of Teaching.* Supervisors should begin improvement efforts with improving the concept of Christian teaching. The creation of a statement of philosophy of church education together with the formulation of objectives and standards will help set the pace for the work. It will require the cooperation of all concerned to get the job of evaluating and improving teaching achieved. Most certainly it will involve self-evaluation on the part of teachers. The approach to the job of evaluation will be shifted primarily from the person of the teacher to the task of ministry, to the principles and practices of good church education. Emphasis will also be placed on teacher growth and development. All workers will work together for the achievement of the goals of Christian education in the church.

There are at least three steps leading to the improvement of instructional practice:

1. Strengthening the leadership
2. Improving the teacher as a person
3. Improving the teacher as a worker

Leadership principles were discussed in Chapter Three. The practicing of these principles will lead to better teaching. Full administrative support of the church and its leaders in providing training sessions, budget for teaching materials and tools, a good library, a strong curriculum, and good facilities will all contribute likewise.

Improving the teacher as a person will be dealt with in a later section of this chapter. Suffice to say that the teacher's spiritual and physical health, appearance, skills, attitudes, morale, and relationships need to be studied to discover needs and places where help is needed.

Methods of improving teacher competencies will also be dealt with further on. Obviously, a strong in-service training program will go a long way toward the improvement of teaching practices. The supervisor will have to study the actual conditions in the classroom. The evaluation devices mentioned above will help him at this point.

In church education, particularly when the departmentalized system is used, department heads and workers can provide valuable assistance to teachers. In some instances the department head is in a better position to do the work of supervising teachers than is the supervisor or Director of Christian Education, because he is much closer to the teacher and the teaching-learning processes.

1. He can assist the teacher with the use of curriculum materials

2. He can provide teachers suggestions about methods
3. He can help teachers evaluate their work
4. He can help teachers evaluate the learning of pupils
5. He can motivate teachers toward training and growth
6. He can conduct department meetings, where problems and opportunities are discussed

Individual differences can be handled in personal conferences. These too will be described in the following section of this chapter. The improvement of teaching can also take place in group meetings of many kinds. These also will be discussed in this chapter later on.

One of the oldest supervisory techniques used in the improvement of teaching is that of classroom visitation and observation. Samplings of instructional performances are secured through this method. Supervisors see in this method an opportunity for improvement rather than that of inspection or rating. Since there is no generally accepted way of teaching applied to all teachers, then the supervisor must assess effects of the influence of teacher performance upon pupils. The primary purpose of observation and visitation, therefore, is to study the teaching-learning process. Objectives, materials, methods, meeting pupil needs, remedying pupil difficulties, and pupil measurement are focused upon.

Robert C. McKean lists three types of classroom visitation: (1) announced, (2) unannounced, and (3) by invitation.[3] Where inspection is eliminated and emphasis placed on problem solving, the first two types of visits are largely made unnecessary. When teachers know they will get help without threat, they will cooperatively plan with supervisors for classroom observation, thus making the third type visit the normal and profitable one. With this kind of freedom and cooperation, drop-in visits can be made at any time.

The frequency and length of such visits are determined by the purpose of the visit. More times may be needed for new and inexperienced teachers and workers. With some problems several visits may be needed. When new materials and methods are employed, more frequent visits may be necessary. The first few visits may serve the purpose of getting acquainted. Subsequent visits will be determined on the basis of need. Some supervisors find *preteaching conferences* helpful in preparing the way for classroom visitation. Purposes of the visit, lesson planning, parts to be played, and anticipated problems might be carefully reviewed in such a conference.

The total teaching process and time-period should be observed. In this way lesson plans and activities may be more fully analyzed and evaluated. Wherever possible, such plans should be studied in advance to make better observation and understanding possible.

During the visit everything possible should be done to encourage relaxation and cheerfulness. Every move by the supervisor in the room should be taken with care so that the teacher and the class are not disturbed or upset. Taking one's seat at the side keeps teacher, class and room in total view. Make every effort to explore the teacher's physical, social and educational needs.

Before the visit is made the supervisor will want to make careful and prayerful preparation for it. A purpose must be determined and a scheduled time decided upon. If previous information on the teacher and class situation is available, it will be wise to review this before arrival. Any previous meetings with the teacher should also be reviewed. Where certain problems are pin-pointed, possible solutions should be considered and made ready for use. It is debatable whether notes should be taken or not. Very likely they will be taken while the situation is fresh in mind. Perhaps at workers' conferences the supervisor can explain his notetaking procedures. Some supervisors use formal observations guides. An example is included in Appendix No. 32. When leaving the room, wait till the lesson is completed and say a pleasant goodbye.

As a follow-up to a classroom observation and visits, careful records should be kept. Such records will not only help the supervisor assist individual teachers but they also provide a wealth of information for teacher improvement in the future.

Some kind of report should be made to the teacher by the supervisor following this visit. This can be done verbally, in a follow-up conference, or in written form. Some supervisors like to write notes of appreciation to teachers along with reports of analyses, evaluations and suggestions for improvement. A formal printed form for this purpose can be seen in the Appendix No. 33.

Still other supervisors use factual descriptions of classroom activities without personal comment, leaving it up to the teacher to make self-evaluations. Two points of view may be discussed, providing two angles of observation. Other devices sometimes used include closed circuit television, tape recordings, time analyses, and discussion flow charts.

Analyses of the data gathered by the supervisor during his visits will enable him to do two things; evaluate (1) teacher functioning, and (2) pupil response. Are pupils free, stimulated, vocal, participating, asking questions, volunteering information, carrying out projects, working together, and enjoying the teaching-learning experiences?

Do teachers over-control? Impose on pupils? Are they open and helpful, warmhearted and spiritual, responsive to pupil needs, and skillful in communication? These and other important questions help focus on possible outcomes.

Teachers need to be brought to realize that supervisory visitation is part of good church education, therefore they should expect it. By being given a voice in the proceedings and by being assured of cooperative activities in problem solving, perhaps in time the visits of a well-trained objective-minded supervisor will be fully accepted and made a part of their professional growth.

Micro-teaching and *micro-learning* are other techniques for self-evaluation and improvement of teaching. These techniques involve teachers in presenting brief lessons to a small group of students for from five to ten minutes, concentrating on the implementation of a specific teaching skill, such as questioning. After teaching the abbreviated sequence, the teaching process is evaluated as the teacher views the video-tape on his own or with the students, teachers and others.

A second teaching segment is then used to re-teach the same lesson, using the critique of the first lesson to improve himself. The lesson is taught to another group of pupils. This is followed by a second critique. This process may continue until the teacher feels he has mastered the skill on which he was working.

This procedure may also be focused on pupil learning. Pupils are asked to criticize the teaching process. This, too, is followed by an evaluation of pupil responses on the part of the teacher and supervisor.

This technique may also be broadened to use the video-tape recorder in (1) recording a full class presentation, focusing on teaching behavior or learning processes; (2)

video-taping class activities to be studied by pupils themselves; (3) video-taping pupil behavior or misbehavior, followed by discussions of possible follow-up; (4) video-taping specific learning situations which are typical and using the replay as a focal point for a workers' conference program or teacher training session; (5) video-taping workshops; and (6) video-taping master teachers and using replay as a teacher training device.

B. Improving and Supervising Individual Workers

1. *Concepts of Supervisory Services.* Studies reveal that the attitude of public school teachers toward supervisory services vary widely, depending on experience, background, and professional competence. Information is not available on the attitudes of church school teachers toward such services. Chances are, however, that reactions in general would be largely similar. Where fear and resistance are removed and the supervisor is able to show the "helping" nature of his work, then favorable and cooperative attitudes develop. But where inspection and rating are over-emphasized, favorable attitudes wane accordingly.

C. T. McNerney listed sixteen suggestions regarding what teachers have a right to expect from the supervisor.[4]

1. An opportunity to participate actively in planning the program of supervision
2. Assistance in interpreting the community background of his pupils
3. Assistance in modernizing his methods and techniques of instruction
4. Assistance in interpreting the results of the evaluation program

5. Assistance in the construction and evaluation of daily lessons plans
6. Assistance in using enrichment materials
7. Assistance in using sensory aids
8. Assistance in the maintenance of school records
9. An opportunity to participate in the activities of professional organizations and state study groups
10. An opportunity to participate in the selection of professional literature for the professional library
11. An opportunity to participate in the selection of new verbal and non-verbal instructional materials
12. An interpretation of his responsibility to participate in non-school community organizations
13. Assistance in the development of cooperative relationships with other departments or levels of instruction
14. Assistance in the procurement of necessary instructional materials
15. An opportunity to use the services of any or all specialists in the school organization
16. Assistance in evaluating his professional growth as evidenced by his increased effectiveness as a director of the educational process

This does not exhaust the possibilities. Church school teachers and supervisors should find this list helpful in guiding their own supervisory program.

2. *The Supervisory Approach.* In working with individual teachers and workers the supervisor should remember that he is a teacher of teachers and workers. The teaching done is not too much unlike that of classroom teaching. John A. Bartky traces the teaching of the supervisor with individuals through five steps: (1) exploratory, (2) motivational, (3) methodological, (4) therapeutic, and (5) evaluational.[5] Such steps do not take place necessarily in that order but are involved somewhere along the line in

supervisor-worker relationships. In working with teachers, for example, the supervisor explores by getting acquainted with the teacher and his background. The teacher has a problem. It may require stimulation to get the teacher to become aware of both the problem and the need for improvement, or to get him to see that the supervisor is ready to help. Following this will come the employment of a method or methods of solving the problem. This becomes of therapeutic value when the teacher realizes that he is getting sympathetic and practical assistance. Both of them then follow up with an evaluation of the solution and the proposed changes involved. Thus, the approach of the supervisor is very individualized in character. It involves a leadership act which practices the principles of problem-solving.

The approach of the supervisor to helping individuals essentially involves the meeting of their needs, recognizing that such needs vary widely with the individuals involved. Without a sensitivity to need supervisors run the risk of becoming authoritarian in attitude and practice, thus creating fears and anxieties among the church school workers. Much time, therefore, should be spent by the supervisor in working with teachers on problems directly related to pupils. Let workers know of the concern felt for any dissatisfactions they might have. Sometimes there are real and unreal sources of irritation, such as no heat, few supplies, etc. Let the workers know that efforts are being made to correct these situations, and improve them. Supervisors might even ask for suggestions on ways of improvement. Most certainly careful checks on sources of dissatisfaction need to be made.

3. *Supervising Personnel Administration.* Selection, placement, and orientation are involved in personnel admini-

stration. Supervisors and administrators need to exercise great care in the selection of workers in the church school. Not only will quality people contribute to the success of the program, proper selection will possibly head off future problems. So time spent in making wise selections will reduce time spent later in helping a teacher or worker do a creditable job.

Supervisors should be in on the planning for recruitment, selection, orientation, and assignment of workers for the simple reason that they are in a position to know the requirements of the job and may be able to suit the worker to it. The act of selecting involves the making of judgments which in turn are based on certain criteria. These criteria should be based on what is believed to be good church education and effective Christian teaching.

Standards for church workers should be held as high as possible. Both spiritual and professional standards should be clearly stated so that all will have a clear understanding on these matters. The creation and development of a job description manual is useful in this regard. Written standards for leadership often make this clear. At times supervisors should evaluate the state of affairs regarding leadership qualifications. Self-rating scales and charts on spiritual life are helpful here. Spiritual qualifications are primary, basic, and essential. Personal Christian experience of Christ as Savior, being filled with the Holy Spirit, and living an examplary Christian life are fundamental. In addition, workers should have the skills and aptitudes needed for their service. Feeling the call of God upon them for Christian service is paramount. Expectations regarding Bible study, prayer, and using the means of grace become important. Some statements on training and preparation should be made clear.

Some churches use teachers' and workers' convenants to accomplish the ends of a Standard. (See for example Appendix No. 34). Guy Leavitt has suggested a questionnaire for use in evaluating and guiding the spiritual life and development of church school workers.[6] Teachers' Self-rating Scales are valuable in guiding teachers to see the importance of deepening and developing one's spiritual life. (See for example Appendix No. 15.) Standards like these will probably be far more acceptable if the whole staff is involved in setting them up. This is true provided the staff is spiritually qualified to begin with.

Some churches use Talent Survey studies to discover prospective workers. (See Appendix No. 35.) Initial information on selection can be secured here. Perhaps a Personnel Committee could be appointed to study this information and prayerfully select candidates considered to be the best qualified.

A personal interview of prospective workers and teachers is imperative. This interview should be conducted on a high level. There should be an exchange of information regarding the position in view. Job descriptions should be presented to the prospective workers along with any sample curriculum materials involved for study and examination. Every effort should be made to impress the prospect with the obligations of ministry and the necessity for self-denial and consecration to get the job done. The candidates should be impressed with the fact that the committee after prayer has felt led to interview him and that they feel he is qualified for the job. Time should be given the candidate to pray about and study the job before an answer is given. Then an appointment can be made to receive his answer at a later date.

Experienced workers should also review their work, be

called on, and either be confirmed or reassigned for the work of the new church year.

Assignments to the job are important. Misassignment creates inefficiency and poor morale. Most common errors possibly include misplacement in a particular age group, large classes, and over-work. Wherever possible, good workers should be assigned to places of great need.

Orientation of new workers is important in personnel administration. Efforts should be taken by supervisors to make them feel wanted and welcome, to make them acquainted with other workers. Here, again, a job description manual proves helpful in providing them guidance in assuming their new duties. Special efforts should be made to impress new workers with the importance of their jobs, that teaching and working in the church school is a ministry. Older workers can provide assistance to new ones by giving advice, counsel and help on the job. In fact new workers can learn much by serving on committees with older and more experienced workers.

A detailed knowledge of the record system is helpful to new workers, not only from the standpoint of statistics, but also from the values of the records in assisting them to come to a greater knowledge of pupils, of the program and achievements. Often an apprentice program will include this aspect of orientation along with that of duties performed.

Not to be overlooked in orientation is concern for the personal needs and affairs of workers. Family and job responsibilities should be taken in consideration as are matters of health and time available. Supervisors should express concern, sympathy and interest in these matters in the interest of better morale and more effective service.

Teacher growth should be encouraged among all workers, new and experienced. An in-service training program is a must for successful churches. This will be dealt with in the next section of this chapter. Concern for professional growth is important, therefore supervisors should plan to make suggestions along this line.

Sometimes people are misplaced in service. Good supervision will recognize this and make plans for possible reassignment. Proper placement means better morale, less frustration, and better results. It will probably be wise for new teachers and workers to be placed on "probation," at least as far as their work is concerned. Problems may possibly be avoided where previous and careful determination of what a job requires is made.

Occasionally it becomes necessary to correct people and situations on the job. This is not easy and demands a lot of study and tactfulness. The goal is to do this without giving offense. Halsey has suggested a list of Ten Commandments of Correction.

1. Try first to get all pertinent facts
   a. Has there been proper placement?
   b. What other circumstances might have caused poor work?
   c. Poor working conditions?
2. If possible, choose a place which is both private and quiet
3. Always begin with a question, but not in the form of an accusation
4. Let the person talk—give reasons
5. Consider carefully all the evidence
6. Fit method of correction to the individual
7. Maintain calmness regardless of other's attitude
8. Close pleasantly; restore self-confidence
9. Follow-up with second interview if necessary
10. Do not use correction too often[7]

Unavoidably, at times it becomes necessary to dismiss incapable and unqualified workers. There are at least two primary reasons for this: (1) ineffective work, or (2) unrighteous living, on the part of the worker. When high standards are lifted for the total program and personnel, this necessarily is held to a minimum. The adoption of high standards and a good training program will often preclude this possibility also.

The policy of annual appointment is helpful with this problem. Where it is clear that changes will be made annually, and that annual approval of all workers will be given by the Board of Christian Education or its equivalent, the task of dismissal becomes somewhat easier. Make all staff positions places of honor by giving recognition and by stressing the ministerial character of all service. New teachers and workers might serve in a co-worker relationship for a time before being given permanent assignments. In the case of elderly teachers perhaps it is possible to start a new class which includes the long-time pupils, then choose another teacher for the rest of the pupils. Perhaps an associate teacher who is competent will motivate the senior teacher to do better. In time the senior teacher could be named teacher-emeritus and be retired.

When it becomes necessary to face frankly the fact of dismissal, careful plans of approach to the worker need to be outlined. Possibly people could be "prayed out" of jobs or be reassigned to other tasks. The Board of Christian Education should assume the burden of dismissal to release pressures from the officers and supervisors. Perhaps check-ups on the job will solve problems and make such dismissal unnecessary. If unsolved, then a committee should be appointed to approach the worker and face him with the situation. Appreciation should be expressed for the work that *was* done. Suggest that it appears that the particular work involved does not appear to be best for the worker, and that the wise thing to be done is to make a change. Perhaps it could be said that the Board has decided to reassign the worker or give the job to someone else. Some typical problems will be discussed later on in this chapter.

4. *Working with Personality Factors.* In working with the supervisory program in a local church, supervisors work with people of varying personalities.

Teachers and workers differ from one another *spiritually.* Some are new Christians, others are mature ones. Some are deeply spiritual, others are carnally minded. Supervisors should be sensitive to this matter because of the extremely spiritual nature of the work of church education. Great influence is brought to bear by workers at this point on the spiritual life of pupils and fellow workers.

Workers differ *biologically.* Some are short, others are tall; some are thin, others are fat. They differ in posture, size, shape, voice, and in dozens of other ways. Appearance does have an effect on one's work. Pupil response, bias and attitudes are often directly affected by these factors. Thus, supervisors should suggest and encourage the best possible appearance on the part of workers. Workers should not be over-pressured or over-worked in the interest of health and effectiveness.

Workers differ *socially.* For this reason one's status and position in the community and church life often affects directly his influence and work for the Lord. Economic situations and affairs sometimes have a bearing here. Such things affect teacher and pupil attitudes. Methods are often influenced by the worker's background. He works or teaches as he has been influenced and/or taught in the past. Sometimes this interferes with present cultural and educational adjustment and stymies progress. Social problems often dictate among workers their ways of handling class problems.

Workers differ *psychologically.* Some can use new methods; others fear them. Some can take classroom visits, others resent them. Individual differences demand varying approaches by the supervisor to improve efforts. Attitudes, feelings, and motives all play a large part in the work.

Since all workers differ, the challenge that comes to the supervisor is to work with these differences creatively to realize the goals of Church education. Attempts on the part of the supervisor to "type" a teacher or worker should be avoided. This, however, appears to be a common practice in some circles. Some are typed according to the four characteristics mentioned above, namely, spiritual, physical, social and psychological. Others can be viewed as physically ill, relatively intelligent, queer, lonely, frustrated, moody, and relatively perverse. Still others can be thought of as submissive, adaptable, self-directed, unadjusted, and even defiant at times. Perhaps one of the most commonly used classifications of workers' personality in church education involves a view of the worker as primarily one who works best among children, youth, or adults. The spiritual or lack of strong spiritual qualities is also involved at this point.

The tendency in church education is to strive toward the goal of the "Ideal Teacher" or "The Master Teacher." Other than in Jesus Christ this kind of worker or teacher is simply not to be found. Church workers in spite of this are in general superior people but at the same time are still human. A supervisor, while holding the standard high, should at the same time be sensitive to the human weaknesses and strengths, even sins, of the workers within his responsibility. He tries to take advantage of their strengths and protects them from their weaknesses. He tries to set up a teaching-learning situation which lends itself to the accomplishment of optimum results with the least possibility of failure. He applies therapeutic remedies wherever possible. He seeks to mold the staff into a deeply spiritual, highly effective and fruitful enterprise to the glory of God.

By creating a good personal relationship, by his willingness to listen, to understand, to sympathize, by making himself available for counseling, by much prayer, by maintaining high standards, by hard work and good example, and many other ways the supervisor may be able to improve personality factors among the workers. Special problems will be dealt with later on.

Not only the understanding of the multiple nature of personality is important for the supervisor but he must also be willing to accept people as they are and strive to improve them according to the purposes of Scripture and Christ-like character. Traits, needs, interests, attitudes, aptitudes, and temperament should all be molded according to the ideals of Scriptural Christianity. In doing this supervisors cannot manipulate people but they can pray, provide a good example, stress obedience and the leadership of the Holy Spirit, and motivate with the ideals of good church education. The fruit of the Spirit and ideals of Christlike character serve as guides here.

All of these matters can be brought to the attention of workers in workers' conferences, through the use of standards and rating scales. (See Appendixes No. 2 and 15). For further discussion of teacher personality the reader is referred to a discussion in one of the author's previous publications, dealing with physical, mental, moral, social, personality, and spiritual elements.[8] Again, Guy Leavitt has offered what he calls a Personality Profile Test for use in self-evaluation. (See Appendix No. 36).

5. *The Supervisor and Problems of Teaching.* Many studies have been made of determining areas of work in which teachers want and need help. Some of the more commonly listed areas include:

1. Improving teaching methods and techniques
2. Determining teaching objectives
3. Using curriculum and materials and resources
4. Meeting needs and individual differences among pupils
5. Handling pupil behavior and discipline problems
6. Meeting the needs of atypical pupils
7. Evaluation
8. Making better use of visual aids
9. Understanding pupils
10. How to study the Bible and Sunday school lessons
11. How to pray

Many other similar problems could be listed. Supervisors must wrestle with these problems and help meet teacher needs. A good leadership training program will deal with these and many other issues. This matter is discussed more fully in the next section.

Suggestions on the way some of the more common problems can be handled is illustrated as follows:

Personal Needs	*Improving Teaching Methods*
1. Workers' conference programs devoted to spiritual life and service	1. Study and reading
2. Discussion on good health and appearance	2. Observation and evaluation of the work of a good teacher

3. Discussion of morale improvement
4. Discussion of a Christian personality profile

Improving Curriculum

1. Help select materials
2. Demonstrations, exhibits, and displays
3. Workshops
4. Laboratory exercises
5. Field trips
6. Travel
7. Audio-visuals

3. Visitation of other teachers and church schools
4. Workshop participation
5. Attendance at conferences
6. Guided practice teaching
7. Discussion of teaching-learning processes
8. Experimentation with new methods

Changing Environmental Conditions

1. Change teaching position
2. Beautify facilities
3. Travel
4. Recreational programs
5. Participation in projects
6. Surveys of needs

In the face of the present day demands in church education newer forms and models for church education have been designed. These, too, help in solving problems of teaching and improving the whole process.

There are new models for grouping people for teaching and learning. For example *intergenerational groups* cluster people of a variety of ages. Ungraded and broadly graded classes cluster people across wide age spans. Family clustering provides opportunities for people who live together to meet over a period of time for study and fellowship. Special interest groups can meet for specific purposes to accomplish specific goals. Such groups may include parents, boards, committees, vocational groups, handicapped people, unreached people, and people in crisis life situations.

Models for staffing educational programs include team teaching, part-time teaching according to individual skills, and alternate use of two or more teams in team teaching situations. Rotations of teachers and leaders are utilized.

Teaching can take many shapes. *Contract teaching* involves an agreement between teacher and learner whereby written plans are made regarding what and how study takes place. *Individual study* allows the student to set his own goals and teachers provide resources and plans. This might involve use of learning centers, reading centers, activity centers, work tables and film centers.

Learning centers are designated areas in the classroom where materials and activities are made available for study by individuals and groups. They would include such matters as collages, reading, mural making, movies, Bible study, field trips, drama, music, worship, recreation, nature centers and special days.

There are various models for how learning takes place. *Action-reflection* involves activities followed by theological reflection. *Discovery learning* involves posing questions and problems and seeking Christian solutions. Models on *uses of time* involve using other times than Sunday for learning. Still other methods for improvement are listed as follows:

Discipline and Behavior

1. Set standards of conduct
2. Adopt a code of ethics
3. Establish sensible regulations
4. Seek the causes of misbehavior
5. Be alert to background problems of pupils in the home
6. Strive for interesting teaching
7. Relate content to pupil interests
8. Use variety, many visual aids

9. Be patient and prayerful
10. Point out the "sin" in misbehavior
11. Pray with pupils before punishing them
12. Seek parental cooperation
13. Do not expect too much of pupils
14. Be efficient in routine matters
15. Stress good teaching as a preventative
16. Give assignments; use projects
17. Give pupils responsibilities
18. Ask "good pupils" to be a buddy
19. Be clear on what is expected
20. Frequently cite good examples
21. Try changing the situation rather than the pupil
22. Be firm without being harsh
23. Remove sources of discomfort and disturbance
24. Eliminate all possible mannerisms
25. Develop a sense of humor

Individual Differences

1. Be aware that all pupils differ
2. Record class behavior and study it
3. Watch for signs of poor health
4. Be alert to any handicaps present, such as poor sight, hearing, etc.
5. Be alert to differences relating to sex
6. Watch for evidences of social problems
7. Stress good teaching as a means of meeting all needs
8. Provide good curriculum materials which appeal to all pupils
9. Make room for creativity among the pupils
10. Be receptive to pupil ideas
11. Encourage a spirit of experimentation
12. Make special provisions for rapid learners, special guidance, extra assignments, research
13. Love those who feel insecure

14. Encourage pupils who are overdependent
15. Accept all pupils as full members of the class
16. Pray much for each one

6. *Methods of Assisting Individual Workers.* In the discussion above some methods of improving workers have already been described, such as classroom visitation. There are many others. Following is a list of some additional ways of working with individual workers to effect improvement and thereby to carry out supervisory responsibilities.

1. Help teachers select and formulate teaching-learning objectives
2. Counseling and guidance
3. Individual conferences and interviews
4. Taking advantage of casual meetings to help
5. Demonstration teaching
6. Help teachers with lesson planning
7. Visitation to other schools and churches to observe
8. Help teachers with evaluation efforts
9. Provision for a good library
10. Planned travel and study
11. Helping new teachers to get oriented and started
12. Helping more experienced teachers with needs and problems
13. Directed reading
14. Attendance at conferences, workshops, etc.
15. Join church education professional organizations and agencies
16. Formal study

Outstanding among the methods listed above is that of the personal conference. Here a face-to-face and heart-to-heart situation prevails and it has great possibilities for good. The purpose of such a conference is to provide for specific and detailed attention to individual problems of the workers. The procedure involves a threefold process which leads to a possible climax or solution to the problems under consideration:

1. Preparing for the conference
2. Conducting the conference
3. Conserving the results of the conference

Preparation for the conference is largely the responsibility of the supervisor himself. He will need certain vital information about the worker to be interviewed. Some have found that a personnel blank of some kind which is kept on file will provide the director with basic information which might prove helpful to him in the approach to an understanding of the worker and his problem. A sample of this kind of blank is provided in the Appendix No. 31. In addition to this, the supervisor will need to collect materials on the problem to be discussed. Further material may be collected when he actually observes the situation or the problem involved.

Further preparation should be made in advance of the conference itself. In fact, if possible, the supervisor should work out a plan of procedure. The plan might include such items as probable reactions to proposed criticism or new ideas, plans to make the most of these reactions, or careful suggestions for improvement and solution of the proposed problem. No supervisor should enter this kind of conference "cold." Workers should be encouraged to submit problems in advance in order to make this kind of preparation on the part of the supervisor possible.

In the second phase, that of *conducting* the conference,

the supervisor should seek first to set up a friendly atmosphere. Make the conference personal by dealing with personal qualities of the worker, his skills and faults. It should also be impersonal, in that personal feelings on the part of the supervisor and worker are subservient to the interests of securing improvement of the work. Criticisms should be both constructive and remedial, favorable and unfavorable.

While defects will be carefully noted, the supervisor should be as generous as possible with favorable comments. By all means he should seek to develop the teacher and worker for general leadership.

The third phase is *conservation.* The supervisor should keep a good record of results. In some instances, important conclusions should be made available to groups. Whatever changes are proposed, the supervisor should give definite assistance in carrying them out. He should keep a careful check on progress of any activities involved from changes suggested. During the conference itself, the supervisor will find it helpful to keep a record of problems at large which might be suggested or discovered and which might serve as points of discussion in group conferences which are to come.

7. *The Supervisor and Problem Teachers.* To say that there are "problem teachers" may invoke criticism, but the fact remains that teachers not only *have* problems but at times *are* problems. There is a wide variety of teachers who fall into this category. Following is a list with suggestions on what to do to help such teachers.

The New Teachers

1. Support them in learning efforts
2. Provide frequent conferences with them

3. Be patient and wait for growth
4. Provide a job description for them
5. Inform them about rules and regulations
6. Inform them about the record system
7. Draw them into social affairs
8. Visit good teachers to observe
9. Take more training
10. Meet their needs
11. Make them feel welcome
12. Help them get acquainted with their fellow workers
13. Help them with teaching-learning processes

Experienced Teachers

1. Help evaluate teaching efforts
2. Help determine placement
3. Provide with resources
4. Assist in use of curriculum
5. Introduce innovations to them
6. Suggest new ideas
7. Urge them to experiment
8. Urge them to evaluate more
9. Suggest good reading matter
10. Draw on experience and knowledge
11. Use good ideas whether old or new

Uncreative Teachers

1. Encourage them to discover more effective teaching methods
2. Challenge them to experiment
3. Study the work of creative teachers
4. Provide opportunity for pupil creativity
5. Utilize special talents
6. Give praise for creative work
7. Help them develop pupil interests
8. Report on results of creative work
9. Prepare results

10. Suggest creative projects; set goals
11. Place of goals in creative work
12. Place a premium on creative work

Reluctant Teachers

1. Be patient with them
2. Long-range plans for improvement
3. Set high standards
4. Recognize desirable methods used
5. Show worth, purpose of projects
6. Serve on committees to study methods
7. Cite results of use of good methods
8. Observe use of good methods with pupil reactions to them
9. Use demonstration lessons
10. Panel discussions on new procedures
11. Be receptive to new ideas
12. Review sources of information where evidence is overwhelmingly favorable to new procedures

Abnormal Teachers

1. Be alert to physical needs
2. Watch for signs of mental illness
3. Watch for signs of radicalism in spiritual life
4. Watch for signs of pupil unrest, misbehavior, disorganization
5. Watch for signs of emotional disturbance
6. Watch for signs of fears, anxieties, obsessions, and compulsions
7. Watch for signs of bad temper

Unsatisfactory Teachers

1. Watch for lack of spiritual experience and growth
2. Watch for signs of incompetence
3. Watch for signs of uncooperative spirit

4. Watch for signs of physical or mental illness
5. Watch for signs of immorality
6. Find and remedy causes of unsatisfactory work
7. Suggest further training and reading
8. Observe successful teachers
9. If cause is hopeless, say so
10. Deal frankly with each one personally
11. Discuss this problem in the Board of Christian Education meeting

Lazy Teachers

1. Make them feel important
2. Try to discover causes for laziness
3. Express appreciation occasionally
4. Are there family problems?
5. Has confidence been lost?
6. Stress evaluation and improvement
7. Suggest good reading materials
8. Draw into committee work where improvements are considered
9. Stress high standards for the work
10. Appeal to duty plus sense of fulfillment
11. Watch for signs of illness
12. Adopt standards for work and attendance

Colorless Teachers

1. Find and play up strong points
2. Give recognition of services
3. Discover and use special interests
4. Draw into social affairs
5. Use role playing techniques in teachers' meetings and conferences
6. Make use of special abilities

Disagreeing Teachers

1. Grant good requests cheerfully
2. Be patient and offer assistance

3. Find and remedy cause of disagreement
4. Do not accept disagreement as a personal offense
5. Show that honest disagreement is welcome
6. Talk through disagreements until an agreement can be reached
7. Stress God's glory above all
8. Make *group* decisions
9. Tactfully reveal consequences of unwise procedures
10. Adopt standards for work set by the teachers themselves

Many problems cannot be handled alone by supervisors. The combined prayers, advice, wisdom, and help of administrators and friends may be needed. As far as possible the supervisor should be able to recognize the symptoms of inefficiency, improper and inadequate performance and diagnose the causes of them. Causes are many but possibilities might include (1) acute or chronic illness, (2) temporary or minor illness, (3) discomforts, (4) distractions, (5) disturbances, (6) trouble at home or in business, (7) resentment, (8) shallow spiritual life, (9) failure to get along with others, or (10) unhappy relationships with pupils and parents. Failures in class duties may be due to (1) fear, (2) lack of training, (3) timidity, (4) lack of confidence, (5) discouragements, (6) personality deficiency, (7) professional incompetence, (8) lack of spiritual power and prayer, (9) poor lesson planning, (10) poor study habits, (11) lack of objectives, and many others.

C. Group Methods for Improvements and Supervision

1. *Morale Factors.* No group process can operate at optimum effectiveness without a framework of good spirit and feeling among the workers, a favorable climate. This

involves morale factors. Morale is that somewhat intangible process involving the mental and emotional reactions of a person to his job. In the church school this can be seen in what teachers and workers feel and believe about their work.

Morale factors can be kept high when first things are put first. Where evangelism and the joy of the Holy Spirit prevail there is a vitality about the quality of spirit among the workers, an enthusiasm and excitement is engendered as workers see and feel the power of God through the Gospel working in hearts and lives. Christian love contributes to this kind of climate also by encouraging better human relations and deepening motivations. Radiant enthusiasm and devoted labor give a high sense of fellowship and direction to the program. The exercising of faith and confidence in the power of Christ to change hearts and lives contributes to a high state of morale. Other contributing factors would also include a strong program of congregational support of the leadership, an effective leadership training program, the establishment of worthy goals, and strong service efforts.

In general the quality of morale can be determined by observing how people act. If one sees loafing on the job, tardiness, absenteeism and adverse criticism, dissatisfactions prevail. Large teacher and worker turnover may be an indication of low morale. Criticism of fellow workers and of the church in general may indicate low spirit. Health and personal problems also contribute. On the other hand where there is cheerfulness, promptness, enthusiasm, dependability and cooperation, signs of good morale prevail.

Weldon Crossland has listed some attitudes and actions that mar and undermine morale in the church.

The indifference or timidity of the minister
The remembered frictions, mistakes and quarrels of the past
Factionalism, which fragments and destroys the unity of the church
Ultraconservatism, that stops the growth of the congregation
The failure to set worthy objectives which challenge and unify the congregation
The lack of a well-rounded program through which the congregation renders its Christian service
The plague of a "church boss", whether ministerial or lay, whose dominance stultifies the leadership growth of the church
A defeated spirit, which fails before it tries[9]

Crossland then proceeds to list twelve factors expressed by laymen as contributing to high morale.

Consider the minister as the chief morale builder
Regard the preaching and practice of Christian stewardship in its true meaning as the foundation philosophy of all worthy leadership
Exalt the church as priority No. 1
Choose long-range goals
Encourage leaders to specialize
Hold regular board meetings
Publicize committee achievements
Install officials impressively
Publish the names of officials occasionally
Feature Layman's Sunday
Deepen the personal religious life of laymen[10]

Perhaps it is possible to add some suggestions to this list, leading to the identification of the marks of good morale:

1. Morale is giving one's best to the ideals of the Kingdom of God
2. Morale is the will to overcome all obstacles
3. Morale is the determination to succeed
4. Morale is courage, faith and integrity maintained in the face of trouble
5. Morale is living up to the highest standards of church education
6. Morale is loyalty to and support of fellow workers
7. Morale is persistent service
8. Morale is a strong sense of responsibility
9. Morale is a strong sense of belonging
10. Morale is belief in the ministry of church education
11. Morale is feeling that one has a part in this ministry
12. Morale is willing to make that extra effort

Some of the very important things that supervisors and administrators can do to maintain and improve good morale would include:

1. Build up the ministry of the laity
2. Keep the ministry of church education before the church and community
3. Maintain a high state of spiritual life
4. Maintain a strong devotional quality in the work
5. Provide good and beautiful facilities
6. Orient adequately all new workers
7. Recognize achievements of pupils and workers
8. Give workers a part in policy-making
9. Support the efforts of all workers with good administration and supervision
10. Practice high standards
11. Manifest faith and confidence in all workers
12. Spend time in problem-solving
13. Give credit where it is due

14. Stress freedom, initiative, creativity, and experimentation
15. Make duties and responsibilities clear
16. Be receptive to suggestions and new ideas

There are certain "job satisfactions" that all church school workers want, assuming, of course, that the spiritual conditions are good. These include (1) pleasant working conditions, (2) a sense of belonging, (3) fair treatment, (4) a sense of achievement and growth, (5) recognition of contributions, (6) participation in policy-making, (7) maintenance of self-respect, and (8) encouragement. Supervisors and administrators should manifest a careful and prayerful concern about all of these matters and do everything within their power to satisfy and provide such satisfactions.

Staff morale can be sampled by asking for suggestions on how positions and conditions can be improved. If suggestions are freely given, the morale may be high. It might be determined also by how freely workers bring their tensions and problems out into the open. Watch absenteeism, tardiness, and worker turn-over. Listen carefully for subconscious revelations during conversations.

If good morale is absent or seems to be disintegrating, set about immediately to (1) determine causes, (2) cooperatively study and plan remedies, and (3) set the plans in motion. Attack these problems head-on and frankly. Do not confine efforts to vague, sentimental appeals and evangelical exhortations.

2. *Human Relations Factors.* Christian love should characterize the spirit and actions of workers and co-workers in the church school. Attention, however, needs to be given to the many details and mechanics of group rela-

tions. Great attention has been given to this factor in the literature. The promotion of staff harmony is based largely on three general things: (1) consideration for the feelings and wishes of those involved in decisions and actions, (2) faith in the value and ability of each worker, and (3) the attitudes and methods of dealing with workers.

Human relation factors are closely related to the morale factors mentioned above and contribute directly and favorably to them. Christian love and the principles of group dynamics would indicate that the following items would be helpful in contributing to a state of good human relations in the church school:

1. Treat people the way they wish to be treated
2. Be willing to help teachers and workers
3. Listen to workers in order to understand them
4. Make changes slowly, preferably those which workers prefer first
5. Make workers feel needed and important
6. Stress the high call to Christian service and ministry
7. Be sincerely interested in workers; like them
8. Talk directly to workers, not at them
9. Criticize only in private
10. Stress the positive in making corrections
11. Be firm but courteous on basic issues
12. "Smile"—you are on candid camera!
13. Remember names and use them
14. Ask people to do things, don't boss them
15. Ask teachers' permission to visit classrooms
16. Make an effort to improve working conditions
17. Help teachers in difficulties with pupils, parents and other workers
18. Consult workers involved by decisions and actions
19. Meet the workers on social occasions often
20. Share all praise and recognitions with workers

21. Make decisions in terms of effects on people, not arbitrarily
22. Work to reduce conflict and competition
23. Assume that others like you
24. Overlook faults and be willing to see your own
25. Practice *lagniappi*—something extra
26. Be prompt, kind and thoughtful
27. Help workers with their spiritual hindrances and problems
28. Decrease staff conflicts by making group decisions
29. Air differences as a step toward progress
30. Do not allow issues to become personal matters
31. Harness criticism
32. Pray much

Some things to avoid in getting along with workers might include some of the following items:

1. Do not make promises you cannot keep
2. Do not keep people waiting
3. Do not shirk your own responsibilities
4. Do not assume an air of superior ability, knowledge, or authority
5. Do not give unsolicited advice on personal matters
6. Do not argue
7. Do not belittle workers or predecessors
8. Do not get angry

In the course of his work the supervisor is related to many individuals and groups. At some time he will be required to interact with the whole church, the administration, office workers, staff people, teachers, department heads, Board of Christian Education, many committees, bus drivers, church members, parents, pupils, and community people. How he meets all these people will reflect his educational philosophy, his personality, and his acceptance of the importance of good human relations attitudes.

3. *Working Together.* The principles of group dynamics are well known and must be brought into play in staff relationships where cooperation is necessary. Pastors, administrators and supervisors must not use the "power over" concept of getting things done. Rather, work as a group. It is not personal authority but *group* accomplishment that counts. It is "power with" a group, where purposes, and problem-solving are shared. Decisions thus become group decisions. All will be given a chance to express themselves, then decide as a group what is best.

It takes time and effort for groups, in Sunday school for example, to learn to work as a unit. Boundaries for action should be clearly drawn by the Board of Christian Education so that limitations will be clearly understood, and then full freedom given to act within this framework. There must be *time* for thinking, working and praying together. It will be wise for the supervisor to suggest that the group start out with problems that are familiar and rather small before larger projects are undertaken. Experience will add to future efficiency. When disagreements exist, talk them through, call for reasons on both sides, then seek for consensus. Put emphasis on *what* is right rather than *who* is right. Veto only when there is a chance of violating Christian principles.

Staff meetings can be improved by organizing meetings around problems involving the staff and the improvement of the total work. Plan agenda carefully and publicize plans for the meeting in advance. Consult the entire group about the best time to have meetings and provide enough time to discuss business, plans and problems. Try not to close meetings without drawing conclusions for action. Be sure to keep good records and share the minutes of all meetings.

It is not wise for supervisors and administrators to try and coordinate group actions alone. It would be better to do this through some kind of an executive committee or group of officers. Design programs around the needs, problems, and interests of the workers. Where committees are used, define clearly their functions.

4. *Group Methods of Improvement and Supervision.* Supervising workers and teachers in groups demands techniques which are not only different but of a wide variety. Group work takes on a character of its own. Members of groups act very differently in the group situation than when dealt with privately. There may be actually what is called a "group mind" or feeling. Group work can exert favorable influences on individuals within its membership by means of its spirit, work, and even its size. There is that intangible thing called "school spirit" or the "we" spirit that may issue in that extra effort above that which is normal.

Supervisors find themselves in the position of either giving direct leadership to groups or indirect leadership through others. The first type is far better. Direct leadership can be given better in the smaller group meetings whereas the latter is given in the larger group meetings. Group methods, both direct and indirect, both large and small, are numerous. Large group meetings are called primarily for administrative and instructional purposes to impart information, give inspiration, establish common purposes, transact business, and for fellowship. Such meetings should be well-planned and conducted, involve participation, and result in achievement of goals. Small groups involve departments, classes, and more direct involvement of members. More specific purposes direct the work of small groups. Tasks may be short or long. Much creative work can be done in these groups. Human relations and communication are very important in such meetings.

Space does not permit us to discuss the merits of each type of meeting. Instead, supervisors and workers will find the following lists suggestive and can possibly evaluate and improve the situations in typical local church educational settings.

Purposes for conducting meetings might include:

Large Group Meetings

1. Planning retreats
2. Workshops
3. Curriculum studies
4. Faculty meetings
5. Workers' conferences
6. Conventions
7. Institutes
8. Leadership training schools
9. Panel discussions

Small Group Meetings

1. Individual conferences
2. Classroom conferences
3. Office conferences
4. Casual conferences
5. Observational visits
6. Department meetings
7. Orientation of new workers
8. Class meetings
9. Study groups
10. Seminars
11. Committee work
12. Teacher training classes
13. Group counseling
14. Intervisitation
15. Laboratory schools

Purposes for conducting group meetings are broad and inclusive. Major reasons might include the following:

1. To integrate, unify and coordinate the workers
2. To inspire and instruct workers

3. To make workers aware of principles and problems
4. To develop morale
5. To evaluate general practice
6. To make plans
7. To gain understanding for and support of new ideas and programs
8. To renew interest and faith in what is good
9. To reward merit by recognition and praise
10. To capitalize skills and enthusiasm
11. To provide a clearing house for the exchange of ideas on common problems and programs
12. To exchange information
13. To inform the church about plans and programs
14. To report successes and failures
15. To promote professional growth of workers
16. To initiate types of supervision
17. To cultivate the acceptance of supervisory ideas and practices
18. To exemplify the principles of good teaching
19. To deepen fellowship
20. To offer times of united prayer
21. To share spiritual victories
22. To think and meditate

Basic principles for operating group meetings are well known. The agenda, objectives and operation of these meetings should be the outgrowth of the planning of the group itself. Programs are centered in the needs, interests and problems of the workers. Advance planning is helpful and essential, as well as advance scheduling and publicity. Total participation contributes to the success of the meetings which should be conducted in comfortable and informal settings. Consensus becomes the basis for drawing conclusions and reaching agreements, followed by action and check-up for carry over into practice.

Sometimes activities and plans eagerly discussed and

adopted in group meetings bog down, and progress is retarded in translating the new ideas and activities into practice among the workers. This calls for techniques in supervision and improvement which might be termed *transitional activities.* The building up of confidence and sharpening of understanding and skills is necessary before the perceived outcomes can be realized. Workers will need help in putting sound ideas into practice. Following is a list of possible suggestions, making transitional activities both possible and acceptable.

1. Start out on a small scale
2. Experiment first, then watch results
3. Role playing and dramatization of new techniques
4. Use of audio-visual aids to illustrate and instruct
5. Study case histories
6. Conduct brainstorming sessions
7. Lesson planning demonstrations and conferences
8. Use of a professional library
9. Bulletins and other documentary aids
10. Field trips
11. Local research
12. Directed reading
13. Demonstration teaching
14. Directed observation
15. Inter-visitation
16. Formal study
17. Use of consultants
18. Leaves of absence
19. Use of bulletin board
20. Self-rating and evaluation

5. *Leadership Education.* Many churches, particularly the most successful ones, attack the problems of improving the teaching-learning process, and the total program for

that matter, through a formal *leadership education program.* Such a program has two phases: (1) the training of new workers, and (2) in-service training of current workers. It has been estimated that there are about two million workers in the church with about one-half million being added as replacements annually. The average term of office is from three to four years. This reveals a large turn-over. Lack of training and proper supervision are probably outstanding reasons for the prevalence of these conditions. Thus, there are two primary goals of a good leadership training program: (1) to improve working conditions, and (2) to improve the quality of the work done.

Much improvement of leaders and workers can be secured during the routine operational aspects of the educational program, in the conducting of small and large group meetings listed above, and in the personal attention of the supervisors and administrators. In spite of this there should be periods when formal study and training are provided by and in the local church. Such training can be provided in (1) one local church, (2) in a group of churches of the same denomination, (3) in a cooperative community-wide school, or (4) professionally designed teaching situations such as laboratory schools and training centers, colleges and seminaries. Curricula for these schools may (1) be locally designed, (2) secured from denominational headquarters, (3) found in the provisions of outside professional organizations, such as the Evangelical Teacher Training Association, Wheaton, Illinois, and correspondence schools, or (4) secured through independent professional church educators, such as professors and publishing houses who provide such services. For details concerning the planning and conducting of leadership schools the reader is referred to a former publication by the author and others.[11]

Adult education and *membership training* are two additional and important aspects of a church program of education. Adult education concerns making available Christian studies on an elective basis to members and friends of the church. The curriculum might consist of Bible study, doctrinal studies, ethical studies, social studies, and many others, subject only to the choice of participants. Membership education involves study and training for membership in the local church body itself. Basic studies in Christian experience, church history, doctrine, polity, and ethics are included, making it possible for candidates for the Christian life and church membership to become qualified.

Beyond the matter of leadership training is that of *leadership development.* A continual training program with personal supervisory attention will contribute to this. Self-confidence and the deepening of service skills should be developed as time passes. Willingness to lead can be encouraged by beginning where people are. Show them that it is permissable to make mistakes. If they do, no one will be penalized. Encourage pioneering and creativeness as desirable activities.

Authority can be shared. Allow workers to make suggestions, help set up objectives, rules and regulations. Draw on their experience and talents.

Assumption of responsibility can be encouraged through the use of group prayer, setting of standards, emphasizing objectives, making available adequate resources, and calling for reports of progress. Ask people to do things *with us* rather than *for us.* When workers help set up policies they will be more inclined to assume responsibility for them. Help workers identify problems which *they feel are important.* Encourage the making of decisions by means of consensus rather than by simple majority. Analyze the work to be done and this will help define responsibilities and will also suggest the allocation of duties. A survey of proposed jobs, giving people a chance to express likes and dislikes, and job preference, is also helpful. Psychologically, to ask people to assume responsibilities during group meetings makes it harder for them to say no. It is wise to give responsibility progressively rather than all at once.

Workers can be assisted in executing responsibility by having groups set deadlines for the completion of work. Where responsibility is assumed, give the person authority to carry it out. It is helpful also to keep open for suggestions from workers on how work can be improved. By all means keep the workers informed about progress. Be sure also to recognize exceptional contributions and give credit where it is due.

Some conditions which discourage the assumption of responsibility include lack of discipline, little or no vision, lack of standards and resources, lack of a sense of belonging, a sense of inferiority, disorganization, bad morale, and inadequate procedures. Supervisors and administrators must not overload workers, nor give the impression that workers are being *used* merely to achieve a good record.

Creative work needs stimulation. Reports of success, the use of outside speakers, in-service training, adequate equipment and supplies, a good library, stimulating conferences, open and inspiring discussion, and reading all contribute to a desire to be more creative. Try to develop among workers a desire to improve, a willingness to try something new. Make them to be dissatisfied with current results. Set up clear objectives. Encourage them in freedom to try new methods and recognize those who actually do these things. Urge workers to attend meetings where new ideas can be found. Help them develop methods of evaluation so that progress can be measured.

D. The Evaluation and Improvement of Individual Growth and Development

1. *Priority of Individual Development.* In considering the matter of evaluating individual growth and development we come to the very heart of the educational program of a church. Here we are concerned with product, the production of Christians and their development as Christlike people. The teaching-learning process is not only concerned with structure and process but also outcomes in terms of what happens to individual pupils.

Actually, the ultimate test of any educational program is what happens to pupils. If what happens is the wholesome development of Christian personality, if pupil behavior is influenced and molded increasingly toward Christian standards, if Christian attitudes are being formed, and if necessary knowledge and skills are being acquired and put to proper use in Christian service, the program of educational improvement may be considered to be successful. Even when structure and process are being evaluated, pupils are affected indirectly and derive educational benefits. In fact that is the real motive for strengthening structure and process. Thus, if the supervisor desires to know to what extent his program has been successful, he must provide some means of evaluating the growth and development of pupils.

Questions are often raised concerning the possibility of

the evaluation and testing of Christian growth.[12] While it is admitted that there are great difficulties presented to measurement in this area, due to the great subjectivity of Christian character and personality, yet many Christian educators are very optimistic regarding the possibility of measurement. Reference can be made to the aspect of subjectivity in any kind of measurement. Sampling is about the best anyone can do, even in secular education. Thus, even in the face of the self-evident lack of precision in measuring any human trait, efforts to measure are better than nothing and most certainly superior to complete reliance on subjective observation only. It is commonly agreed that there are four general areas in the program of Christian personality growth where measurements should be attempted: (1) growth in knowledge of the Christian faith, (2) growth in Christian attitudes and Christian personal qualities, (3) development in church education structure, and (4) the status of educational practice in terms of the teaching-learning process.

Early studies in evaluation tended to limit themselves to so-called objective factors in measurement. The feeling was then that such matters as personality, character, and spiritual life were too subjective in character to be adequately measured. Recent developments in the behavioral sciences, however, have tended to modify this attitude. Studies in these fields have pointed up the importance of attitudinal and emotional factors, not only in social relationships, but also in personal ones as well. Such factors have a direct and practical bearing on intellectual, physical, and even practical affairs. This has led to a more open-minded attitude toward measurement of subjective factors in human lives.

The evaluation of pupil growth and development is essentially a process of making value-judgments about pupils' achievement and behavior as they progress through the church school and later on in life. The basis of these judgments should be dependable information as to the status of the learners and the progress they have made toward desirable Christian education goals, with due regard for the abilities and needs of the individual. Consideration should also be given to environmental influences which affect the rate and direction of growth, such as the home background, community, and cultural influences.

2. *The Approach to Evaluation of Individual Growth.* Previous consideration was given (in Chapter IV) to an outline of the variety of methods used to evaluate results in the three program facets involved—structure, process, and product. It remains now for attention to be given to the use of these measures.

There are at least three methods of securing information about the status and growth of the learner:

1. By observation of behavior
2. By testing knowledge, skills, abilities, attitudes, and character traits
3. By measuring characteristics and behavior through use of standardized devices and testing procedures

The evaluation of observed behavior is largely a subjective procedure in which value-judgments are used. Tests and measures are more exact and objective ways of observing behavior, not involving value-judgments, but concerned with the more quantitative matters. Judgments as to quality or merit of behavior as revealed by measurement are based on comparison of test results with some established Christian norm or standard, primarily the Bible and/or Christian ethics.

There are two aspects to the evaluation approach of individual growth and development: (1) comparison of personality growth to the Christian standards revealed in the Word of God, and (2) learning to diagnose learning difficulties.

3. *Criteria for Evaluating Individual Growth.* The selection of means of appraising the educational product depends directly on one's concept of the nature and scope of outcomes. In Christian and church education, workers are concerned with the development of the whole person as well as the development of specific facets of personality, such as knowledge, attitudes, and skills. Such knowledge will issue in a clear statement of goals as well as content to be taught. This statement in turn depends directly on one's concept of what good church education is and what the derivative goals are. Previous discussion regarding these matters was given in Chapter IV.

The ultimate criteria for use in evaluating Christian experience, maturity, personality and growth are to be found in the Word of God. Any evaluation of these matters, therefore, becomes a matter of analyzing the Word and then comparing pupil commitment and progress with the standards revealed. We turn first to the matter of Christian character.

The character of Christ is the goal for the individual (Matt. 5:48; John 15:4). An analysis of the character of Jesus is revealed in the Scriptures. He was like God (John 14:9). His Godliness was expressed in all areas of His life and conduct. (Luke 2:52) Jesus increased in wisdom and stature, and in favor with God and man. The pattern for men, therefore, is to become increasingly more Godlike. Spiritual maturity is another way of expressing it (I Cor. 14:20; Eph. 3:19; 5:18; 4:13). With Christlikeness as the objective the individual has a "personality goal" toward which he should strive. Church education, then, is not so much concerned with native tendencies and capacities as it is with the ultimate development of the individual toward the personality goal.

Christian behavior has a Bible-based standard. Christian living is pictured as a "walk" with God. It is a manifestation of the very personal presence of God through the Holy Spirit. The character of the Holy Spirit is to be expressed in the daily walk of the Christian. This is known as the fruit of the Spirit and provides a new dimension for education, a divine dimension, not present in other forms of education. This dimension is exceedingly important, for without it the ideals and character goal of Christian education cannot be accomplished.

Personality consists broadly of knowledge, attitudes, skills, and personal qualities. Basic facets of knowledge would include an intellectual mastery of the Bible, church history, Christian doctrine, Christian ethics, and principles of morality. Skills encompass the development of the ability to observe and practice religious habits, such as prayer, Bible study, church attendance, and others. Ability to observe and practice certain character and moral habits, such as friendliness, honesty, responsibility, self-control, etc., is also included. Values and attitudes are far more subjective. Attitudes toward God, others, the church, society, and self, along with a value-system for making judgments, are involved in this facet of personality. Personal qualities would encompass the depth of Christian experience and the manifestations of individuality in common everyday living. All of these attributes need to be thrown against a background of Christian expectancies and standards. It is apparent from this illustrative listing of personality attributes just how complex personality is and how difficult it is to measure.

As previously indicated teachers are concerned with bringing about changes in the lives of pupils—changes in knowing, feeling, and doing. Sunday school teaching is often characterized predominantly by intellectual changes. These are important, of course, but the whole person should be changed in his life situation if witnesses are produced. The whole person should be patterned after the character and personality of Jesus Christ (Eph. 3:16-19). The feeling element is very important. Unless attitudes change it is hard for changes in ideas and actions to take place. There must be a feeling-tone to both teaching and learning.

4. *Means and Methods of Evaluating Individual Growth.* A vast amount of literature on this subject is available in general and secular education. In church education not a great deal is available. Church educators will have to carefully sift out methods from secular sources deemed valuable and useful. There are a number of ways it is possible to classify methods used. One of the more common ones is to divide methods arbitrarily into two categories: (1) measures of educational achievement, and (2) measures of character, personality, and behavior.

In appraising educational achievement one should be concerned with many factors—rate, scale of difficulty, quality, and area mastery. At least three types of classifications according to use are evident: (2) survey tests which measure achievement, such as subject matter mastery, Bible for example; (2) diagnostic tests which compare the relative status of a pupil or class with respect to outcomes previously determined, and (3) prognostic tests which seek to predict probable success in a given field of learning. Church education has access to few sources suitable for its program other than in the category of survey tests, primarily of Bible knowledge mastery.

Secular educators have developed many ways of studying character, personality traits, conduct, and behavior, including items personal in nature, such as interests, attitudes, appreciations, self-control, social and emotional adjustment, and morals. To these classifications the Christian will find it necessary to add that of Christian commitment. Some attempts have been made to devise measuring instruments in these categories.

Following is a list of some more common methods classified according to the two categories suggested above and which might be found useful in church education.

Educational Measures

1. Standardized tests
   a. Achievement
   b. Interest inventories
   c. Intelligence tests
2. Written objective tests
3. Essay written tests
4. Case studies
5. Catechisms
6. Cultural activities, such as art, music, poetry, etc.
7. General observation

Measures of Character, Personality and Behavior

1. Standardizes
   a. Personality and adjustment tests
   b. Attitude scales
2. Problem-situation tests (problem solving)
3. Behavior records
   a. Check lists

   b. Rating scales
   c. Codes of personality traits
   d. Codes of behavior
4. Statements of opinions and interests
5. Logs and diaries
6. School records
7. Questionnaires on habits, interests, activities, etc.
8. Interviews, conferences, and personal reports
9. Personal testimonies
10. Stenographic records, minutes
11. Direct observation
12. Sociogram procedures (group study)
13. Tests of attitudes and beliefs
14. Check lists of reading materials
15. Choice of motion pictures, radio, and TV programs
16. Observation on adult behavior following early training

5. *Assistance in the Evaluation of Individual Growth.* At best evaluating individual growth and development is very subjective. Some general methods of doing this would include securing pupil opinions, studying conversational flow in classes, and observing the quality of group life, personal relationships, and teacher-pupil relationships. Care must be taken in selecting and using materials available from secular sources. Careful adaptation of principles and content need to be made, if at all possible.

6. *Diagnosing Learning Difficulties.* Diagnosis involves the interpretation of the results gathered from evaluation and testing for the purpose of determining strengths and weaknesses in the educational project. From previous discussion it has been proposed the one's concept of church education, his formulation of goals and the use of evaluation devices will assist in diagnosis of status. Now it remains to deal with the question of discovering evidences or symp-

toms of difficulty in learning. Efforts should be made to discover the causes of poor and unsatisfactory learning. The scope would include the total personality.

The teacher is the key person in evaluating efforts. He is closest to the learner and the teaching-learning process. Teachers can not only observe results themselves but are also in a position to help pupils in self-evaluation. Following is a list of suggestings showing possible ways in which a teacher can measure the behavior of pupils as a basis for effective instruction.

1. Study pupil backgrounds through observation and study of records
2. Observe pupils at work—spirit of class, individual differences, interests, maturity, etc.
3. Study academic life of pupils
   a. By investigating studies already covered
   b. By giving periodic tests over study content
4. Observe pupils at work—habits, spirit of sharing, working together, etc.
5. Watch for evidences of quality in spiritual thinking and experiences
6. Give special attention to pupils with special needs
7. Confer periodically with parents and public school teachers
8. Watch for evidences of moral deviation and physical and emotional difficulties

As teachers evaluate their children they are also evaluating themselves as teachers. Studies on the improvement of materials and methods may issue in better teaching and learning.

Teachers need to be aware regarding possible reasons why pupils are not making satisfactory growth. The total personality may be involved as well as more limited and specific reasons. Following is a suggested list of personality factors where difficulties may arise.

Physiological Factors

1. Poor sight
2. Poor hearing
3. Poor health
4. Motor difficulties
5. Physical fatigue

Emotional Factors

1. Immaturity
2. Withdrawal
3. Aggressiveness
4. Tensions
5. Fears
6. Timidity

Spiritual Factors

1. Lack of Christian experience
2. Carnal tendencies
3. Weak prayer life
4. Neglected devotional life
5. Low morale
6. Lack of Christian love and fellowship

Intellectual Factors

1. Low level of intelligence
2. Verbal difficulties
3. Peculiarities in modes of thought

Environmental Factors

1. Lack of cooperation between home and church
2. Bad home conditions and spirit
3. Economic insecurity
4. Inadequate facilities
5. Drab surroundings
6. Lack of Christian love and fellowship
7. Poor "housekeeping"

Instructional Factors

1. Poor preparation
2. Lack of readiness and interest
3. Poor methods
4. Poor materials
5. Lack of motivation
6. Overcrowded classes
7. No evaluation
8. Weak objectives and classroom practices
9. Disorderly conduct
10. Drop-outs

Few diagnostic instruments are available to church educators. The use of the record system, observation and some of the tests and measurements suggested mentioned above may prove to be helpful. In cases involving psychological difficulties church workers will need to use great care, caution and wisdom in making use of professional services available.

7. *A Testing Program.* Due to the paucity of testing materials available and also because great doubt is cast upon the use of secular materials in church education, even when adaptation is possible, it is doubtful whether it is possible to set up a formal testing program for a local church. For those, however, who are interested perhaps the following is suggestive.

1. Give a basic intelligence test to determine mental ability
2. Use vocational and interest inventories among youth and young adults
3. Give a basic personality test
4. In classwork use Bible Content Tests, Attitude Tests, Social Distance Tests, rating scales, interest inventories, and tests of beliefs
5. Have teachers study record system and use general observation of pupils' background, behavior and abilities
6. Watch for deviations in physical, moral and social life
7. Carefully appraise spiritual experience, devotional life and service activities
8. Administrators and supervisors could measure structure and process in the total church education program

One church set up the following test pattern to measure spiritual maturity. A battery of tests was used called a "Spiritual Inventory Battery."[13]

1. General Bible Test—Ruth Beechick, Southwestern College, Phoenix, Arizona
2. 100 questions on Bible Doctrine by Norman Wright, Talbot Seminary A Bible-doctrine test based on Gospel Light Curriculum Pre-school through grade 8
3. 20 Questions to measure dependence/independence factors, based on J. Dwight Pentecost's book *Pattern for Maturity*
4. 100 items on application of doctrine to life

Perhaps it would be helpful to bear in mind the purposes of the use of tests. The general purpose of testing in to improve instruction. At least five immediate purposes can be cited in secular education: (1) placement, (2) diagnosis, (3) assessment, (4) predicting, and (5) evaluation. Placement is used to classify pupils according to subject matter achievement or grade level. It is possible that Bible achievement tests in church education could be used for better grouping of pupils for teaching purposes, but this would call for far more flexibility in pupil groupings in Sunday school, for example, than currently exists.

Diagnosis reveals pupil weaknesses, such as gaps in knowledge, understandings, and skills. Presumably it will pinpoint individual remedial work and/or revise methods of teaching. It points to causes rather than results. Bible and personality tests would prove helpful in diagnosis in Christian teaching.

Assessment refers to the evaluation of the effectiveness of teaching methods, issuing in pupil progress—growth, development, or change. Here the concern is comparison of the individual or group *after* instruction either with himself (or itself) *before* instruction. Thus, the amount of change is highlighted. Bible tests would fit in here.

Prediction refers to the appraisal of future achievement based on a measure of present performance. This type of test is almost unknown or almost totally unused in church education.

Evaluation stresses comparison of present status with some general or administrative standard. As previously noted we have found much use for this kind of testing. Church educational standards are the basis of this kind of testing.

E. The Evaluation of Supervision

1. *Evidences Among Workers and the Program.* Supervision, like everything else in the church educational program, should be evaluated. When one considers that the supervisor is a teacher of teachers and workers, then his work is actually a part of the teaching-learning process as a whole. Evidences of how well the educational objectives have been achieved and how much progress has been made toward overall improvement of the workers and program will help determine the effectiveness of supervision. What are these evidences?

Among Workers

1. Improved quality of leadership
2. Improved quality of teaching
3. Cheerful assumption of responsibilities
4. Openness to new materials and methods
5. Greater knowledge of pupils and fellow workers
6. Improved skills
7. Deeper fellowship
8. Increased participation and involvement

9. Unity and cooperation
10. Improvement of the supervisor himself in spirit and practice
11. Worker morale favorable and high
12. Acceptance or rejection of the work of supervision
13. Growth in creative activity
14. Deeper quality of spiritual life

In the Program

1. Improvement in pupil growth and development—saved souls, and changed lives
2. A definite philosophy of church education
3. Clear objectives
4. Better curriculum materials
5. Better use of materials
6. Well-balanced curriculum
7. Deeper appreciation for worship
8. Larger outreach
9. Increased evangelistic results
10. Greater interest and support on the part of parents and friends
11. Larger community impact
12. Greater understanding of the educational task of the church
13. Deepening of the quality of age-group programs
14. Better facilities and equipment
15. Better use of faciltities
16. Greater financial support
17. Better school atmosphere

2. *Self-evaluation.* It is not only important for the supervisor to be evaluated but also for him to evaluate himself. He should assess his own growth and development as well as that of others workers. The keeping of a log or diary is helpful on determining how time was spent

and what happened. The maintenance of a good filing and record system will yield valuable information. Actual case studies are thus made possible. Some kind of rating scale which lists desirable supervisory characteristics is helpful. (See Appendix No. 38).

In the final analysis the supervisor will want to determine if supervisory goals were achieved, if processes were sufficient, and if educational outcomes were adequate and what part he had personally in getting all of this done. The reaction of teachers and other workers to him personally and to his efforts will reveal actual feelings and attitudes.

Educational supervision is important to the continuing upgrading of teaching and learning in the church school. While this office is relatively new in the church, more constructive worker-supervisory relationships and approaches to evaluation indicate further developments which will enhance the stature and increase the potential contribution of the supervisor.

The Psychological Corporation, 304 East 45th. St., New York City 10017, has published a test on "How Supervise?" This would be useful in training and upgrading supervision, in evaluating results, and in counseling.

Questions for Class Discussion

1. What is teaching? What is learning?
2. What is the place of classroom visitation? In the supervisory program?
3. How does a supervisor plan for classroom visitation?
4. What does the supervisor do during classroom visitation?
5. Outline the main points of a plan to develop a policy of visitation.
6. What is the place of the individual conference in the program of supervision? Its purpose?

7. What should be the focal point of every supervisor-teacher conference?
8. Write brief summaries of lessons observed or taught.
9. How can favorable attitudes toward group conferences be developed?
10. What group processes are involved in drawing conclusions and in reaching agreements in group conferences?
11. Select a troublesome instructional problem and prepare a plan for building a group conference around it.
12. Discuss the needs of youth.
13. Discuss the advantages and disadvantages of using secular tests and measurements in church education.
14. Outline standards or criteria by which evidences of improvement can be discovered.

Questions for Local Church Use

1. Discuss the nature of teaching and learning.
2. How can wholesome teacher attitudes be built toward observational visits in Sunday school classes?
3. What are the purposes of visiting Sunday school classes to observe?
4. How may an individual conference be a means of growth for supervisors and teachers?
5. How does one motivate workers to take courses in a leadership training program?
6. What is involved in setting up and operating a training program?
7. What is good discussion?
8. How do teachers discover pupil needs?
9. What is the value of attending a Christian education convention?
10. Can we set up a testing program in our church school?
11. Develop a check list or rating scale for use in the church school.

12. Plan a year's calendar of workers' conference themes.
13. Develop a good leadership training library and reading lists.
14. What can be done to help slow and gifted pupils?
15. How can Sunday school teachers be encouraged to do professional reading?

Notes for Chapter Six

1. Donald M. Joy, *Meaningful Learning in the Church* (Winona Lake, Indiana, Light and Life Press, 1969), p. 56. This book is recommended also for study of the details of the learning process (see Chapter 8).
2. Wayne R. Rood, *The Art of Teaching Christianity* (New York, Abingdon, 1968), p. 22.
3. Robert C. McKean, *The Supervisor,* Washington, D.C., Center for Applied Research in Education, Inc., 1964, p. 83.
4. Chester T. McNerney, *Educational Supervision* (New York, McGraw-Hill, 1951), p. 92.
5. John A. Bartky, *Supervision as Human Relations* (Boston, D.C. Heath and Co., 1953), p. 143.
6. Guy Leavitt, *Superintend with Success* (Cincinnati, Standard Publishing Co., 1960), p. 89 (see Appendixes).
7. George D. Halsey, *Supervising People* (New York, Harper and Brothers, 1946), pp. 152ff.
8. H. W. Byrne, *A Christian Approach to Education,* rev. ed. (Mott Media, 1977), p. 125.
9. Weldon Crossland, *Better Leaders for Your Church* (New York, Abingdon, 1955), p. 120.
10. Ibid., p. 121ff.
11. Consult H. W. Byrne, *Christian Education for the Local Church,* rev. ed. (Grand Rapids, Michigan, Zondervan, 1973), Chapters 3 and 4. See also Crossland, *Better Leaders.*
12. See *Evaluation and Christian Education,* Bureau of Research, National Council of Churches, 1960, p. 2; also consult Frank

McKibben, *Guiding Workers in Christian Education* (New York, Abingdon, 1953), p. 137.

13. Rev. Andre Bustanoby, Temple Baptist Church, 1601 W. Malvern, Fullerton, Calif. Described in *Christianity Today,* No. 21, 1969, p. 22.

Appendix No. 1

List of Some Statements of Objectives

General Sources

David R. Krathwohl, *et al, Taxonomy of Educational Objectives,* New York, David McKay Co., Inc., 1956. Shows the classification of educational goals

Robert F. Mager, *Preparing Instructional Objectives,* Belmont, California, Fearon Publishers, 1962. Guidelines for preparing a statement of educational objectives.

Church Education Sources

Objectives in Religious Education (1930), Paul H. Vieth, New York, Harper, 1930.

Jr. High Objectives (1953), National Council of Churches of Christ in the U.S.A., New York

Objectives of the Christian Education of Senior High Young People (1958), New York, National Council of Churches

Consult *Basic Principles* (1947) and *Christian Faith and Life at a Glance* (Revised, 1958)—United Presbyterian

Consult *The Church's Teaching Series* (1949–51), 6 volumes, The Protestant Episcopal Church

Consult *Foundations for Christian Teaching in Methodist Churches* (1960) The United Methodist Church

Consult *Objectives of Christian Education* (1957), *Age-Level Objectives of Christian Education* (1958), and *The Functional Objectives of Christian Education* (1959), Philadelphia, Lutheran Church of America, 1957, 1958, 1959

Consult *Christian Education within the Covenant Community—the Church,* 1958, Presbyterian Church in the U.S.

Consult *A Statement of Educational Principles as Seen in the Light of*

Christian Theology and Beliefs (1957), The United Church of Christ

Consult "The Great Objective", American Baptist

Consult *The Objectives of Christian Education;: A Study Document,* New York, National Council of Churches, 1958

Consult *The Church's Educational Ministry: A Curriculum Plan,* St. Louis, Bethany, 1965

Consult Lois Lebar, *Education that is Christian,* New York, Revell, 1958

Consult H. W. Byrne, *A Christian Approach to Education,* rev. ed., Mott Media

Consult James D. Murch, *Christian Education for the Local Church,* Standard, 1934

Consult Frank E. Gabelein, *Christian Education in a Democracy,* Oxford, 1951

Consult Cornelius Jaarsma, *Fundamentals in Christian Education,* Eerdmans, 1953

Consult C. B. Eavey, *The Art of Effective Teaching,* Zondervan, 1953

Consult, J. Edward Hakes, ed, *An Introduction to Evangelical Christian Education,* Moody, 1964

Appendix No. 2

Standards for Church School Teachers

Standards for Church School Teachers
______________________________Church

1. Attend the worship services of the church unless hindered by reasons approved by a Christian conscience

2. Seek spiritual guidance for his individual responsibilities
3. Allow adequate time, thought, study, and prayer in the preparation of each Sunday session
4. Feel a personal responsibility for the attendance of each pupil on the class role, and for the securing of new pupils
5. Attend the planning sessions for your group and the Workers' Conferences for all church school workers
6. Be present every Sunday before the first pupil arrives. In case of necessary absence, notify your Leader Teacher or Supervisor in advance
7. Accept all opportunities for additional training, such as leadership training courses, demonstration sessions, laboratory schools, etc.
8. Read the (suggested magazine) and other recommended books and periodicals on Christian education each year.

These Standards were adopted by the Board of Christian Education at their monthly meeting ____________ Revised ____________.

My Job and I

A. I am a worker for the Lord.
   1. As a Christian, I am a worker for the Lord. Am I doing the work for which I am best fitted? ______

B. My Evaluation of my Spiritual Qualifications.

1. Am I thoroughly committed to the Christian work entrusted to me, willing to make the sacrifice necessary for success? _____
2. Am I an active, supporting member of my Church? _____
3. In my home life, am I a Christian, as shown in my relationship with the members of my family, my daily reading of God's Word, meditation and prayer? _____
4. In public are my dress, words, actions, and general behavior such as to bring honor to my Lord? _____

C. My Evaluation of my improvement in my job

1. Have I taken the elemental training courses pertaining to my work in the church Sunday school? _____
2. Am I continuing to improve myself as a worker, by further training? _____
3. Do I own and use a personal library pertaining to my work? _____
4. Do I practice self-development through observation, visiting other schools, attending laboratory classes and demonstrations? _____
5. Do I practice self-development through individual reading and study? _____

D. My Evaluation and my Ability as a Leader

1. Do I make the best use possible of suggestions from department workers in the Sunday school? _____

2. Am I on friendly and cooperative terms with the other workers in my church and its Sunday school? ______
3. Am I reliable, dependable, trustworthy? ______
4. Am I consistently on the look out to discover and help train new workers in the church and its school? ______
5. Are my motives in my work above criticism? ______

E. My Evaluation of my Efforts

1. Do I devote at least one hour to my work each week, not counting Sunday or the time given to preparation for Sunday? ______
2. Am I always fully prepared for my work on Sunday morning? ______
3. Am I present at least fifteen minutes before the time for school to begin session? ______
4. Do I make it a rule to begin and to stop on time in my Sunday school class? ______
5. Am I satisfied that I am doing my best in the work for which I have been selected? ______

Sample

A Teacher may ask Himself these Questions:

1. How much interest did my pupils show?
2. What were the points of greatest interest?

3. What parts of the session were the dull spots?
4. What made the difference between the interesting and the dull points?
5. How many pupils took part in some way?
6. At what points was participation liveliest? Dullest? Why?
7. What did this participation reveal to me concerning the pupils who participated?
8. Did the presentation go as I had planned?
9. Did the application and the conclusion take hold of the pupils?
10. Which of my questions stimulated more interest? Which less? Why?
11. Did the lesson lead to a program of action?
12. What have I learned about my teaching?
13. What improvements am I going to make in my teaching next Sunday?

Indeed, if a teacher takes the time and makes the effort to consider carefully the last two questions, answering them with a sincere desire and determination to be a better teacher, the evaluation will be profitable.

Sometimes the very best evaluation is done while talking over with God in prayer these questions and their answers.

No. 2—Sample

Your character is important to your work as a teacher. If you are to develop Christian character in your pupils, you must possess in your own life these characteristics which you desire to develop in others. Here are the questions, designed to help us judge our character. What are your strong qualities? What are your weaknesses? Put a circle around those where improvement is needed.

Are You:	Or Are You:
1. Open-minded, inquiring?	Narrow, dogmatic, not hungry for truth?
2. Accurate, thorough, discerning?	Indefinite, superficial, lazy?
3. Decisive, possessing conviction	Uncertain, wavering, undecided?
4. Cheerful, joyous, optimistic?	Gloomy, pessimistic, bitter?
5. Amiable, friendly, agreeable?	Repellent, unsocial, disagreeable?
6. Tolerant, sense of humor?	Dogmatic, intolerant, selfish?
7. Kind, courteous, tactful?	Cruel, rude, untactful?
8. Honest, truthful, sincere?	Dishonest, hypocritical?
9. Patient, calm equable?	Irritable, excitable, moody?
10. Regular, punctual, on time?	Tardy, usually behind time, incapable?
11. Interested in the Bible?	Little concern for God's Word
12. At peace with God?	Unrepentant?

Lesson Evaluation

A good way to evaluate the lesson preparation is by the seven laws of teachings:

1. Did I know, thoroughly and familiarly, the lesson I was to teach?
2. Did I gain and keep the attention and interest of the pupils upon the lesson?
3. Did I use words understood in the same way by the pupils and by me—language as clear and vivid to them as it was to me?
4. Did I begin with who is already well-known to the pupil upon the subject and with what he has himself experi-

enced? Did I proceed from there to the new material by single, easy and natural steps, letting the known explain the unknown?

5. Did I stimulate each pupil's own mind to action, leading him to anticipate what was coming next, letting him feel that he was discovering the thought for himself.
6. Did I require each pupil to reproduce in thought the lesson being learned, expressing it in his own language?
7. Did I review the past lessons, review the points in this lesson, and summarize them clearly so that no pupil was left with false understanding, but with a complete understanding of the truth?

Appendix No. 3
Sources for Standards

Denominational Sources

Standard of Achievement, Department of Sunday School, Wesleyan Methodist Church of America, Box 2000, Marion, Indiana.

100 Ways to Improve Your Sunday School
The Sunday school standard and self-evaluation for Evangelical Free Church of America, 1515 East 66th. St., Box 6399, Minneapolis, Minn., 55423

14 Steps to Sunday School Improvement
Christian Education Department, Evangelical Free Church of America, 1515 East 66th. St., Minneapolis, Minn. 55423

Measure of an Effective Church
Strategy Handbook accompanies, Free Methodist Church Headquarters, Winona Lake, Indiana 46590

Standards for Free Methodist Sunday Schools
Department of Sunday school, Free Methodist Church Headquarters, Winona Lake, Indiana 46590
Sunday School Achievement Guide
Sunday School Department, Sunday School Board of the Southern Baptist Convention, 127 9th. Ave., North, Nashville, Tenn. 37203
Standard Handbook
National Sunday School Standard, Christian Education Office, Home Department, Christian and Missionary Alliance, 260 West 44th. St., New York, New York 10036
Standard of Achievement
Department of Church School Administration, American Baptist Convention, 1703 Chestnut St., Philadelphia, Pa.
Achievement Guide
Department of Church Schools, Church of the Nazarene, Kansas City, Mo.
Standard of Achievement
National Sunday School Board of General Baptists, Box 101, Malden, Mo.
Achievement Goals for United Brethren in Christ Sunday Schools
United Brethren in Christ Church, Huntington College, Huntington, Ind.

Inter-denominational Sources

The International Standard for the Sunday Church School
National Council of Church of Christ in the U.S.A., Division of Christian Education, National Council, New York City
Standards for the Sunday School
Gospel Light Publications, Glendale, Calif.

No. 4

Sunday School Superintendent's Problem Finder from Leadership Education Audiovisual Kit

NOTE: Executive and administrative activities are those concerned with organizing and running the school. Educational supervision consists of activities concerned primarily with improving the quality of the program and the skill of the workers. In some churches, a director of religious education is responsible for educational supervision; in others, the minister carries major responsibility; in yet others, department or division superintendents serve as educational supervisors. The general superintendent ordinarily carries executive and administrative activities, and, where no one else is responsible, he does what he can on educational supervision as well.

Activities *Whose responsibility/what success*

A. *Executive and Administrative Activities*
(Organizing and running the school)

I. Presiding Activities
1. Presiding over the school
2. Speaking to the school
3. Maintaining discipline
4. Conducting worship programs

II. Promotional Activities
5. Planning and providing publicity
6. Enlisting new pupils

7. Securing punctual and regular attendance of pupils
8. Securing punctual and regular attendance of teachers and officers
9. Calling on absentees

III. Organizational activities
10. Grading pupils in classes and departments
11. Promoting pupils
12. Seeing that records are kept
13. Supplying teachers for all classes
14. Encouraging and helping classes to organize

IV. Providing Facilities
15. Financing the Sunday School
16. Securing needed equipment
17. Securing needed building improvements
18. Keeping equipment in good order
19. Seeing that proper supplies are ordered

V. Program Building
20. Providing social and recreational activities
21. Encouraging presentation of plays and pageants
22. Observing special days and seasons
23. Providing for social service activities

VI. Maintaining Relationships
24. Conferring with the pastor to keep school related to church as whole
25. Working with the Committee on Education
26. Working with associates and assistants
27. Conducting workers' conference
28. Cooperating with other Sunday Schools and agencies

B. *Educational Supervision*
(Improving the quality of the program and the skill of the workers)

I. Program Improvements
29. Building a complete and unified curriculum or program

30. Fostering the Christian Spirit and method in all work
31. Using Standards or guides as a means of evaluating the program and undertaking improvements
32. Studying records as a basis for improvement
33. Guiding workers in selection of courses, materials, types of activity
34. Keeping lesson materials up to date
35. Guiding improvement in worship
36. Guiding improvement in recreational and social life

II. Improving the Leadership
37. Counseling with workers to help improve their work
38. Getting workers to attend conventions, leadership classes, conferences, institutes
39. Guiding workers in the reading of helpful books and magazines, as through a workers' library
40. Conducting workers' conferences on better methods
41. Enlisting and training prospective workers

III. Working with Pupils and Parents
42. Interviewing pupils who have special needs
43. Helping pupils to become church members
44. Visiting in the homes of pupils
45. Guiding pupils toward Christian decisions
46. Conducting conferences with parents to secure cooperation

IV. The Larger Setting
47. Conferring with other workers to keep whole church program unified
48. Cooperating with other churches for mutual helpfulness
49. Cooperating with public schools and other community agencies
50. Relating the work of the church to worldwide Christian enterprise

C. *The Superintendent's Own Growth*
51. Providing for personal devotional life
52. Enriching fellowship with pastor and other colleagues
53. Attending institutes, conventions, leadership classes
54. Keeping up to date through regular reading of religious educational books and periodicals
55. Visiting and observing effective work elsewhere
56. Keeping the experimental attitude by trying out new ideas

No. 5

Sunday School Standards

Working a Successful School—Isa. 62:10

by
Dr. H. W. Byrne

Introduction

1. Plans for building a good Sunday school must be understood
2. Specifications must be faithfully followed

I. Organization
A. Principle—church control—Ep. 4:11-13
B. Practice
1. Board or Committee on Christian education
2. Church election of workers (may be delegated)

3. Active pastor; study reports to the church
4. Sunday School Council or Executive Committee (business)

II. Administration
   A. Principle—I Cor. 14:40
   B. Practice
      1. Adequate slate of workers
      2. Manual of Duties
      3. Adequate staff of teachers
      4. Good record system
      5. Good attendance of teachers
      6. Finances
      7. Annual installation service
      8. Annual banquet
      9. Workers' and teachers covenants
      10. Self-rating scales
      11. Parent-Teacher Organization
      12. Publicity and promotion
      13. Annual calendar
      14. Retreat

III. Curriculum
   A. Principle—2 Tim. 3:16, 17
   B. Practice
      1. A Bible-based program
      2. Emphasis on missions, stewardship, temperance education
      3. Teaching processes
      4. Stress on home Bible study
      5. Worship, planned
      6. Recreation
      7. Service
      8. Christian family life
      9. Expanded program for children, youth, adults
      10. Special Days

IV. Leadership Training
  A. Principle—2 Tim. 2:15b; Rom. 12:1, 2
  B. Practice
    1. Annual survey leadership needs and personnel
    2. Workers' conference (9 times)
    3. Workers' training program
    4. Leadership library
    5. Reading
    6. Apprentice training
    7. Training calendar
    8. Audio visual resources
    9. Supervision
    10. Lay training for service—stewardship, Bible study, teams

V. Evangelism and Missions
  A. Principles—Great commission—Matt. 28:18-20; Luke 19:10b
  B. Practice
    1. Prayer and responsibility lists
    2. Definite plans for evangelism
    3. Christian life class
    4. Home missions
    5. Foreign missions
    6. Visitation
    7. Follow-up
    8. Organized Cradle Roll, Extension and Home Departments

VI. Attendance and Outreach
  A. Principle—Go—Matt. 28:18-20; Acts 6:7; 5:42
  B. Practice—goals; new Sunday schools; cooperation outside

VII. Facilities
  A. Principle—Amos 9:11—Solomon's Temple
  B. Practice—Good quarters; survey space, equipment; plans; materials

VIII. Supervision
- A. Principle—2 Tim. 2:15c
- B. Practice—Employ DCE; Stress morale, quality, skills; measurement

No. 6

Points to Consider in Evaluating Curriculum in Christian Education

Compiled by Professor Margaret M. Swain,
Alderson-Broadus College

Objectives

a. Does the curriculum have a clear pattern of objectives (or goals) it is attempting to follow throughout which includes the following areas:

Persons and their relationship to God
Persons and their relationship to Jesus Christ
Persons and their relationship to the Bible
Persons and their relationship to the Church
Persons and their relationship to themselves
Persons and their relationship to others

b. Are the objectives theologically acceptable to the judging groups? Are they clearly related to Christian motivations?

c. Is there an educational and continuous approach to evangelism?

d. Do objectives and material cultivate a response to the Gospel?

e. Are the objectives balanced in the curriculum with a sequence of pattern, and are they co-ordinated throughout as well as being clearly recognized in the material?

Content

a. Is the content (or message) of the material basically related to the Bible and central in the message and use of the Bible?
b. Does the content meet real life experiences of people "where they are?"
c. Does the content lead persons to live out the objective in daily life and conduct?
d. Does the content meet individual needs and ages so it can be comprehended by them?

Educational Factors

a. Does the curriculum take into account the laws of growth and development?
b. Does it meet the needs of each age group with opportunities to develop real-life experiences and activities, thought and insight (otherwise is it pupil-centered)?
c. Is the role of the teacher one of a stimulator, guide and counselor?
d. Do the materials stimulate teachers to creative thinking and planning instead of just transmitting ideas and having materials memorized.
e. Is there concern shown for change in attitudes and actions as well as the development of knowledge and skills?
f. Are specific changes in pupils listed in terms of thoughts, feelings, attitudes, and actions?

Methodology and Supplementary Materials

a. Do the methods suggested develop leadership?
b. Are the methods such as to give pupils opportunity to learn

and express themselves, rather than accepting passively what a teacher says? (Or are they pupil-centered?)

c. Are they methods which produce an informal, relaxed atmosphere in growth?
d. Are creative activities, coming from the pupil's planning and thinking, encouraged and shown how to be done, rather than just "busy work?"
e. Are many supplementary sources and materials suggested?

Unit Organization

a. Is each lesson incorporated in a larger pattern or unit?
b. Is each unit teaching a definite objective with certain goals?
c. Is each unit explained so the teacher can adapt the objectives to the needs of his particular pupils and group?
d. Is each unit suited to the needs, interests, and experiences of the age group it is meant for?
e. Do the units tie together and establish a coherent way of evolving out of the preceding one?

Evaluation of Progress

a. Are suggestions given for evaluating pupil progress towards the objectives in attitudes, skills, and the ability to apply principles of Christianity?
b. Are suggestions given for pupils and teachers to evaluate their work together?
c. Is growth toward the desired objectives emphasized, rather than the giving of awards?

Literary Qualities

a. Are the stories and materials well-written?
b. Are the style and vocabulary suitable to the age groups?

Helps for the Teachers

a. Are there ample helps and resources given with ways suggested as to how to do the teaching?

b. Is there provision made for the teacher's spiritual enrichment and knowledge?

Home Experiences Utilized

a. Does the curriculum work in and through home experiences?
b. Is there home material available to co-ordinate the teaching of attitudes and knowledge?

Mechanical Setup

a. Is the type and size of material suitable to the age groups?
b. Is the art work good with suitable concept for age groups?
c. Is there durable binding?

No. 7

Evaluation Outline for Curriculum Materials and Activities

Objectives

1. Have clear, worthy, attainable objectives been set up to guide the teacher?
2. Do the objectives of the particular age or unit of work harmonize with the objectives for the program of religious education as a whole?
3. Do the objectives clearly reflect the needs, interests, and capacities of the pupils? Are the goals child-centered?
4. Have all the materials, activities, and experiences been selected with respect to these objectives?
5. Is the attainment of these objectives measurable?

Subject Matter

6. Is the subject matter suited to the accomplishment of these objectives? Is there too much or too little content?
7. Is the subject matter used adapted to the interests, needs, and capacities of the pupils? Does it also center in the social life about the pupils?
8. Does the subject matter possess intrinsic interest for the pupils? Is it definitely related to their present-day religious needs and experiences? If not, can its use be justified on other bases?
9. If pupil study must be motivated, is a method for motivation suggested? Is the supervisor able to aid the teacher in developing proper motivation?
10. Does the subject matter of the course adequately deal with the various sources and types of religious thought and experience? Is it wide in scope of interest and rich in value?
11. Is the content of the course properly related to the courses preceding and following it? Is it related to a total curriculum?
12. Does the subject matter have possibilities of being effectively related to other elements of the program such as worship, service? Are these possibilities utilized?
13. Are activities suggested in connection with the subject matter; Do these activities naturally grow out of or lead into the subject matter?
14. Is the material broken into proper units or "lessons" for study? Is there too much material or too little material for the lesson period?
15. Do the units of content have proper sequence? Is the course marked by progress from beginning to end?
16. Is the material of each unit well organized? Is there a teaching outline? Are the explanations and directions for the teacher clear and helpful? Are they too detailed? Not sufficiently explicit?
17. Are there adequate suggestions of course materials? Is the

teacher's material rich in illustrative and informational materials?
18. Is such material as is placed in the hands of the pupils interesting and well written?
19. Is its organization clear and helpful to the pupils?
20. Is the vocabulary within the understanding of the pupils? Is it in good literary form?
21. Are the directions and suggestions for the pupils phrased within their understanding?
22. Is the subject matter made available to pupils and teachers in attractive and durable form?
23. Are the textbooks well made? Is good paper used? Is the mechanical structure or construction of high grade?
24. Do the literary construction and diction conform to the highest standards?
25. Are tables of contents, indexes, and other devices provided to enable the teachers to use materials easily?
26. Are all maps, drawings, tables, and pictures of high grade and usable character?
27. Are drawings and pictures in pupils' texts of good quality and artistic value, in keeping with the nature and importance of the subject?

Activities and Experiences

28. Are the activities, situations, and experiences selected with definite relationship to clearly defined objectives?
29. Do they have intrinsic worth in themselves? Are the experiences and situations typical and real?
30. Are the activities, experiences, situations pupil-centered? Are they of definite interest and value to the pupils?
31. Are they definitely related to the on-going processes of the lives of the pupil, the school, and society?
32. Are they related to a regular outline, program or course that provides continuity and progress?
33. Are they carefully graded to the limitations and capacities of the pupils?

34. Do the activities represent a variety of interests, values, skills, and relationships?
35. Do the experiences, selected include the various major areas of life? Do they extend the pupil's thought and activities into the normal round of life activities?
36. Are the experiences selected rich in meaning, capable of expansion, effective for class treatment?
37. Are the various interests of individual pupils taken into account? Is provision made for dealing with individual differences?
38. Where activities and experiences are introduced into the class period is there sufficient aid given in the teacher's guide to provide definite assistance in making the experiences or activity profitable? To what extent is the supervisor able to supplement meager course guidance?
39. In the use of all activities, experiences, and life situations are suitable teaching methods and techniques employed? Do the teachers' manuals, guides, or outlines provide adequate teaching helps?
40. Are adequate material supplies and facilities available when such are needed? Are they in good condition? Are they accessible to the teachers and pupils?
41. Are the activities carried through to completion? Are the objectives and values sought realized?
42. Are the pupil experiences and life situations explored fully? Are they carried through to definite conclusions, solutions, principles, and applications to conduct?
43. Is care exercised to aid the pupils to summarize the results of activities, projects, the study of like situations? Is the work of a given unit, term, quarter, or course conserved to the larger units of training?
44. Do the activities and experiences permit of some method of measurement of results? Do the teacher's manuals, guides, or outlines suggest measurement devices or tests? Is the supervisor able to give definite assistance in the evaluation of results?

CORRELATION PATTERN FOR CHRISTIAN EDUCATION IN THE LOCAL CHURCH

Sheet 27, *Correlated Christian Education In The Local Church,* Harvest Publications

	Under Two's	Twos'n Threes	Kinder-garten	Primary	Junior	Junior High	Senior High	Older Youth	Adults	Golden Age
Sunday School	X	X	X	X	X	X	X	X	X	X
Extended Session	X	X	X	X	X					
Pastor's Instruction					Grades 6, 7 & 8					
Membership Training					X	X	X	X	X	X
Training Fellowship					X	X	X	X	X	X
Children's Hour		X	X	X						
Leadership Training							X	X	X	X
Vacation School		X	X	X	X	X	X	X	X	X
Summer Camp					X	X	X	X	X	
Boys' Organization					X	X	X			
Girls' Organization					X	X	X			
Women's Organization								X	X	X
Men's Organization								X	X	X
Parents' Study Group								X	X	X
Music Organizations				X	X	X	X	X	X	
Inquiry Class							X	X	X	X
Day Camp			X	X	X					
Family Worship	X	X	X	X	X	X	X	X	X	X
Released Time				X	X	X	X			
Week Day School		3 yr old	X							

No. 8

Evaluating Christian Education in the Local Church (For the Small Church)

By
Dr. H. W. Byrne

Phase I—Where are we now?

I. GROWTH

A. Purpose

1. To see the trends in growth or loss
2. To compare gains or losses with the potential in the community

B. Procedures

1. For gains or losses*

(*You may want to make more detailed charts on the comparative growth of Sunday school departments and/or classes)

Make a chart on Sunday school enrollment for the past five years.

Year	*Enrollment at the end of Sunday School Year*	*Average attendance for the year closing*

Make a graph on Sunday school growth for the past five years.

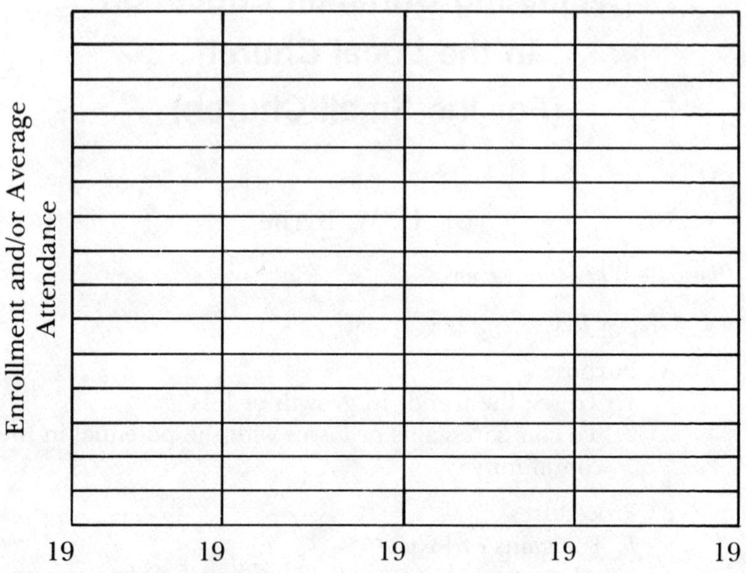

2. Our Potential
   a. Is our community increasing in population?
   b. Or is it static or decreasing?
   c. Do we have enough compassion and concern to reach out for the unreached?
   d. Do we know the number of prospects?Their location?
   e. Have we taken a religious census?
   f. Do we maintain a regular visitation program and do we systematically and regularly assign prospects to appropriate departments and classes?
   g. Do we receive reports on all visits made?
   h. Has our numerical growth been in proper proportion to our total possibilities?

i. If our enrollment has declined, what are the reasons? Why do we have drop-outs?
j. Do we follow up absentees?
k. Could we have reached more persons if we had prayed more earnestly, planned more wisely, and worked more diligently?

C. Spiritual Results
1. How many Sunday school scholars have been converted?
2. How many Sunday school scholars have joined the church?
3. Are spiritual needs being met?
a. Among older pupils?
(1) Do we love and know our Bibles better?
(2) Is there real interest in and enthusiasm about matters of moral and spiritual concern?
(3) Is genuine Christian love manifested for one another and other people?
(4) Are we witnessing for Jesus Christ?
(5) Are we interested in service?
(6) How many have been called and dedicated to special Christian service?
(7) What is the general spiritual tone of the church?
b. Among children?
(1) Do they like to attend our Sunday School?
(2) Do they seem to enjoy what goes on?
(3) Are they learning not only to repeat Bible verses but to put them into practice?
(4) Are we able to see wholesome signs of character development in their lives?

II. ADMINISTRATION

A. General Administration
1. Do all of your workers have a clear and adequate concept of the nature of Sunday school work?

2. Do they know what your objectives are?
3. Do you give sufficient attention to planning your work?
4. Do officers and teachers have the number and kinds of meetings that are needed for doing the best work?
5. Are your meetings well planned and well conducted?
6. Is the total program adequately financed?
7. Are you satisfied with your curriculum materials?

B. Organization
1. Do your departments and classes have room for growth?
2. Are departments and classes too large?
3. Have you provided for special groups, such as the homebound, mentally retarded, handicapped, etc.?
4. Are your pupils properly grouped and graded?
5. Do you have a definite plan of visitation organized?
6. Do you have adequate time allocated for Bible teaching?

C. Leadership
1. Do you have enough workers?
2. Do you make an annual study of leadership needs and where to find workers?
3. Is there a proper ratio of workers to enrollment?
   a. Total number of workers _____
   b. Total pupil enrollment _____
   c. Ratio of workers to pupils. One to _____
   (Divide pupil enrollment by workers)
   (Standard: Preschool 1 to 5) (Children 1–8)
   (Youth 1–10) (Adults 1–25)
4. Have you provided for Associate Superintendents and substitute teachers?
5. Are your leaders committed fully to the Lord?
   a. Are they dedicated to Bible teaching?
   b. Do they have a concern for persons?

c. Are they dependable?
d. Are they willing to work hard?

6. Are your workers adequately trained? What are your plans?

Phase II—Plans

III. PLANS FOR HELPING PEOPLE

A. For helping Sunday School Members

1. What will your Sunday school do this year to improve the quality of teaching-learning experiences?
2. What will you do to involve more members in outreach and to improve the effectiveness of outreach?
3. What will you do to involve members in more meaningful individual, family, and corporate worship?
4. What will you do to involve members in more meaningful witnessing?
5. What will you do to involve members in learning experiences in addition to those provided by Sunday school?
6. What will you do to involve members in ministering to church members and immediate prospects?

B. For helping unenlisted church members (inactive people)?

1. How many people fall into this category? (Church members not in Sunday school)
2. Check the ways you plan to help them this year

______ Pray for them

______ Minister to their needs (visit, show friendship, help in crisis)

______ Give them opportunities to participate in ministry to others (distribute food, visit sick, visit old people, read to blind, etc.)

______ Provide resources to encourage individual and family worship (literature)

_____ Share Christian experiences with them (prayer, testimony, etc.)

_____ Encourage them to share their own Christian experiences as opportunities arise

_____ Provide resources for Bible study and encourage participation in regular study (classes share materials, home Bible classes)

_____ In the case of parents, provide materials for use in the Christian education of their children

_____ Invite them to participate in the activities of the church, with special emphasis on the Sunday school (special programs, socials, etc.)

_____ Other ways you will help them

C. For helping unsaved persons in your community
 1. Try to determine the number of such persons
  a. Number _____
  b. Do you know them personally?
  c. How many of these persons are listed in your prospect file? _____
  d. How many natural opportunities do you have to witness to them each week?
  e. How many opportunities should you make?
 2. Check the ways your Sunday school can help them

_____ Pray for them

_____ Show interest in and respect for them as persons as well as potential church members (genuine interest, visitation, leave literature)

_____ Demonstrate Christian love and friendship (help meet their total needs)

_____ Share Christian experiences with them (witness, literature, etc.)

_____ Provide resources for Bible study and encourage each person to study regularly (at home, guide them)

_____ Appeal to their interests and invite them to participate in the activities of the church, with special emphasis on the Sunday school
_____ Other ways you plan to help them

D. For helping unaffiliated members (indifferent)
   1. How many indifferent members of your denomination live nearby?
   2. Check the things your church should do for them
      _____ Pray for them
      _____ Demonstrate genuine interest in them as persons as well as potential church members
      _____ Minister to their needs in a spirit of Christian love and Friendship
      _____ Provide resources (reading materials)
      _____ Share Christian experiences with them (same as before)
      _____ Encourage them to share their own experiences as opportunities arise
      _____ Provide resources for Bible study (quarterlies and guides)
      _____ In the case of parents, provide materials for use in the Christian education of their children (reading materials)
      _____ Invite them to participate in the activities of the church, especially emphasizing Sunday school
      _____ Other ways you plan to help

E. For helping persons of other denominations not involved in the life and work of any church
   1. How many of these are in your community?
   2. Plans to help (same as for those above)

F. For helping children not in Sunday school
 1. Number of children under 13 who are not in Sunday school but living in your community ______
 2. How many of these are assigned to the proper Sunday school departments and/or classes as prospects? ______
 3. Check things your church can do for them
 ______ Pray daily for them
 ______ Minister to their needs and to the needs of their families
 ______ Provide transportation to Sunday school
 ______ Witness to their parents
 ______ Provide lesson course material to be used at home by those who will not attend Sunday school
 ______ Cultivate the friendship of the child and his parents
 ______ Other ways to help

G. For helping people with special needs (handicapped, sick, blind, etc.)
 1. What groups with special needs are found in your community?
 2. What should your Sunday school do for them this year?

H. Plans for helping active church members
 1. What can we do to encourage church members to worship meaningfully and regularly at church services and in their homes?
 2. How can we help members to witness faithfully for Christ?
 3. How can we encourage and help members to minister to the needs of persons around them?
 4. What can we do to help members be good stewards?
 5. How can we stimulate members to grow in Christian knowledge and in Christian skills?

6. In what ways can we lead members to avail themselves of the help offered by other church program organizations?

Phase III—Evaluation

IV. LEADERS' SELF-EVALUATION

A. Call and commitment

1. Am I in the position that I have accepted because I believe God wants me there?
2. Am I seeking, by God's help, first to be, and then to do what this position requires?

B. Effectiveness

1. Am I doing my best?
2. Am I willing to give time to my responsibilities?
3. Am I setting a good example for other workers?
4. Am I well-prepared for my responsibilities?
5. Am I co-operative?
6. Am I willing to follow up absentees?
7. Am I personally acquainted with pupils?
8. Am I willing to visit my pupils?
9. Am I willing to be on the job at least 15 minutes early?
10. Am I willing to notify my superior when absent?
11. Am I winning pupils to Christ?
12. Am I willing to help meet the needs of pupils?
13. Am I able to handle the Bible well?
14. Am I able to relate to people?
15. Am I using sound teaching methods?
16. Am I making my teaching relevant to life?
17. Am I convinced my pupils are learning? Growing?

C. Personal Growth

1. Is my personal devotional life strong?
2. Do I attend worship services of the church regularly?

3. Do I attend workers' and teachers' meetings provided for my growth?
4. Do I read books and other literature helpful to my growth as a worker?

D. Training
1. Do I recognize the need for further training for the task God calls me to?
2. If I acknowledge the need, am I willing to pay the price in time and effort to get more training?

Appendix No. 9

Suggestions for Research Projects

1. Select three outstanding supervisors and analyze the bases of their success.
2. Analyze three conferences with teachers and decide what was good about them, what was bad, and how they could be improved.
3. Make a case study of successful leadership in some local industry, business or public agency. What can you learn from this study that may prove to be helpful in the church school?
4. Examine several issues of church education journals to see if there are evidences of interest in research, evaluation and experimentation.
5. Try to discover to what extent Sunday school pupils study lessons at home.
6. What do pupils like or dislike about the Sunday School?
7. What do pupils like or dislike about their teachers and leaders?
8. What kinds of help do teachers desire most from supervisors?

9. Make a case study of the work of the supervisor in terms of how he spends his time.
10. What are the current problems of supervisors?
11. What are the functions frequently or regularly preferred by supervisors?
12. Study supervisory responsibilities of the department head.
13. Take some of the attitude scales developed in the educational field and use them among church school pupils, such as Mooney Problem Check Lists.
14. Study teaching characteristics of teachers to determine evidences of teaching competence.
15. Discover and define the difficulties that teachers experience in attempting to provide desirable conditions for learning.
16. Make a survey of common instructional practices in any selected grade in attempting to provide best instruction.
17. Develop a set of principles of modern teaching practices and compare Sunday school classroom practices with them. Cover such categories as (1) the teacher, (2) the pupils, and (3) the environment.
18. Make a survey of classroom practices in the use of teaching aids, visuals, etc.
19. Using criteria for good Christian education facilities, evaluate the buildings, facilities, and equipment of a church.
20. What community resources are useful in church school work and how should they be used?
21. Compare assignments procedures among children and youth in the typical church school.
22. Study resistance to leadership training programs in typical churches.
23. Study the usual practices in selecting Sunday school teachers.
24. Describe and evaluate programs of teacher training in selected church schools.
25. Study the most effective and least effective supervisory procedures as reported by Sunday school teachers who have supervisors.

26. Study the effects of leadership training on classroom practice.
27. Make a study of the frequency, causes and possible solutions to discipline problems in the Sunday school.
28. Study the attitudes toward the use of new and audio-visual media in the church and Sunday school.
29. How are the needs of workers on the job determined?
30. How are the needs of teachers on the job determined?
31. How is orientation for new workers provided?
32. How is in-service training for workers provided?
33. What should be stressed in the professional growth of workers?
34. Compare the work of the church done by the workers with ways they were taught or how they were handled by their parents.
35. Study how supervisors and workers view each other in church work.
36. Create a list of acceptable personality characteristics of church workers.
37. Make a study of the felt needs of teachers.
38. Make a study of the personal problems faced by teachers and workers.
39. Make a study of the discipline problems faced by the workers.
40. Record class behavior and study it to note individual differences.
41. Make a study of the common problems of Christian teachers with their possible solutions.
42. Study what and why pupils like their workers and leaders.
43. Compare how supervisors view their work with how teachers view them.
44. Compare the results of pupil growth and development in the schools *with* supervisors with those in schools *without* supervisors.

No. 10

Survey of Adult Programs Through the Church

Clifford V. Anderson
Bethel Theological Seminary

1. List program emphases provided for adults on left hand side of paper
2. Place the agencies or types of activities across the top of the paper.
3. After completing the listing of needs/interests or program emphases and the agencies in the church which touch the lives of adults, evaluate the contribution of the agency in meeting the program emphasis with the following symbols:

   A MAJOR purpose and emphasis
   B Secondary emphasis
   C Some emphasis

4. Study the results:

   What needs are not now being met? Where can these be programmed?
   Any evidence of over emphasis?

(*See chart on following page.*)

	Sunday Morning Services	Sunday Evening Service	Midweek Service	Sunday Church School	Women's Society	Men's Brotherhood	Training Fellowship
Worship	A	B	C				
Bible Study Knowledge	C	B	A	A	C	C	A
Missions and Social Service				C	A	A	C
Social Action and Citizenship				C	A	A	B
Family Education			C	C			B
Friendship and Fellowship	C	C	C	C	A	A	C
Leadership Training			B		C	C	A
Evangelism	A	B		A	B	B	

No. 11

Check List on Worship

Locating Worship Difficulties and Defects

General Worship Outline

Provision for Worship

1. Does each department or grade have at least 15 minutes for worship; either in one period, or at intervals as in the Beginners' and Primary Departments?
2. Is this period kept entirely free from such distractions as announcements, training in singing, and addresses unrelated to the program?

Quality of programs

1. Are the programs of worship carefully prepared in advance?
2. Does your worship program usually have a central thought, with which the Scripture readings, hymns, music, prayers, and other elements in harmony, thus giving unity to the whole?
3. Are the hymns expressive of Christian sentiment, and of such character as to stimulate dignified worship?
4. Is each program carried on in a spirit of sincerity and reverence, free from whispering, talking, disorder, and inattention on the part of pupils and teachers?
5. Are the programs of worship such as to exalt better ideals of living and acts of service?
6. Are needless comments, announcements, interrup-

tions, and distractions which would interfere with the spirit of worship avoided during the period?

7. Is the arrangement of the room conducive to an atmosphere of worship?

Gradation of Materials

1. Are ideas and feelings so expressed that they may be clearly understood and appreciated by the department in which they are used? Are the interests, needs, and experiences of the pupils considered in the selection of themes and materials of worship?

Leadership

1. Does the Leader make the personal preparation necessary to enter with purpose, sympathy, understanding, and poise into the service of worship?
2. Do those who lead in music and singing express the spirit of reverent devotion in keeping with the theme?
3. Do those who lead in prayer express ideas and feelings natural to the members of the group

Pupil Participation

1. Is there general participation by the members of each group in the various parts of the program?
2. Do the members take part in their worship programs with evident enjoyment?
3. In departments of intermediate age and over, do pupils have a definite share in planning and conducting the programs?

Training

1. Is provision made for training in the singing of hymns, sharing in Scripture responses etc., apart from the periods of worship?

2. Is provision made for giving the pupils an understanding of hymns, responses, art masterpieces, and other materials in worship?
3. Is provision made for the training of individuals and groups in the leadership of worship?
4. Is the church worship interpreted for the members of the schools so they may take part therein with understanding and appreciation?
5. Is provision made for encouraging and aiding pupils to form their own private devotions?

No. 11 (Continued)

Check List of Worship Defects

I. Centering in Leadership

1. Leaders are frequently untrained in the art of conducting worship
2. Make inadequate preparation for each service
3. Fail themselves to enter into the worship experience
4. Possess only a superficial understanding of theory and technique of worship
5. Become mechanical and familiar with worship materials
6. Lack necessary leadership skill, poise, and self-control
7. Frequently intrude their personalities and mannerisms into the experience to its detriment

8. Are technically trained in music but do not understand the relationship of music to worship
9. Are given training in leading worship at the expense of the worship experience itself
10. Follow too rigidly a set plan, failing to utilize unexpected opportunities and spontaneous responses.

II. Centering in the Worshiping group

1. Worshipers are frequently untrained in the nature, purpose, and value of worship
2. Fail to make the effort to master materials and forms of worship
3. Are frequently unaware of the responsibility they bear in making worship effective
4. Fail to cooperate with their fellows by promptness, quietness, and control of conduct
5. Are encouraged frequently to sit passively while others worship for them.

III. Centering in Materials

1. The materials are often of inferior grade
2. Provide little or no expression of the worshiper's thought and feeling
3. Are frequently of an ungraded character
4. Are not arranged in a psychological or climactic manner
5. Represent a meager range of materials
6. Represent too frequent use of the same materials
7. Contain too much new and unfamiliar content
8. Frequently become and end rather than a means to an end
9. Are not unified or correlated about a theme

10. Do not include seasonal emphases
11. Are lacking in value and richness because of failure of interpretation
12. Include extraneous matters having no place in a worship experience.

IV. Centering in Ritual and Form

1. Ritualistic forms and materials are often used as ends rather than as means of worship
2. Are used either too exclusively or too infrequently
3. Are used with groups wholly untrained or unprepared for such use
4. Are used in incongruous settings
5. Are frequently insufficiently varied in character to provide full range of worship experiences
6. Are used with groups, mature and immature, who have not been led to understand their meanings.

V. Centering in Time Element

1. The time is sometimes too long or too brief to lead to a satisfactory worship experience;
2. For the worship experience is not appropriately placed with respect to other elements in the total program or to the time of the day;
3. For training in worship is inadequate.

VI. Centering in Control-Management

1. Worship services and experiences are seriously disrupted by late arrival of worshipers
2. Are interfered with by teachers and other leaders moving about and engaging in other activities during worship

3. Are ineffective because habitual inattention, unresponsiveness, and misbehavior on the part of participants are permitted.
4. Are interrupted by attention to ventilation, bringing in charts at critical moments
5. Are lessened in value because choir and orchestra members and other leaders are so seated as to detract from worship
6. Are ineffective because leaders fail by their lack of poise and self-control to suggest quiet and reverence.

VII. Centering in Physical Conditions

1. The physical conditions under which worship is conducted are not suitable or appropriate for worship
2. Are lacking in appropriate stimuli for effective worship
3. Lead to noise and confusion because worshipping room is not sufficiently segregated from other groups
4. Often include equipment that is noisy and ill-adapted for worship
5. Represent unpedagogical features with respect to light, ventilation, space and seats
6. Are lacking in aesthetic values conducive to rich worship experiences

VIII. Centering in the Total Program

1. The total worship program for any age group frequently is unrelated to the total worship program of the church

2. Represents overlapping and duplication in the various unrelated services provided by different organizations and leaders
3. Is not harmoniously and intelligently adjusted to the major preaching worship service of the church.
4. Frequently includes for elementary ages Junior Church services totally unrelated to departmental programs of worship
5. Often fails to include opportunity for training in worship
6. Fails to emphasize proportionately formal and informal worship experiences
7. Fails to make integration with other elements, such as, instruction, service, etc., for a given age group.

Cooperative Study of Worship Problems

1. What are the relative values of the formal worship services and the informal spontaneous worship experiences for the various age groups?

2. In view of the trend toward larger classes and the unified program, should departmental worship services be dropped in favor of class worship experiences?

3. Is the formal worship service for the Primary and Junior groups sufficiently important to justify the building of a children's chapel?

4. When, if ever, and under what conditions, should pupils of the elementary departments worship with adults in the church or church school?

5. Should worship services be provided for the inter-

mediate, Senior, Young People, and Adult groups in the church-school hour, or should these groups be expected to worship under the "church" hour? Under the leadership of the minister?

6. What should be the nature and objectives of the Sunday evening young people's devotional service as it relates to the total worship program for these young people?

7. To what extent is the "Graded Church" idea to be accepted. How will it affect the total worship program for each age group?

8. What are the evidences that the enrichment of graded worship, such as, increased ritual, more beautiful surroundings, more skillful leadership, is making worship more vital and meaningful to the lives of the worshippers? How may the outcomes of worship be measured?

Comment:

Certain fundamental principles and policies are involved in these questions which will need to be formulated and adopted before the solution of many detailed problems can be formulated. They will need to be settled largely in the light of local conditions and leadership.

No. 12

Survey Schedule of Social and Recreational Activities

I. General Provision:

1. Is the church as a whole informed regarding the importance of social and recreational activity as an element in the program of religious education? Has definite effort been put forth to provide the officers and constituency with such knowledge?
2. Has the church formulated a definite attitude toward and developed a policy concerning such activities as a whole?
3. Has the church assumed definite responsibility for this phase of the program by appointing a committee assigning the responsibility to the committee on education, appointing officers, or providing equipment and finance for social and recreational activities?
4. Has a definite program been outlined covering these phases of the church life?
5. Have the social and recreational facilities, programs, and activities of the community been studied to determine their extent, quality, and acceptability, to prevent undue competition and overlapping and to supplement them at such points as may be necessary?

II. General and specific objectives:

1. Has a general objective been formulated by a repre-

sentative authoritative body in the church to guide in the development and promotion of a program?

2. Has effort been made to bring all concerned into an understanding of and acceptance of this objective? Does it serve to guide all workers in their detailed activities?
3. Have specific objectives been formulated to indicate the detailed nature and scope of the program proposed? Are these objectives understood and used by all leaders?
4. Are all the objectives restudied periodically, especially in the light of experience?
5. Are these objectives used also as a means of measuring results?

III. Scope of the Program:

1. Is the general scope of the program determined by the needs and interests of the groups to be served and by the degree to which these are met by other agencies in the community?
2. Are the various types of social and recreational activity chosen with respect to the full range of possible emphases and the knowledge of the particular needs of the groups ministered to?
3. Is full opportunity provided for the different age groups to participate in the various heedful types of social and recreational activity? Are any groups neglected? Do any groups fail to find opportunity for expression along lines needed or desired?
4. Is there definite recognition of the significance of the spirit of fellowship in all the relationships of the various groups in the entire program of the church and church-school life? Is effort made to intensify and enrich this fellowship at every opportunity?

IV. Quality of Activities:

1. Are the social and recreational activities planned with a view to development of character or the moral and spiritual outcomes?
2. Do leaders appreciate the values to be sought through the various types of activities introduced into the program?
3. Are social occasions maintained on a high level? Are pupils permitted to engage in "rough house" conduct, play questionable games, or express un-Christian attitudes?
4. In all athletic events and activities is a proper emphasis placed upon fair play, clean sportsmanship, rather than upon winning? Are undue rivalry and competition eliminated?
5. Are the social programs and associations free from clanishness, snobbishness, and unwholesome class or race distinction?
6. Are all the activities closely related to the total program of instruction, worship, service, etc., offered to the respective groups?
7. Are pupils prevented from engaging in certain recreational activities that endanger health or from carrying certain activities to excess?

V. Pupil Participation and leadership

1. Are all pupils encouraged and given opportunity to participate in a full range of activities?
2. Do the pupils actually engage in activities, games, social hobbies rather than have others perform for them?
3. Do pupils help select, plan, and carry forward various types of social and recreational activity?

4. Are pupils encouraged in the development and pursuit of special interests, hobbies, skills?
5. Are pupils given adequate opportunity to develop leadership abilities through the direction and leadership of their own activities?
6. Are pupils led to see and attain a balanced all-around development?
7. Are pupils stimulated and aided to enrich their limited conceptions and practices in social and recreational life?

VI. Leadership and Supervision

1. Is definite adult supervision provided for all activities? Is too much or too little supervision exercised?
2. Does the leader guide the pupils into worthwhile and profitable activities?
3. Is the leader skillful in making the most of social fellowship values of all contacts, relationships, and activities?
4. Is adequate leadership provided for the various types of social and recreational activity?
5. Does the adult leader seek to develop the pupils in qualities of self-control, initiative, resourcefulness, and leadership?
6. Do special leaders in these activities understand the total program of religious education and seek to relate their work to that of other leaders of the same pupils?

VII. Physical Equipment

1. Has the church made suitable physical provision for the various activities included in the program?
2. Are there adequate social rooms in the church available to the various groups needing them? Is their

use supervised? Are they neat, clean, and well cared for?

3. Is there some place provided in the church or nearby in the community for the rougher games? Is it free from furniture and other equipment unsuited for such activity?
4. If there is a gymnasium in the church, is it well equipped? Is its use supervised? Are similar facilities in the community used?
5. Are outdoor facilities for games, hikes, picnics, etc. available and used?

No. 13

Observation Outline for Service Training and Activity

I. A Definite Program of Service Training and Activity:

1. Have the church and school a definite consciousness of the nature and importance of service service training and activity in the total curriculum of religious education?
2. Does the program of religious education include a well-developed plan by means of which the pupils may share in worth-while service enterprises and receive adequate training in service?

3. Does such a plan provide for all age groups? Does it give to each individual and and group a sense of sharing in a representative and worth-while service program?
4. Does the program include a comprehensive outline of activities and emphases? Are the varied interests of particular groups, the church as a whole, and life outside the church and community adequately represented?
5. Does the program include long-time continuous activities that train in habits of faithfulness and dependability? Does it also include suitable projects of limited duration and scope to cultivate interest and develop specific attitudes and skills?
6. Is the program of service training and activity graded to meet the needs, interests, limitations, and resources of the various age groups in the church school?
7. Are the training and service activities effectively correlated with the other elements in the total curriculum? Do the activities grow out of the contribution to class discussion and study? Are service projects and problems frequently made the theme of worship or otherwise related to the worship experience?
8. Is the service plan properly related to the service program of the church so that the pupils become increasingly interested in and capable of taking part in the major enterprises of the church?

II. Quality of Service Activity:
1. Are service activities selected according to high standards, worthy purposes, and urgent needs?
2. Are real worth-while challenging activities always

selected instead of those that "just give the pupils something to do"?

3. Are the service activities of such character as to relate the pupils to the large and more permanent service program of the local church?
4. Are service enterprises and projects selected which have the largest possibilities of yielding information, developing desirable attitudes, arousing Christian motives, awakening wholesome appreciations, and cultivating useful habits and skills in service?
5. Is there a proper balance between those service activities which relate to the local field and those that have to do with lands and peoples throughout the world?

III. Pupil Participation:

1. Are the pupils made intelligent through investigation, stories, discussion, regarding the reasons for service activities, or are they just told what to do?
2. Do pupils have a full share in choosing the type of service enterprise or the ends toward which they shall work, and in determining the manner in which it shall be carried forward?
3. Is every opportunity for pupil determination, leadership, and participation utilized?
4. Is care exercised to make sure that all pupils participate in some manner, that leadership is distributed and that pupils receive training in proportion to their needs and capacities?
5. Do pupils take part in service activities enthusiastically, with evident enjoyment? Are their associations in service characterized by a splendid spirit of fellowship?

IV. Giving:

1. Is giving in the various classes and departments related to the plan of stewardship and to the total giving program of the church? Are pupils led to feel that they are sharing vitally in the financial program of the church as a whole?
2. Does the plan of giving lead to the development in the pupil of the habit of regular systematic giving? Is a pledge or subscription card and envelope, or an adequate substitute, used to develop this habit and disposition?
3. Is care exercised to make sure that every pupil in the school is effectively related to the program of benevolence, including local church and world-wide activities?
4. Is giving associated with worship experiences rather than made a matter purely of business and secretarial concern?
5. Is the major emphasis placed upon the spirit in which giving is engaged in, rather than upon the amount of the gift?

V. Adult Supervision:

1. Are the various service projects properly supervised? Is such supervision exercised without dominating the activities?
2. Does the teacher or leader definitely guide pupils into profitable activities, into economical and effective ways of carrying them forward? Is he effective in leading pupils to see the values inherent in the various procedures? Is he able to lead them to profit by mistakes, to encourage them to carry projects through to completion?

3. Does the leader aid in distributing responsibility evenly among members of the group?
4. Does the leader hold the pupils to the matter in hand, preventing them undertaking too much, losing interest, discontinuing projects before they are completed?
5. Is the leader capable of estimating the results, does he know when the activities and training are effective?
6. Does the leader bring the pupils into contact with information, resource material, groups, situations, relationships from which they can receive guidance in solving problems and executing projects?

VI. Training Outcomes:

1. Is a positive outgoing good will toward others developed on the part of each pupil? Is that good will expressed in interests, attitudes, appreciations, sympathies, and understanding concerning those who have been the object of study and expression?
2. Have pupils developed a general and world point of view? Have they become committed definitely to the ideal of world friendship? To what extent have they shown appreciation of the ideal of world brotherhood and international good will?
3. Have they acquired an understanding of the possible contributions of other peoples and races? In what ways do they show an appreciation of these contributions?
4. To what extent have strong abiding motives for service been developed in each pupil? What evidence is there that these motives will carry beyond the immediate service activity which called them into being?

5. To what extent have the pupils developed ability to carry forward projects of their own, to assume responsibility for leadership, to take their share of work and discharge it effectively?
6. To what extent are the pupils being led at appropriate years to consider enlistment and preparation for full-time vocational service in the church and Kingdom program?
7. To what extent are the pupils being led at appropriate years to volunteer and prepare for lay service in the church and community? To what extent has the challenge to such service been presented to them? To what extent are opportunities for preparation for such service being offered to them?
8. Are the pupils increasingly identifying themselves with the program and activities of the local church, the denomination, and the Kingdom?

No. 14

Lesson Plan for First Year Junior (Length of Session, One Hour)

The Kingdom of Love—Matt. 5, 6, 7

Aim:

To help the pupils to discover the heart of Jesus' message in the Kingdom of love and to lead them to consecration to the ideals of the Kingdom.

Materials:

Construction paper; pictures for illustrating hymn; notebooks; scissors; paste; pencils; "The Children's Bible" (Each pupil has his own.)

Procedure:

Pre-session

Finish booklets illustrating the hymn, "We Would See Jesus," "Lo, His Star is Shining." Preparation of notebooks for section of the New Testament

1. Conversation; stories; supervised study; pictures; dramatization.

   What is the Kingdom?

   a. Ruled by a King
   b. Made up of people who are loyal to the King.
   c. Governed by laws, policies, or rules (why are there rules for a game? laws of a country?) The Kingdom of Love (Jesus' purpose was to help God to establish this Kingdom, not just in one country, but throughout the world)

2. Rules of the Kingdom of Love (to be developed in class discussion)

   a. Love God
      (Supervised study: "The Children's Bible" Page 312. "The Two Great Commandments" Matt. 22:35–40 in the Bible.)
   b. Love your neighbor as yourself
      (Same as above to be studied)
   c. Have your treasure in heaven, not on earth.
      (Tell the story "How to use Money" from "The Children's Bible," Pages 313, 314)

d. Help those in need.
   (Tell the story of Grenfell)
e. Love your enemies.
   (Study the parable of the Good Samaritan and, if time permits, tell the story of Stephen, possibly dramatize the story of the Good Samaritan.)
f. Be modest, not proud
   (Study from "The Children's Bible", Pages 327, 328 "Jesus Tells How One May Become Great". Tell the story "King Robert of Sicily" in "Tales of a Wayside Inn" by Longfellow)

3. Does this Kingdom make a difference in life?

   a. In Jesus' Day
      "Except ye . . . become as little children" See Mark 10:13–16. Jesus makes Zacchaeus his friend. (Tell the story in "The Children's Bible" Page 328)
   b. In our day
      What kind of world would this be if everyone should live by the rules of the Kingdom? Who are some people who have lived by these rules?

No. 14 (Continued)

My Teaching Plan

Lesson Topic: ______________________________

General Theme and Purpose of the Quarter: __________

____

My Teaching Aim for this Lesson:
Materials I need for teaching (Bibles, pupil's quarterly, maps, etc)

How I plan to begin the lesson (Note: appeal to the intellectual interests of the pupils)

Main points which I shall emphasize:

1.

2.

3.

4.

(Note: Show truth which satisfies needs—urge acceptance and show the way of truth)

How I plan to encourage class participation:

How I plan to close the teaching session:
(Note: here appeal to the will; decision; action)

Carry-over
Assignments

This is a suggested form for teachers' use in planning their teaching sessions. For best use follow this written lesson plan.

No. 15

Teacher Self-Rating Chart

1. Worship:
   a. Do you attend at least one worship and preaching service a Sunday unless hindered by some real reason? .... 5 ____
   b. Do you make the worship service of your department one of real worship for yourself, and so conduct yourself that you will be willing to have the pupils follow your example? .... 5 ____
   c. Do you practice personal fellowship with God, with at least some moments of each day dedicated especially to this purpose? .... 5 ____

2. Lesson Preparation:
   a. Do you devote a minimum of at least one hour a week to lesson preparation, getting thorough understanding of the content for yourself and for your individual pupils? .... 12 ____
   b. Do you make a written teaching plan to use in the presentation of your lesson? 8 ____

3. Cooperation:
   a. Do you relate your work to the whole church program, and are you interested in other church activities of your pupils? .... 5 ____

b. Are you open-minded in giving and receiving suggestions in conferences with your officers? .... 5 ____

4. Personal Relationship to Pupils:

a. Do you keep personal information about your pupils, such as addresses, phone numbers, birthdays, etc., and such other information about their work as will give at all times an accurate picture of each individual? .... 5 ____

b. Are you a real friend to your pupils greeting them on the street, playing with them when the opportunity offers, visiting them when sick, and taking an interest in their affairs? .... 5 ____

c. Do you visit the homes of your pupils at least once a year, and is each absence checked by yourself or some responsible person? .... 5 ____

5. Faithful Attendance:

a. Do you regularly attend the monthly workers' meetings and all departmental meetings? .... 10 ____

b. Are you always present 15 minutes early in order to meet the first comers to your class? .... 10 ____

c. Do you always give ample notice of necessary absence? .... 10 ____

6. Growth in Efficiency:

a. Do you read regularly at least one good magazine on your work? .... 2 ____

b. Do you make use of available library facilities, reading at least one good book a year on your work? . . . . 2 ____
c. Do you complete one or more courses in a leadership training class each year? . 6 ____
Total Possible Score . . . . 100 ____

It is suggested that visiting the corresponding grade in public schools is very helpful for growth in efficiency. Better still, visit some other Sunday School Class

No. 15 (Continued)

A Check-Chart for Teachers

Preparation

1. Do I plan my work far enough ahead?
2. Do I spend enough time upon each lesson?
3. Do I set a goal for each quarter (some definite objective I want to reach?)
4. Do I make suggestions to my class for outside reading and preparation, so that each lesson is not approached "cold?"
5. Can I state, in a simple sentence, what I am setting out to do in each lesson?
6. Does every member of the class have adequate preparation materials and helps?

Teaching Methods

1. Do I strive for variety:
   a. By alternating between the discussion and lecture methods? Others?
   b. By using charts, maps, posters, blackboards?
   c. By arranging for dramatization of some of the lessons?
2. Do I open the class period with prayer?
3. Are my opening statements challenging, interesting, clear and heard by all?
4. Do I stick to the lesson? Do I apply it to life?
5. Do I summarize in an endeavor to tie together all loose ends, so as to make one definite, lasting impression?
6. Do I link my thoughts and lessons together, so as to make a complete picture?
7. Do I do all the talking?
8. Do I argue?
9. Do I listen to the opinions of others?
10. Am I attempting to do the teaching rather than presenting the teachings of Jesus Christ and the Bible?

The Class

1. Is my class made up as nearly as possible of people of the same age and interests?
2. Is my classroom attractive and comfortable?
3. Is my class too large? Too small?

The Teacher

1. Do I start and close the period on time?
2. Do I use all the time to advantage, or do I waste time?

3. Am I friendly?
4. Do I make my class feel at home?
5. Do I get my students acquainted with each other?
6. Am I personally concerned for the spiritual welfare of every pupil:
   a. Do I pray for them?
   b. Do I encourage them to come to church?
   c. Do I try to help them outside of the class period?
   d. Do I keep check on their spiritual welfare?

No. 15 (Continued)

An Efficiency Test for Teachers

If you as a Sunday school teacher can answer yes on 18 or more of these 25 points, you are a "jewel of a teacher." But, if not, do not be discouraged—try harder!

1. Are you faithful in attendance, rain or shine?
2. Do you arrive 15 minutes before school opens to talk to your pupils?
3. Do you sit with your class during opening worship, gladly taking part?
4. Do you mark records promptly, getting them to the secretary without class interruption?
5. Do you have a clear, over-all view of the entire quarter's lessons?
6. Can you put into one brief sentence your teaching aim for each Sunday?
7. Do your pupils understand that the lesson is from the Bible, not from a red or green quarterly?

8. Do you use a vocabulary your pupils can understand?
9. Do you ask questions and encourage your pupils to do some of the talking?
10. Have you already started preparing the next week's lesson by Tuesday of each week?
11. If something funny happens in class, do you join in the laughter and use the incident to get back to the lesson?
12. Can you put a talkative pupil in his place without his resenting it?
13. Do you send out birthday cards, Christmas cards, get-well cards to your pupils?
14. Do you know the hobbies and heartaches of your pupils?
15. Do you call in the homes of your pupils once a year, and do you call immediately on a pupil who has been absent for two successive Sundays?
16. Do you pray daily for your class and departments?
17. Before teaching, do you refer to a Bible map so that you know the geographical details concerning each lesson?
18. Do you attend departmental parties and the Sunday school picnic with enthusiasm?
19. Are you faithful in attendance at church services and midweek activities?
20. Do you occasionally read magazines and books on Christian education?
21. Do you vary your teaching methods so that your pupils are not just sure what you might do next?
22. Is your Christian life clean and exemplary in that you are not doing things you would be ashamed for your pupils to know about?
23. Do you evaluate your work and analyze pupil reaction each week, noting mistakes and successful results?

24. Are you seeking to lead your pupils to Christ as Savior, Friend and Lord?
25. When you get discouraged and are ready to give up the class, do you go to the Lord for His encouragement and strength?

—From *Christian Life* magazine, February, 1953

No. 16
Observation of Questioning

1. Does the teacher give evidence of having carefully formulated certain key questions in advance of the session?
2. Is the teacher skillful in wording questions clearly and concisely? Are wordy, ambiguous questions avoided as well as short, fragmentary questions?
3. Is he capable of knowing when his language or sentence structure is confusing to the class? Can he reword questions quickly?
4. Does the teacher permit interruptions in the form of pupil questions? Does he stimulate independent questioning by the pupils?
5. Does he use thought and drill questions in right proportion? Are they concerned with proper materials? Does he vary the pace?
6. Does he give opportunity for pupils to think through to an answer before repetition or reassignment of question?

7. Does he distribute the questions fairly among the members of the group? In terms of individual differences?
9. Does the teacher avoid answering the questions himself? Avoid repeating them except in legitimate cases? Insist upon clear, intelligent answers? Avoid repeating the pupils' answers?
10. Does the teacher attempt either at once or later to clear up misunderstanding or strengthen imperfect grasp of material?
11. Does the sequence of questions indicate a definite teaching plan? Are the questions logically arranged? Is there movement toward a conclusion or climax?

No. 17

Observation of Directed Discussion and Problem-Solving

I. General

1. Is this the best method to employ with this particular lesson, problem or situation?
2. Is the issue or problem of sufficient importance to justify the time and effort of the class session? Is there a reasonable chance of worth-while outcome being realized?
3. Does the teacher maintain in the class a spirit of fellowship? Is there a give take, a willingness to be corrected, or to have statements challenged?

II. Preparation

1. Is the teacher skillful in "setting the stage"? By creating an interest in the problem? By referring to some familiar experience or incident connected with the problem or topic?
2. Do the pupils share in suggesting and choosing the problems to be solved or topics to be discussed?
3. Does the teacher arouse the proper mental attitude? Are the pupils alert and attentive, or passive and unresponsive?

III. Analysis

1. Does the teacher show skill in directing the analysis of the problem or topic, in suggesting possible leads, in getting the problem in its entirety before the group?
2. Is he ready in suggesting sources of information and skillful in stimulating pupils to find others?
3. Does he hold the class to the discussion of the main issue and prevent profitless dispute?
4. Are pupils led to evaluate statements made to discriminate between conflicting arguments, to suspend judgment?
5. Does the teacher encourage the pupils to insist upon reasonable verification of statements made?
6. Is he skillful in using summaries, outlines, to organize the facts presented?

IV. Search for Solution

1. Is he capable in stimulating the class to suggest principles of solution, to criticize and evaluate them?
2. Does the teacher refrain from drawing inferences from the data and discussion? Is he patient in encouraging the pupils to improve their first crude inferences?

3. Is he alert to note those principles of solution which are correct, founded on the facts and data gathered?
4. Does he aid the pupils in making concrete tests of the suitability of the principle to the problem under discussion?
5. Does he aid the pupils in formulating a concise statement of the principle of solution?

V. Application
1. Does the teacher lead the pupils to face the feasibility of their solution? Will it work?
2. Does he stimulate the pupils to make varied suggestions as to ways of applying the solution, trying it out?
3. Is the teacher alert to sense the adequacy of their suggestions, to estimate the extent to which they understand outcomes of discussion?
4. If the discussion is not finished within the period, is there definite provision for re-opening the discussion or for outside work?

No. 18

Observation of Story-Telling

I. Selection
1. Does the teacher have a clean-cut aim or purpose in using a story? Is the story the most effective teaching procedure by which to realize the objective?
2. Is the particular story used adapted to the aim?
3. Has the teacher made a good selection from the

standpoint of the value of the story? Is it wholesome, worthy story? Does it deal with positive moral and spiritual values?

4. If the teacher has created his story, is it well-constructed? Has he observed the principles of story construction? Used good incidents, employed choice language?
5. Is the story adapted to the teaching period? Too long? Too short?
6. Does the story possess life interest for the pupils? Lie within their appreciation? Does it avoid artificial scenes, action and personalities?

II. Preparation

1. Does the teacher lead up properly to the use of the story? Does he "set the stage" for it by relating it to the class discussion, problem, or interests of the pupils?
2. Does the teacher have command of himself? And the situation before beginning the story?
3. Does the teacher give evidence of having mastered the story? Has he made thorough preparation himself?
4. Does the teacher secure the attention and interest of all before starting the story?
5. Does he anticipate interruptions by questions or misunderstandings by explaining in advance any difficult names of unfamiliar customs or places?

III. Technique of Telling

1. Does the teacher assume a comfortable, natural pose? Does he avoid any physical strain, excessive movement or restlessness?
2. Does he use a well-modulated, pleasing distinct tone

of voice? Does he make sure that all the pupils hear distinctly?

3. Is his personal appearance free from novel and unusual features that distract or annoy?
4. Are his gestures spontaneous, natural, and effective? Does he avoid forced, mechanical, too numerous motions of arms and body?
5. Does he enter heartily and effectively into the telling of the story, capitalizing the dramatic elements? Does he imitate, impersonate, and mimic well? Does he avoid extremes in these expressions?
6. Does he use only choice language, avoid hackneyed and overworked phrases? Is he careful not to use slang?
7. Does the teacher permit the story to "teach its own lesson"? Does he refrain from "tacking on a moral"?
8. Does he encourage the pupils to discuss freely the incidents and personalities of the story, expressing their own reactions to it? Is he alert to correct wrong impressions or make clear misunderstandings?
9. Does he have in mind criteria by which to judge the effectiveness of the story?
10. Is there any attempt to use in real life the feelings aroused? Any outlet for expression of sentiments developed?

No. 19

Observing Drill-Memorization Procedures

I. Purpose and Value

1. Does the teacher have a clear-cut objective in mind in planning the drill or memorization period?
2. Has he considered the relative effectiveness of this method as compared with other methods that might be employed?
3. Has he made careful selection of materials? Do they have value in relation to other learning activities and to life situations?

II. Preparation

1. Has the teacher led the pupils to an understanding of the nature and purpose of the exercise?
2. Has he developed in them a real desire to master the process or the material? Has he properly motivated their approach to the task?
3. Does he have the material properly arranged? Is he ready for work? Does he conserve time?
4. Has he carefully estimated the time and periods that will be required?

III. Skill in Directing

1. Does the teacher manifest a mastery of the principles of drill and memorization?
2. Is he alert to note ineffective efforts and misapplied energy?
3. Is he able to sustain interest, arouse zeal, and motivate the activity of pupils?

4. Does he avoid waste of time on his own part? On the part of pupils?
5. Does he use good judgment in the length of time devoted to this purpose? Has he planned carefully for follow-up periods of drill or memorization?
6. Has he led the pupils to an intelligent appreciation of the nature and content of the material being memorized or the value of the skills to be acquired?
7. Is the teacher skillful in relating the memory activity to other phrases of the program? Is the memorization thought of as an end in itself or as a means to an end?
8. Does the teacher aid the pupils in applying the results of the period? Does he aid them to make use of the materials memorized and skills acquired?

No. 20

Outline for Observing Dramatization

I. Selecting and Building Dramas

1. Is the dramatization project closely associated with other elements of the program? Does it grow out of or lead into other activities?
2. What objectives does the teacher have in view in using this method? Has he considered the preferability of some other means of achieving the objective?

3. If a prepared drama is to be used has the teacher carefully studied its suitability for his purpose and group?
4. If the pupils are to create their own drama does the teacher give careful guidance to the choice of theme and content?
5. Does the teacher manifest knowledge of the principles by which dramatic activity should be developed?

II. Directing the Production
1. Does the teacher give evidence of having a plan of procedure?
2. Does he encourage initiative, originality, and spontaneity on the part of the pupils?
3. Is he quick to appreciate valuable suggestions on the part of the pupils? Is he skillful in leading them to more finished and seasoned suggestions?
4. Does he lead the pupils in a thoughtful analysis of the plot, in wise choice of characters, in suitable divisions of the plan to acts and scenes?
5. Does the teacher show skill in balancing the emphasis between training in appreciation, development of skills, and mastery of content?
6. Is he appreciative of the time element, both as to the total time required to carry the project through and as to the amount of time each period that should be devoted to it?
7. Is a spirit of play and cooperation maintained throughout the project?
8. Does the teacher distinguish between dramas for educational and developmental purposes and those for exhibition purposes? Does he guard against the latter objective defeating the former?

III. Securing Results
1. Is he able to carry the drama through to a successful conclusion?
2. Has the teacher any means of testing the results of the project?
3. Is there evidence of enriched attitudes, strengthened habits, finer appreciations, vitalized knowledge, and broader sympathies growing out of the dramatic activity?
4. Is the teacher skillful in relating the outcome of dramatic activity to the total educational program and experience of the pupils?
5. Is he careful to prevent overenthusiasm for villainous characters?
6. If the drama is produced as a contribution to other groups, does he strive for a finished piece of work?

No. 21

Observation Schedule for Supervised Study and Activities

I. Supervised Study
1. Is the physical setting appropriate for supervised study? Is it free from noise and interruption? Does the teacher show skillful management of the conditions of the room?
2. Are suitable materials and equipment available to the

pupils? Are they encouraged and directed in their use of the same?

3. Does the teacher keep the pupils at work? Is he able to develop and maintain interest? Does he lead them to an aggressive attack upon the work?
4. Does he give guidance and assistance without dominating the pupils' work or without becoming indispensable to progress on the part of the pupils?
5. Is the teacher quick to discover those pupils who need assistance? Does he distribute his time equitably on the basis of real needs?
6. Does he show skill in determining when the pupils need periods of supervised study? Does he properly relate these periods to the balance of the program?

II. Directing Activities

1. Is the teacher capable of distinguishing between free but worth-while activity and "puttering around" on the part of the pupils?
2. Can the teacher keep individuals and groups at work quietly? Is he skillful in directing their activities and leading them to real achievement?
3. Does he develop in the pupils the ability to outline units of activity, formulate plans and carry them through and acquire skill in evaluating results?
4. Does he aid pupils in overcoming difficulties, in persisting with activities that are exacting and problematic?
5. Is he quick to discover natural leaders, skillful in giving opportunity for expressing leadership abilities? Does he avoid neglecting those who show little ability but need development?

No. 22

Observation Outline for Lesson Assignment

1. Does the teacher show clear understanding of the characteristics of good lesson assigning?
2. Does he plan the lesson assignment in advance?
3. Is he capable of revising his plan in the light of progress of the class during the session?
4. Does he give specific instructions? Does he meet patiently and intelligently questions arising from the students?
5. Does the teacher use any check to discover if the pupils understand the assignment?
6. Does he suggest aids and sources of help in doing the work?
7. Does he check carefully upon the results? Does he fail to call for the results of the work done by the students?
8. Is he careful to strengthen the pupils' habits and abilities in outside study?

No. 23

Check List on Class Management

I. The Management of Physical Conditions:
   1. Is the physical setting such as makes possible the type of class session intended?

2. Is there a sufficient number of seats? Are they adapted to the size of pupils?
3. Are seats arranged so that the light does not strike the pupils in the eyes? Can all the pupils see the teacher and blackboards, bulletin boards, maps, and other equipment?
4. Is the room orderly and neat? Is it suggestive of serious study? Is it clean?
5. Is the proper temperature maintained? Is there a thermometer in the room? Is it observed by the teacher?
6. Is there an adequate supply of fresh air? Is definite responsibility for ventilation assigned to someone?
7. In case folding doors, screens, curtains, or other devices are used to isolate the class, are these devices in condition to be used effectively? Are they used regularly?
8. In case the class meets in a room with other classes, are the pupils seated so they can all hear the teacher and each other? Do they face toward or away from distractions?

II. Handling Materials and Supplies:

1. Are the materials kept in a closet or cabinet? Are they kept on the piano, on a chair, or on the floor?
2. Is material equipment such as blackboards, maps, reference books in usable form, conveniently located and available to teacher and pupils alike? are blackboards firmly supported? Are eraser and chalk provided?
3. Is material passed out and collected in an orderly manner?
4. Is the teacher skillful in stimulating the pupils to take

good care of their material? Do pupils aid in keeping the room neat and clean?

5. Is time conserved in handling supplies, passing from one type of activity to another?

III. Economy of Time and Effort:

1. Does the teacher begin the class work on time? Does he move according to schedule? Does he close on time?
2. Are routine records cared for without loss of time?
3. Does the teacher plan carefully the various items of management such as getting the pupils into working position, distributing supplies, getting the working material arranged?
4. Does the teacher give evidence of having endeavored to reduce all detailed matters to routine procedure?

No. 24

Observation of Pupil Activity

1. Do pupils readily suggest problems and experiences for class discussions? Are they alert to discuss problems suggested by the leader or other members of the group?
2. Do they actively engage in analyzing problems, in discovering the issues involved in given situations and experiences?
3. Are they ready to make suggestions as to solutions,

sources of information, methods of dealing with the situations?

4. Do they respond by reporting personal experiences, by volunteering information, calling to mind stories, other people's experiences, etc., that bear upon the problem?
5. Do they profit by previous experiences of problem-solving?
6. Are they quick to discern and accept clear evidence or valuable information? Do they refrain from sulking when their ideas are rejected?
7. Do they refrain from too ready acceptance or rejection of statements, proposals, suggestions?
8. Are they willing and able to change and reconstruct their ideas and principles of solution as they work through a given problem?
9. Do they recognize an acceptable solution when it is stated?
10. Are they quick to see how the solution can be applied? Do they make suggestions as to its meaning for life?
11. Do they show any disposition to test their solution before finally accepting it?

No. 25

Supervising Schedule on Teaching Method

This schedule is intended to call attention to items in method that supervisor and teacher may desire to confer together on. The supervisor or teacher may keep references on as many points as desired for later conferences or for special study, but some specific items should be agreed upon for supervisor's visitation. This form will be checked after the less—not in the classroom, but from notes made in the classroom.

General Approach:

1. Was there a definite aim by the teacher for the class period? What was it?
2. Was the aim well chosen? Was it Christ-centered? Was it related to previous experiences of the group or to those planned for a later time? Did it meet real needs of those present?
3. What was the general plan of the lesson hour?
4. Did the lesson material further the objective?
5. Was provision made for pupil sharing in determination of goals and plans of procedure?

Equipment:

6. Did pupils have texts or sufficient guide sheets or regular material for their participation?
7. Were teacher and pupils handicapped by lack of readily accessible material? Were Bibles available? Was denominational or missionary material used?
8. Was there provision for visual education by blackboard, maps, charts, studies, pictures, or other materials? Were they utilized to advantage?
9. Were materials used by class conserved for future use or for use by other groups?
10. Was there any attempt to enrich the immediate situation by use of community materials? Library? Public school? Other organizations? Individual?

Procedure:

11. To what general type did the lesson belong? Question-answer? Problem-project? Discussion? Appreciation? Drill? Life-experience? Dramatics? Story-telling? How far were different methods used?
12. What laws of learning were recognized? Disobeyed? Was a readiness created for that which was to be learned? Was there apparent satisfaction in the experience of the hour? Was there self-activity?
13. Who did the purposing? planning? executing? judging? projecting future activities? Teacher alone? Pupils? Both?
14. Was time given for study and thought on the part of the pupils? Was supervised study used to advantage? Were pupils directed to source materials?
15. Were pupils responsible for work outside the class? Were assignments used in class in such a way as to stimulate interest in doing them well?
16. Could the lesson plan have been changed with better results?

Elements of strength: In what measure were the following achieved?

1. All of the pupils were stimulated to participate in class experience.
2. The pupils were made conscious of the meaning of religious values, and a desire to interpret them in their own lives was created.
3. The pupils were given a clearer conception of the meaning of religion and thereby helped to become more interested in carrying out some specific Christian objectives.
4. The text and other materials used provided suffi-

cient data as a basis for clear thinking and the solution of problems from the religious point of view.

5. The pupils were helped to differentiate between types of motives for conduct and to recognize the Christian ones.
6. The lesson was related to the experiences of the pupil and their experiences definitely enriched and enlarged. New appreciations were stimulated.
7. The pupils were taught to hold hasty judgments in control.
8. Pupils raised problems that led to further study with more series intent.
9. The pupils were led to realize religious values in literature, art, and nature.
10. Children were led to give religious interpretation to a common life-experience.
11. Some one idea was emphasized sufficiently so as to carry over into daily life.

Elements of weakness: To what degree were the following factors evident?

1. Wrong method of teaching was used and laws of learning were ignored; that is, the teacher taught a development lesson when his class was ready for a practice lesson or perhaps for a review lesson; or he gave a review of a topic when practice or drill was needed.
2. No provision was made for pupil study, source materials were not available.
3. There was too much dependence placed upon memory and not enough thinking stimulated, therefore, little opportunity for problem-solving.
4. Pupil responses were not well distributed. One or

two did more of the talking. Teacher seemed unable to meet needs of all.

5. There was not proper differentiation between relative significance of facts.
6. The lesson was not lifted to a spiritual level. There was no consciousness of God, nor of the will of God, nor of inner obligation because of religious purpose.
7. Pupils did not feel the responsibility of criticizing their own conclusions nor were they expected to apply them to life situations.
8. There was time wasted on incidental matters and thereby losing main issues.
9. Teacher was not able to change plans and adapt himself to crisis which arose.
10. Teacher did not utilize vital life-situations to lead up to the lesson.

No. 26

Pupil Response

Church school ____ Grade ____ Date ____
Time ____ Boys ____
Enrolled ____ Girls ____ Enrolled ____
Teacher ____
Observer ______ Lesson ______ Course ______
Time teacher has had class ______

In the following questions give illustrations and incidents where possible.

General Situations:

1. How far is interest indicated by regularity of attendance, increase, promptness?
2. Describe conditions of orderliness, courtesy, controlled behavior, self-government, that suggest serious interest, class pride, individual problems, etc.
3. How far does the class seem to assume responsibility for success or failure, or progress in class undertakings?
4. What physical conditions seem to affect the responses of the group?

Situations affected by teaching methods:

5. How far does the teacher dominate the situation? In what ways is democratic participation invited and provided for?
6. What part does the class have in determining objectives and plans and in evaluating achievements?
7. In what ways are the pupils caused to think? Independently, thoroughly, systematically, concretely, experimentally, etc? In terms of religious principles?
8. What opportunity is given for questions? Does the method of teaching stimulate further inquiry? Are the pupils interested in each others' questions? How far are these religious questions?
9. Do they relate personal experiences voluntarily? What religious experiences are most common? Do they apply religious principles to their own situations without teacher prompting? Do they have special problems?
10. What provision is made for working out their ideas? In handwork, projects, dramatizations, ordinary life situations? What religious interests are shown?

11. Describe the conditions of attention. Consistent, spasmodic, voluntary, involuntary, indifferent, coerced, fluctuates from one topic to another.
12. What emotional responses does the teacher seem to arouse most frequently? Love, hate, anger, indignation, sympathy, humor, irritation, etc.? To what degree are they wisely stimulated and associated?
13. Does the teacher control discipline without distracting from the progress of the lesson? What problems of disturbers are there in the class? Is personality respected in controlling individuals?
14. Distinguish between the motives the teacher is trying to stimulate and those that actually operate in the class and seem to carry on. Indicate any definitely Christian motives that seem to be controlling.
15. Does the class seem to reflect any attitudes of the teacher? What personality influences are strongest?
16. What system is there for distribution of responses? Check the distribution.

Subject matter and goals affecting responses:

17. How far is there a spiritual point of view in the class? How is it manifest? What tendencies to superficiality, flippancy, seriousness, practical outcomes?
18. To what degree is the view of religion abstract, concrete, life-centered, God-conscious, conventional, influenced by ideas of Jesus, influenced by church standards and customs, related to social issues, influenced by the character of some leader or leaders?
19. How far does the class course of study meet their life needs? In what ways does the teacher seem conscious of such? In what ways are the pupils desirous of solving life-problems? Does the course of study aid or handicap this?

20. What signs are there of inter-Sunday interest? What preparation? What follow-up? What wider reference is stimulated than that in immediate lesson material: In what ways?
21. How much do the pupils use the Bible? To what degree does their religion seem Bible-based?
22. Does the class generalize on principles? Do they recognize God's law? How far are they stimulated to search for examples of conduct, or principles?
23. Does the interest in class studies seem to be related to intrinsic values in the material and goals, or is it mostly teacher-propelled?
24. With what phases of their studies do they show most interest? Bible studies, missions, biographies, social problems, personal problems, theological questions, church relationships, etc.?
25. What carry-over interests are developed in relation to religious literature, religious enterprises, world problems, realization of personality for self and others?
26. How far does class summarize findings of a study period, project the next study, recall results of one time for another, make progress and desire progress?

No. 27

Schedule for Analysis of Routine and Environmental Conditions

The following analysis that you are invited to make is of factors that may be of significance for the best conduct of a church school. Some of them the administrative officers should accept responsibility for and some of them are the direct responsibility of the teachers or group leaders.

A conference is called for ______ at ______ o'clock at which time teachers, officers, and the supervisors will exchange notes and talk over some ways of improving our present school situation. Turn all suggestions in to ____________ by ____________ who leads the discussion on this. Our school is always evaluating its work and trying to improve. Whenever anyone suggests a place for improvement he assumes our group is capable of improvement.

Let us examine our worship periods, our assemblies, departmental meetings, class sessions, and other organization meetings Sunday or week-day in this church. Make comments brief and explicit. Refer to numbers in outline below.

Physical conditions:

1. Ventilation. 2. Heat. 3. Light. 4. Cleanliness. 5. Attractiveness of rooms. 6. Satisfactory tables and chairs. 7. Plenty of equipment for good work. 8. Reference material conveniently located. 9. Shelves and cupboards in good order, and used to advantage. 10. Provision for wraps. 11. Toilets. 12. Drinking foun-

tains. 13. Rearrangement of seating. 14. Repairs needed.

Orderly procedures:

15. Entrance and exit of pupils, and change from assembly room to class. 16. Arrangement of ushering. 17. Distribution of materials. 18. Marking of reports and gathering of secretarial data. 19. Offering. 20. Ritual conducted reverently and meaningfully. 21. Understanding of what is expected so that co-operation is practicable. 22. Music as an aid to reverent attitudes. 23. Problem children and problem adults. 24. Plans made in time for adjustments.

Economy of time:

25. Teachers on time, and ready to welcome their groups. 26. Worship and assembly periods planned for agreed times and kept to such. 27. Teacher begins without delay. Has plan for each session which pupils understand and have agreed for the common good. 28. Class business has its place but does not interfere with class instruction period. 29. Discipline does not waste time. 30. Teacher does not give too much time or attention to one or two persons. 31. Recitation on work done out of class given a fair proportion of time. 32. Assignments ready without need for writing out long details on a blackboard, or taking considerable time to explain them. 33. Materials needed for dramatization, handwork, projects, etc., planned in advance. 34. Sufficient time allowed to do what ought to be done. 35. Habits that persist.

Stimulating environs:

36. Building as a whole and separate rooms arranged to best advantage. 37. Organ, pianos, hymn books, music

used to create religious atmosphere. 38. Pictures and decorations evaluated as to effect on observers. 39. Special loan features capitalized. 40. Symbols of religion appropriate. 41. Approach to church outside neat, attractive, aesthetic. 42. Colors all in good taste. 43. All literature used in good form. 44. Religious atmosphere, reverence, kindliness, thoughtful meditation, expected and aided by all.

No. 28

Schedule for Guiding Observation in Matters of Discipline and Classroom Management

I. General Conditions

1. In what ways do physical conditions aggravate problems of discipline and classroom management?
2. Was there sufficient attention to the methods of ushering and care of latecomers?
3. What provision was made for creating atmosphere supplying quietness, reverence, self-control? Did they seem to recognize that conduct should show respect for church and its objectives?
4. In what ways was the group made conscious that their behavior was a part of their desire to act in a Christian way?
5. To what extent did the teacher assume that individu-

als would exercise self-control, and to what extend did he provide for self-government by the class?

6. Did the worship or assembly service prior to the class period produce the right tendencies to controlled behavior? Was the program interesting? too long? poorly graded?
7. Did the music or other items of the program assist in content or tend to excite the group?
8. How far did boy and girl relationships cause problems of control?

II. Personality and Teaching Skill

1. What instances were observed of pushing, chewing gum, scraping of chairs, slamming books, shuffling feet, looking out window, playing with extraneous things, reading funny papers, paper wads, leaning back in chair, flapping handerchiefs, ostracizing a stranger, etc.
   a) How were these cases dealt with?
   b) Why did these cases of misconduct seem to demand discipline?
2. How was discipline affected by the teacher's personal condition?
   a) Did the teacher appear to be in good physical condition?
   b) Was she neat and attractive in personal appearance?
   c) Was there any outstanding feature of her personal appearance which wad distracting?
3. How was discipline affected by the teacher's firmness, forcefulness, prepossessing manner, fairness, decisiveness, calmness, patience, courage, good nature, persistence, scholarship, tact, and expectancy of good conduct?

4. In what way was discipine affected by the teacher's understanding of the pupils?
   a) In what ways did the teacher reveal a knowledge and appreciation of the background and history of individual pupils?
   b) How did the pupils react to this appreciation of their problem?
5. In what way did the executor of the program affect discipline?
   a) How thoroughly prepared was the teacher for the lesson?
   b) To what extent was the program suited to the needs and understanding of the group?
   c) To what extent was interest maintained throughout the lesson?
   d) How widely and how evenly distributed were the responses of the group?
   e) How far did failure to provide for difference in the abilities of the pupils affect restlessness and cause distractions?
   f) To what extent was the program broken into by rollcall, collection, records, business, etc.?
6. Criticize the forms of discipline.
   a) Examples—teacher, pupil historical characters.
   b) Approval of good conduct—merits, prizes, praise, favors, special privileges, etc.
   c) Punishment—threats, force, deprivations, social stigma.
   d) Substitution of other motives and activities.
   e) Disregard of offenses.
   f) Withdrawing or modifying stimuli that produces the offense.

No. 29

General Record of Observation for a Class Visitation

Schedule for Supervisors and Visiting Teachers

Instructions for recording observations:

1. Familiarize yourself with this blank before entering the classroom. It is often better to take notes and fill in the form after the visit rather than during the class period.
2. Be brief. Use good descriptive adjectives and phrases.
3. Be scientific. Do not read into the situation. Give facts and keep interpretation of facts separate. Do not try to prove anything. Record what takes place.
4. Give accurate reference numbers in any comments to avoid misunderstanding.
5. This schedule is intended to aid in a conference to improve teaching and learning and should be a fair analysis of the situation.

Grade__________ Teacher__________ Date__________
Lesson Topic__________
Attendance: Boys__________ Girls__________ Church__________

A. Physical conditions:
   1. Ventilation________ 2. Temperature________ 3. Appearance________
   4. Seating arrangements________ 5. Handicaps________
   Comments__________

B. Routine:
1. Record making________ 2. Distribution of materials________
3. Entrance and exit of pupils________ 4. System in procedures________
Comments________

C. Personal factors in teacher
1. General appearance________ 2. Voice________ 3. Mannerisms________
________ 4. Use of language________
5. Personality: a) Tact________ b) Sympathy________ c) Self-control________
d) Patience ________ e) Poise ________ f) Humor ________
g) Animation____ h) Reserve________ i) Self-confidence________
6. Attitudes: a) Religious convictions ________
b) Interest or duty________ c) Autocratic or democratic________ d) Willing to learn________
e) Co-operative________
Comments________

D. Pupils' behavior:
1. Attention________ 2. Interest________ 3. Manners________
4. Punctuality________ 5. Regularity________ 6. Initiative________
7. Co-operativeness________ 8. Self-Control________
Comment________

E. Teaching:
1. Aim________ 2. Preparation________
3. Plan________ 4. Adaptation ________
5. Type of procedure: a) Talk or lecture________ b) Story________
c) Review________ d) Drill________ e) Questioning________
f) Project________ g) Supervised study________ h) Socialized recitation________ i) Dramatization________
j) Other________
6. Class participation: a) Discussion________ b) Study________
c) Handwork________ d) Project________ e) Prayer________
f) Independent thought________ Comment________

F. Materials used:
1. Course________ 2. Teaching aids________
3. Pupil's books________ 4. Effective use________
5. Reference materials________ 6. Equipment________
Comments________

G. Out-of-class work:
1. Carry-over activities________ 2. Regular meetings________
3. Occasional________ 4. Home visitation________
5. Correlation________
Comments________

H. Results: Give illustrations to indicate satisfactory or unsatisfactory reactions along such lines as, (a) practical application of lesson, (b) reverence, (c) emotional attitude, (d) motivation of conduct, (e) co-operation in a social undertaking, (f) use of knowledge, (g) search for facts, (h) new appreciations, (i) relation to the church or some religious cause, (j) self-control, (k) worthy desires.

____

____

____

—Chave, Supervision of Chr. Ed., p. 79

No. 30

General Record of Observation for a Class Visitation

Schedule for Supervisors and Visiting Teachers

Instructions for recording observations:

1. Familiarize yourself with this blank before entering the classroom
2. It is often better to take notes and fill in the form after the visit rather than during the class period
3. Be brief. Use good descriptive adjectives and phrases
4. Be scientific. Do not read into the situation. Give facts and keep interpretation of facts separate. Do not try to prove anything. Record what takes place.
5. This schedule is intended to aid in a conference to improve teaching and learning and should be a fair analysis of the situation.

Grade________ Teacher________ Date________
Lesson Topic________
Attendance: Boys________ Girls________ Church________

A. Physical conditions:
   1. Ventilation________ 2. Temperature________ 3. Appearance________
   4. Seating arrangements________ 5. Handicaps________
   Comments________

B. Routine:
   1. Record making________ 2. Distribution of materials________
   3. Entrance and exit of pupils________ 4. System in procedures________
   Comments________

C. Personal factors in teacher:
   1. General appearance________ 2. Voice________ 3. Mannerisms________
   ________ 4. Use of language________
   5. Personality: a) Tact________ b) Sympathy________ c) Self-control________
   d) Patience________ e) Poise________ f) Humor________
   g) Animation________ h) Reserve________ i) Self-confidence ________
   6. Attitudes: a) Religious convictions________
   b) Interest or duty________ c) Autocratic or democratic ________
   d) Willing to learn________ e) Cooperative________
   Comments________

D. Pupils' behavior:
   1. Attention________ 2. Interest________ 3. Manners________
   4. Punctuality________ 5. Regularity________ 6. Initiative________
   7. Cooperativeness________ 8. Self-control________
   Comments________

E. Teaching:
   1. Aim________ 2. Preparation________
   3. Plan________ 4. Adaptation________
   5. Type of procedure: a) Talk or lecture________ b) Story________ c) Review________
   d) Drill________ e) Questioning________ f) Project________
   g) Supervised study________ h) Socialized recitation________
   i) Dramatization________ j) Other ________
   6. Class participation: a) Discussion________ b) Study________
   c) Handwork________ d) Project________ e) Prayer________
   f) Independent thought________ Comments________

F. Materials used: 1. Course________ 2. Teaching aids________ 3. Pupil books________
   4. Effective use________ 5. Reference materials________ 6. Equipment________
   Comments________

G. Out-of-class work: 1. Carry-over activities________ 2. Regular meetings________
   3. Occasional________ 4. Home visitation________ 5. Correlation________
   Comments________

______from Frank McKibben, *Guiding Workers in Christian Education,* p. 108

No. 31

Church School Teacher and Officer Information Blank

1. Occupation (school teacher, housekeeper, etc.) ______
2. Male ______ (Female ______ 3. At what age did you begin to teach? ______
4. Your present age ______ 5. Department ______
6. Officer? ______ 7. Teacher? ______ 8. Years in present S. S. position ______
9. What schools have you attended?

Elementary-No. of years? ______

High School-No. of years? ______

Business College-No. of years? ______

Teachers' College-No. of years? ______

College-university-No. of years? ______

Other school ______ No. of years? ______

10. Check the following courses you have had in college or university:

Educational Psychology ______

School Management ______

History of Education ______

Principles of Teaching ______

Organization & Adm. Church Schools ______

Principles of teaching religion ______

History of religion ______

Biblical literature ______

Missions ______

Bible History ______

Other courses ______

______

______

______

11. Indicate courses taken at the following schools:
    (a) Courses taken in local church training school:
    Course ____________________No. of lessons ______
    Course ____________________No. of lessons ______
    (b) Courses taken in Community training school or summer school:
    Course ____________________No. of lessons ______
    Course ____________________No. of lessons ______

12. How many years have you taught in the following schools?

Sunday school–Years ______
Public or private school ______
Week-day Religious school ______
Daily Vacation Bible School ______
Other school ______

13. List some books on religious education recently read: _

____

____

14. What religious educational periodicals or magazines do you read regularly? ____________________

____

15. What conventions, institutes, training classes have you attended regularly? or recently? ______________

____

16. What do you consider to be the types of service you are best qualified to undertake? ______________

____

No. 32

Guide for Observing a Church School Session

I. How to Observe

A. Things for the supervisor or observer to remember

1. It is difficult for the teacher to teach children in the presence of observers or supervisors.
2. The teacher is quite conscious of being observed and evaluated

B. Suggestions for supervisors and observers

1. Arrive early
   a. Give the teacher time to explain to you the purposes and plans for the lesson before the pupils arrive.
   b. Remember that this is only one session in a series.
2. Remove hat and wrap and stay in an inconspicuous place during the entire session unless requested by the teacher to move.
3. Remain quiet; do not laugh at comments or actions of pupils.
4. Take time to talk to the teacher after the class session.

II. What to Observe

A. The physical conditions

1. Is the room inviting and attractive? Heat? Cleanliness?

2. Is the room adequate in size? Well lighted? Ventilated?
3. Are the chairs, tables, and other furnishings appropriate for the age group?
4. What provision is made to create an atmosphere of beauty, worship, work, and friendliness?
5. Is there a place for work (or play) materials so that pupils can have access to them?
6. Is there a place for the teacher to keep his supplies?
7. Are pictures appropriate for the age group? To the unit being used? Are they appropriately placed?
8. Is there a place for wraps for both teachers and pupils?

B. Routine factors
1. Does the teacher arrive early? How much?
2. Does the teacher remove his hat and wrap and get busy on arrival (saving visiting with others until after the session)?
3. What method is used to get started? Taking roll? Seating and passing? Offering? Distributing supplies: Handling materials and apparatus?
4. Do the pupils and teachers feel at ease and at home with each other?
5. Are individual needs and interests recognized?
6. Is there a spirit of cooperation among the pupils? Between the teachers and pupils?
7. Do the teachers speak in quiet voices? Meet interruptions calmly? Enter into the pupils' conversation and work joyfully?

C. Discipline and order
   1. Means?
   2. Skill? Occasions

D. Class Procedure
   1. Is there evidence of a definite aim or purpose to the lesson?
      a. Can you detect the kinds of knowledge or information which the teacher planned to give to the class?
      b. Can you detect what attitudes and feeling responses the teacher tried to encourage?
      c. What applications to the student's life and conduct were made during the course of the lesson?
   2. What evidences of the use of materials or subject matter did you observe?
      a. Were stories used?
      b. Were pictures or object lessons used?
      c. What kind of prayers were used?
      d. Music?
      e. Handwork or other forms of expression material
   3. What methods were used?
      a. What types of teaching were used? Storytelling? Questions? Drama? Discussions, etc.?
      b. Were assignments made?
      c. Was a review of the previous lessons given?
      d. How was the interest of the students engaged?
      e. Do all participate in the lessons?
      f. How were the following used in the session?
         (1) Bible

(2) Other books
(3) Stories
(4) Conversation

4. What general principles of teaching were violated, if any?
5. How did the teacher use questions?
6. Did the teacher use any methods of evaluation, such as tests, examinations, rating scales, standards, etc.?

No. 33

Supervisor's Chart

Thank you for your hospitality. I was glad for the privilege of visiting your class in order to learn to know your pupils better and to become better acquainted with the work being done in your department.

I liked a lot of things about your class on ______. Among these were:

______ Your personal appearance, which was very neat and showed thoughtful consideration for your important work.

______ The pleasant, friendly atmosphere which you create in your classroom.

______ The manner in which you interest and gain the attention of your pupils and the way in which they respond to you.

______ The evidence that you meet the children at other

times than during your class session—by visiting them in their homes or seeing them in other places

______ The resourceful way in which you had prepared for many activities through which your pupils might learn the Christian way of life and the necessary skills and information by which to live the good life.

______ The obvious fact that you study books and magazines which will help you to do a better teaching job in your work of helping to build the kingdom of God.

I did think your work would probably be more effective if you:

______ Would have your class sessions a little more carefully planned, with your aim a little more accurately thought through.

______ Would have more variety of method in your class sessions. (Perhaps you do change your methods from Sunday to Sunday—this helps your pupils to come to your class in an expectant mood.)

______ Would provide for more activities (purposeful ones, not too difficult) through which your pupils can gain knowledge and Christian skills.

______ Would plan your questions so they would require more thought for answering—avoid questions that can be answered with one word, except on written quizzes.

______ Would improve the physical appearance of your classroom—look about and see what you yourself could do about it.

______ Would give more attention to the ventilation, temperature, seating, lighting, and other physical comforts of your pupils.

_____ Would arrive earlier in your classroom and plan for some interesting pre-session activities for your pupils.

A personal note:

Signature __________

No. 34

Teacher's Agreement

(Sample)

In consideration of my appointment by the __________ Sunday School and of the opportunity offered me to participate in the sacred work of teaching the religion of our Lord and Master, as a teacher in the Sunday School, I agree on my part that:

1. I will accept and faithfully perform the duties of that office from this date to the following December 31.
2. I will make it a practice to attend the sessions regularly, and if for any real reason I am prevented from coming, I will notify my department superintendent, or the general superintendent, and help to provide a substitute who is mutually acceptable. If I am absent more than 10 Sundays in the year, or 3 Sundays without notice, I understand that my office shall be considered vacant.

3. I will make it a practice to come on time to the sessions, which I interpret to mean that as a teacher I am to be present at least 10 minutes before the opening of the session.
4. I will prepare thoroughly for each session, maintain discipline, help to create an attitude of reverence and a spirit of loyalty and cooperation, and, with the help of God, set a good example in Christian living.
5. I will cooperate with the officers of the school, my department superintendent, and my fellow teachers; I will welcome constructive criticism and helpful suggestions, and will at all times abide by such rulings as may be made for the best interests of the whole school.
6. I will regularly attend the meetings of teachers and officers, known as the workers' conference, and participate in the work of the conference.
7. I will broaden my knowledge of and experience in my task through reading and study. I will read regularly a magazine dealing with my work, study good books, or take a training course—all three if possible.
8. I will make a careful study of the "Self Rating Chart" used in our school and make a conscious effort to measure up as high as possible in each of the points.
9. In case I find it impossible to continue my services for any reason, I will notify the superintendent in writing at least two weeks in advance.

Signed ____________________

The __________ day of __________ 19_____

__________, __________
(City) (State)

No. 35

Let Me Help

Date________________

Name________________________ Home Phone______ Bus. Phone______

Home Address___________________ Bus. Address___________________

Profession or Occupation__________ Hobbies_______________________

What I Would Like To Do Most In My Church__________________________

I think____________________would be best for_____________________
name position

INSTRUCTIONS: Please check both columns, HAVE SERVED (H) OR WILING TO SERVE (W)

H	THE CHURCH	W	H	SPECIAL SERVICES	W	H	SUNDAY SCHOOL	W
__	Trustee	__	__	Picnic Chairman	__	__	Superintendent	__
__	Financial Secretary	__	__	Social Chairman	__	__	Assistant Supt.	__
__	Secretary	__	__	Bus Driver	__	__	Departmental Supt.	__
__	Treasurer	__	__	Use My Car	__	__	Secretary	__
__	Librarian	__	__	Handcraft	__	__	Treasurer	__
__	Literature Committee	__	__	Cook, Waitress	__	__	Board of Education	__
__	Library Committee	__	__	Publicity	__	__	Teacher—Children	__
__	Usher or Greeter	__	__	Nurse	__	__	Teacher—Youth	__
__	Steward	__	__	Doctor	__	__	Teacher—Adult	__
__	Communion	__	__	Auditor, Accountant	__	__	Cradle Roll	__
__	Building Committee	__	__	Civilian Defense	__	__	Home Department	__
__	Children's Church	__	__	Associate Teacher	__	__	Missionary Education	__
__	Nursery Director	__	__	Historical Com.	__	__	Usher	__
__	Evangelism Committee	__	__	Telephone Caller	__	__	Librarian	__
__	Christian Ed. Com.	__	__	Public Speaker	__	__	VBS Director	__
__	Christian Ed. Bd.	__	__	Projector Operator	__	__	VBS Committee	__
__	Finance Committee	__	__	Tape Recorder Operator	__	__	VBS Teacher	__
__	Home Visitor	__	__	Recreation Director	__	__	Teacher Training	__
__	Publicity	__	__	Reader for Shut-ins	__	__	Week Day Chr. Ed.	__
__	Radio	__	__	Mimeograph Operator	__			
__	Pastor's Assistant	__	__	Typist	__			
__	Deacon	__	__	Direct Plays, Pageants	__			
__	Deaconess	__						
__	Lay Representative	__						

H	THE CHURCH	W	H	EVANGELISM	W	H	MUSIC	W
—	Class Leader	—	—	Visitation	—	—	Choir Director	—
—	Adult Director	—	—	Personal Witness	—	—	Organist	—
—	Youth Director	—	—	Personal Worker	—	—	Pianist	—
—	Children's Director	—	—	Follow-up Work	—	—	Soloist	—
—	Boys Brigade (Scouts)	—	—	Community Survey	—	—	Choir (Soprano, Alto,	—
—	Pioneer Girls (Scouts)	—				—	Tenor, Bass)	
						—	Trio	—
						—	Quartet	—
						—	Instrument ( )	—

CHURCH AUXILIARY	Pres.		Sec.		Treas.		OTHER INFORMATION
	H	W	H	W	H	W	
Women's Missionary	—	—	—	—	—	—	________
Girls' Missionary	—	—	—	—	—	—	________
Men's Fellowship	—	—	—	—	—	—	________
Sunday School Class	—	—	—	—	—	—	________
Women's Aid Society	—	—	—	—	—	—	________
Youth Fellowwship	—	—	—	—	—	—	________
Young Adults	—	—	—	—	—	—	________

Courtesy EVANGELICAL TEACHER TRAINING ASSOCIATION, 1825 College Avenue, Wheaton

No. 36

Personality Profile Test

QUALITY	DEFINITION	MY ESTIMATE				
		Low		Average		High
		1	2	3	4	
Spirituality	Christianity, always putting God first					
Sincerity	Truth and genuineness					
Dependability	Loyalty, reliability, promptness					
Enthusiasm	Keen interest, zeal, earnestness					
Co-operation	Ability to work with others					
Self-confidence	Feeling sure your ability is equal to demands					

QUALITY	DEFINITION	MY ESTIMATE				
		Low		Average		High
		1	2	3	4	
Well-groomed Appearance	Properly dressed and clean					
Good health	Good physical condition					
Forcefulness	Using firm and decisive action, expression; not hesitant					
Emotional Stability	Ability to maintain poise at all times, even under emotional stress					
Tact	Saying and doing what is effective without offending					
Courtesy	Polite, kind, considerate					

QUALITY	DEFINITION	MY ESTIMATE				
		Low		Average		High
		1	2	3	4	
Friendliness	Cordial, sympathetic					
Persistence	Ability to continue effectively even with strong opposition					
Patience	Being long-suffering					
Use of Good English	Using words effectively in clear, understandable, correct grammar					
Pleasing Voice	Strong, rather low pitched voice, easily heard, but not irritating					

—From *Superintend With Success* by Guy Leavitt, Standard, 1950, p. 93

No. 37

Evaluation of Personality and Spiritual Outcomes of Teaching

Following are some of the characteristics, as given by C. B. Eavey, which the Christian teacher may look for when evaluating the outcomes of his teaching as these should be found in the personality and life of his pupils.

1. The well-taught pupil knows whom he has believed and has made that commitment of himself to the will of God which colors all his outlet and all his motives. He may not feel secure in all aspects of knowledge and understanding but he has a sense of directions. He knows where he is going and why he is going.

2. The man of God has spiritual discernment. He is able to distinguish clearly between temporal and eternal values. The more mature he is the more inclined he is to choose the latter in preference to the former when he must make choice between the two.

3. He is growing more and more into adult capacities of spiritual life and experience being able to thrive on meat instead of the milk that babes in Christ must have for food.

4. The more perfect the man of God the better does he know how to translate the Word of God into daily practice in his life. He constantly narrows the gulf between Christian profession and Christian practice.

5. He is a follower of good works. He maintains an organic union between true piety on the one hand and sound knowledge and genuine culture on the other hand. He uses every talent and every capacity he possesses in God's service with an eye single to His glory.

6. The man of God is loyal to the church of Jesus Christ as a whole. "I am of Paul" and "I am of Apollos" are not his statements, for, in the measure that he is mature, he is not a factionalist.

7. The man of God is not at home in this world. He uses the things of the world as not possessing them. He is a good citizen of his community and he is loyal to his country. His desire, however, is for "a better country, that is an heavenly."

8. The quality of the life of the perfect man of God is rooted in two essential Christian practices—Bible reading and prayer. The more mature he becomes, the more does he practice regular and much reading of the Word of God and the more he does engage in unceasing prayer.

9. The mature man is productive. He assumes responsibility for witnessing to others and for doing the work of Christ and he works diligently for God. The mature person does not play at life as does a child.

10. The higher the level of perfection, the less there is of self in the life of the individual and the more earnestly does he desire and seek that God may have first place in his thought and purposes.

11. Growth in Christian perfection is marked by greater and greater reliance upon the Holy Spirit. More than the immature person, the mature one realizes that it is not by

might nor by power but by the Spirit of God that victories are won and service rendered.

12. The perfect man of God is obedient to God. His commitment to God grown upon him through time and he works more and more into life and action the principles of single-hearted devotion to God. Not for him is the path of ease and self-indulgence. Instead he endures hardships that the perfect will of God may be accomplished in and through him.

No. 38

A Check List for Self-Evaluation for Supervisors

1. Do I let the staff know I need help?
2. Do I rely on the Judgment of all the members of my staff?
3. Do I respect the opinion of all teachers?
4. Do I stand by the teachers and officers in their decisions?
5. Do I demand loyalty to myself or to the whole staff and program?
6. Do I succeed in getting each member of the staff to feel a responsibility for the success of the program?
7. Do I make each staff member feel his job is important?
8. Do I give praise frequently?
9. Do I emphasize the good aspects of a teacher's work?

10. Do I know of the special work people under my supervision are doing?
11. Do I give adequate publicity to the work being done by the teachers on the staff?
12. Do I make all members of the staff feel that they belong?
13. Do I show likes and dislikes for the members of the staff?
14. Do I let people know that I have confidence in them?
15. Do I use "we" instead of "I"?
16. Do I always try to make the other person think I am important?
17. Do I admit a mistake in judgment when results show I have been wrong?
18. Do I allow my feelings to be hurt?
19. Am I always accessible to the staff?
20. Do I keep people waiting?
21. Do I take tactless suggestions without becoming angry?
22. Do I have an adequate system for making sure of engagements and keeping promises?
23. Does the staff come to me for advice on personal matters?
24. Do I bring the total staff into the establishment of goals?
25. Do I succeed in getting all teachers to take an active part in the formulating of Sunday School policies?
26. Do I seek advice in the selection of new staff members?
27. Do I secure the assistance of the staff in making promotions?
28. Do I consult those who will be affected by an action before I take it?

29. Do I always get the facts before I form an opinion about responsibility for an error?
30. Do I help the new workers get adjusted to their duties?
31. Do I promote improved working conditions for the staff?
32. Do I give the teachers a real part in the evaluation of the program?

Bibliography

Church Education Sources

Adair, Thelma and Elizabeth McCort, *How to Make Church School Equipment,* Westminster, 1955

Atkinson, C. Harry, *Building and Equipping for Christian Education,* Bureau of Church Building, National Council of Churches, 1956

Byrne, H. W., *A Christian Approach to Education,* rev. ed., Mott Media, 1977

Byrne, H. W., *Christian Education for the Local Church,* rev. ed., Zondervan, 1973

Chave, Ernest J., *Supervision of Religious Education,* University of Chicago Press, 1939

Crossland, Weldon, *Better Leaders for Your Church,* Abingdon, 1955

Gangel, Kenneth D., Leadership for Church Education, Moody, 1970

Hakes, Edward, ed., *An Introduction to Evangelical Christian Education,* Moody, 1964

Leavitt, Guy P., *How to Improve My Church's School,* Standard, 1963

Leavitt, Guy P., Superintend with Success, Standard, 1960

McKibben, Frank M. *Guiding Workers in Christian Education,* Abingdon, 1953

McKibben, Frank M., *Improving Religious Education Through Supervision,* Cokesbury, 1931

National Council of Churches of Christ, *Evaluation and*

Christian Education, Office of Publication and Distribution, 1960

Smith, Frank W., *How to Improve Your Sunday School,* Abingdon, 1924

Taylor, Marvin J., ed., *An Introduction to Christian Education,* Abingdon, 1966

Wyckoff, D. Campbell, *How to Evaluate Your Christian Education Program,* Westminster, 1962

Secular Education Sources

Adams, Harold P. and Frank G. Dickey, *Basic Principles of Supervision,* American Book Co., 1953

Ayer, Fred C., *Fundamentals of Instructional Supervision,* Harper, 1954

Bartky, John A., *Supervision as Human Relations,* D. C. Heath, 1953

Briggs, Thomas H. and J. Justman, *Improving Instruction Through Supervision,* revised edition, Macmillan, 1952

Burton, William H. and L. J. Brueckner, *Supervision a Social Process,* 3rd ed., Appleton-Crofts-Century, 1955

Harris, Ben M., *Supervisory Behavior in Education,* Prentice-Hall, 1963

Harrison, Raymond H., *Supervisory Leadership in Education,* American Book Co., 1968

Krathwohl, David R., *et al, Taxonomy of Educational Objectives,* David McKay Co., Inc., 1956

Lucio, William H. and John D. McNeil, *Supervision,* McGraw-Hill, 1962

Mager, Robert T., *Preparing Instructional Objectives,* Fearon, 1962

McKean, Robert C., *The Supervisor,* Washington, D.C., Center for Applied Research in Education, 1964

Mackenzie, Gordon N., *et al, Instructional Leadership,* Columbia University, 1954
Pi Lambda Theta, *The Evaluation of Teaching,* Washington, D.C., 1967
Swearingen, Mildred E., *Supervision of Instruction,* Allyn and Bacon, 1962

INDEX

NAMES